THE TRELLIS
COOKBOOK

THE TRELLIS COOKBOOK

CONTEMPORARY AMERICAN COOKING

IN WILLIAMSBURG, VIRGINIA

MARCEL DESAULNIERS

PHOTOGRAPHS BY TAYLOR BIGGS LEWIS, JR.

WEIDENFELD & NICOLSON
New York

Published by Weidenfeld & Nicolson, New York
A Division of Wheatland Corporation
10 East 53rd Street
New York, New York 10022

Library of Congress Cataloging-in-Publication Data

Desaulniers, Marcel.
    The Trellis cookbook.

    Includes index.
    1. Cookery—Virginia—Williamsburg.   2. Cookery,
American.   3. Williamsburg (Va.)—Social life and
customs.   4. Trellis Restaurant.   I. Title.
TX715.D465   1988   641.59755   88-159
ISBN 1-55584-114-7

Manufactured in the United States of America

Designed by Irving Perkins Associates

First Edition

10   9   8   7   6   5   4   3   2

To My Partners:

Connie Desaulniers

John and Julia Curtis

Tom and Mary Ellen Power

ACKNOWLEDGMENTS

As with any cookbook, *The Trellis Cookbook* would not have been possible without the energies, unselfish involvement, and support of many people.

I would like to thank my kitchen staff: especially chef Philip Delaplane, under whose direction The Trellis maintains its standards for quality and innovative food;

Senior assistant chef Jeff Duncan, who along with Phil directs the kitchen staff and is always willing to do more;

Assistant chef Jonathan Zearfoss, my right-hand man, literary consultant, and recipe tester throughout the entire project;

Pastry chef Andrew O'Connell, for his uncanny ability to transform an unrepentant chocophile's dreams into decadent reality;

Assistant chefs Michael Gyetvan and John Twichell; pantry supervisors Gisele Hicks and Clementine Darden; receiving steward Ken Oliver; and all the cooks and apprentices.

I would also like to thank:

Phillip Cooke, of Food Service Associates, for believing that this cookbook would be more than a thought;

Dan Green, C.E.O. and Publisher of Weidenfeld & Nicolson, for all the encouraging words, but most of all for making this book a reality;

Judie Choate, my editor at Weidenfeld & Nicolson, for making the dreaded editorial process a pleasant experience;

Penny Seu, friend and Williamsburg resident, for dotting the i's and crossing the t's;

The Culinary Institute of America, my alma mater;

Rose Levy Beranbaum, Cordon Rose Cooking School, for being so generous with her expertise;

Victoire Desaulniers, good cook—great mother;

The Colonial Williamsburg Foundation, for setting the stage for The Trellis.

Special thanks to the following retailers for making available many of the beautiful plates, glasses, candlesticks, and porcelain pieces used in the photographs.

The Lenox Shop, Williamsburg

The Porcelain Collector, Williamsburg

Shirley Pewter, Williamsburg

CONTENTS

INTRODUCTION

Writing *The Trellis Cookbook* has been like writing the story of my development as an American chef. Most of my life has revolved around food. As a teenager I worked in restaurants around my hometown of Woonsocket, Rhode Island, where I did everything from washing dishes in a banquet hall that seated a thousand to waiting on tables, frying clams, and making spaghetti sauce in a restaurant catering to the race track crowd. My decision to attend the Culinary Institute of America after high school and to make cooking my profession was a natural one.

The Culinary Institute was wonderful. After graduation I moved to New York City and worked in several private clubs with European chefs. Then, just as I thought my career was blossoming, it was interrupted by a tour in Vietnam (not a cook's tour, but a Marine's—the only food I handled was C rations!).

The return to the States and the culinary world offered many challenges for me, and in 1970, I moved to Williamsburg, Virginia, to work for the Colonial Williamsburg Foundation and for Rod Stoner, a fellow C.I.A. classmate.

Rod and I were fortunate to cook for Mrs. Carlisle Humelsine, wife of the president of the Colonial Williamsburg Foundation and hostess *extraordinaire* to the many heads-of-state that visited the Colonial capital. Mrs. Humelsine had an impeccable sense for all things gastronomic, including a prescient knowledge of what would envelop the culinary landscape in the following decade. She insisted on fresh foods served only at their best. She was particular about quality. If avocados were in a recipe and none were ripe, we changed the menu. Quality always came first because menus could always be changed. Mrs. Humelsine's menus were diverse, innovative, and always stylish—forerunners of today's exciting contemporary American cooking.

Since leaving the Colonial Williamsburg Foundation in 1974, travel has been an integral part of my continuing learning experience. I plan my trips to maximize my exposure to the best foods and wine available. In great food cities like New York and San Francisco, I sometimes eat as many as five meals a day.

By teaching and also attending cooking classes, I continue to challenge and refine my skills. I have demonstrated contemporary American cooking in places as diverse as the Ahwahnee Hotel in Yosemite National Park and a barge cruising the Yonne River in Burgundy. I have taken classes in French pastry at Lenotre outside of Paris and studied Italian cooking in Florence under the direction of Giuliano Bugialli. Whether teaching or being taught, these classes have made me aware that all good food, be it French or Italian, classical or contemporary American, has something in common: honesty, simplicity, and faithfulness to quality.

Thanks to my travels, many dishes on the Trellis menu are inspired by a multinational influence. Pasta, for example, is one of our mainstays, but there are many other subtle manifestations of our love for Italian ingredients and Italian-influenced recipes. Roasted peppers, charred over a wood fire, are frequently a component of our menu. Our own dried cherry tomatoes often lend their "twangy" presence to a pasta special. Fresh herbs are constantly at play. The French influence is apparent in the flavor and texture of our soups and sauces as well as in the craftsmanship of our terrines. Another French touch is our penchant for combining different temperatures of foods, especially in salads.

Wine, once so European and now very American, has always been synonymous with food at The Trellis. Even with the Trellis's ninety-two-selection, award-winning wine list, my partners and I have espoused a simple wine philosophy: food and wine should coexist. Furthermore, wine should work together with food to create more than each would on its own. This symbiotic relationship does not mean that selecting the proper wine should be a mystical, complicated, or expensive experience. Most of the wine suggestions in this cookbook are in fact affordable, and available in most wine stores.

The Trellis menu is eclectic and changes seasonally, which allows me to incorporate food at its peak. This same flexibility is illustrated in each recipe of *The Trellis Cookbook* in the Chef's Touch section. Here I offer personal anecdotes, tips on making maximum use of seasonal foods, and the best substitutions in cases of dietary restrictions or the unavailability of products or equipment. The Chef's Touch sections, plus a chapter of basics recipes and techniques, will encourage and guide you in adapting seasonal Trellis meals to your own kitchen and locality.

With the recipes that follow, I hope to share the Trellis personality—its seasonal menus using regional food, its fine wines, its commitment to quality. Please attempt to recapture The Trellis in your own home, then come to Williamsburg and join our table. After all, good food and fine wine go best with good friends.

Marcel Desaulniers
August 1988

APPETIZERS

Grilled Skewers of Snails and Chicken on Red Pepper Capellini

Serves 8

5 large red bell peppers, halved and seeded	1 tablespoon chopped fresh parsley
1 cup water	2¹/₂ tablespoons minced garlic
3¹/₄ cups all-purpose flour	48 snails (two 4¹/₂-ounce cans of 24/26 count), thoroughly washed
2 eggs	
1 tablespoon olive oil	
1 teaspoon salt	3 tablespoons brandy
¹/₂ cup cornmeal	2 pounds boneless and skinless chicken breast, cut into 48 pieces (each piece about 1 inch square)
10 tablespoons unsalted butter, softened	
6 tablespoons minced shallots	
Salt and pepper to season	1 tablespoon fresh lemon juice
12 tablespoons dry white wine	

EQUIPMENT: *Paring knife, film wrap, 2¹/₂-quart saucepan, measuring cup, food processor, rubber spatula, measuring spoons, cutting board, fork, pasta machine, two baking sheets, parchment paper, French knife, two non-stick sauté pans, stainless-steel bowl, wooden spoon, eight 9-inch bamboo or metal skewers, charcoal grill, tongs, 5-quart saucepan, colander, pastry brush*

Cut 3 of the peppers into 32 strips the length of the pepper and ¹/₂ inch wide. Cover with film wrap and refrigerate until needed. Cut the remaining peppers into 1-inch pieces. Place in a 2¹/₂-quart saucepan with 1 cup lightly salted water and bring to a boil over medium high heat. Lower the heat and simmer until all the water has evaporated, about 45 minutes. Cool for 15 minutes, then purée in a food processor fitted with a metal blade. Refrigerate, uncovered, for 15 minutes.

Prepare the pasta dough by placing 3 cups flour on a clean, dry cutting board or similar work surface. Make a well in the center, add the eggs, cooled pepper purée, olive oil, and 1 teaspoon salt. Using a fork, combine the eggs, pepper purée, olive oil, and salt. When thoroughly mixed, begin to work the flour into the center, a small amount at a time. When enough flour has been added so that you can handle the dough, begin kneading by hand. Knead the dough by hand until all the flour has been incorporated, about 10 minutes. Cover the dough with film wrap and allow to relax at room temperature for 1 hour.

Cut the pasta dough into 8 equal portions. Roll and knead each portion of dough through a pasta machine, using the extra ¼ cup flour as necessary to prevent the dough from becoming tacky. Cut the sheets of dough into capellini (see page 315). To prevent sticking, toss the cut pasta with cornmeal, then place the cut pasta portions on a baking sheet lined with parchment paper. Cover the sheet tightly with film wrap and refrigerate until needed.

Prepare a garlic butter by heating 2 tablespoons butter in a non-stick sauté pan over medium heat. When the butter is hot, add 2 tablespoons minced shallots, season with salt and pepper, and sauté for 1 minute. Add 6 tablespoons wine and continue to heat until the wine has evaporated, about 10 minutes. Allow the reduced wine and shallot mixture to cool at room temperature for 30 minutes; then combine with 6 tablespoons butter, the chopped parsley, and ½ tablespoon minced garlic. Season with salt and pepper and keep at room temperature.

Heat the remaining 2 tablespoons butter in a non-stick sauté pan over medium high heat. When the butter is hot, add the remaining 4 tablespoons minced shallots and 2 tablespoons minced garlic and sauté for 1 minute. Add the snails, season with salt and pepper, and sauté until hot, about 3 to 4 minutes. Add the remaining 6 tablespoons wine and the brandy. Reduce the heat and cook slowly for 15 minutes. Cool at room temperature for 30 minutes.

Combine the chicken pieces with the lemon juice and season with salt and pepper. Skewer the snails and chicken pieces, alternating 6 pieces of each item per skewer. The skewers may be prepared up to this point and refrigerated until needed.

Preheat the oven to 250 degrees.

Grill the skewers and red pepper strips over a low charcoal or wood fire, turning regularly, for 4 to 5 minutes. While the skewers are cooking, baste with a small amount of garlic butter. Transfer the skewers and pepper strips to a baking sheet and once again baste with a small amount of garlic butter. Hold warm in the preheated oven.

Cook the pasta (see page 315) in 3 quarts boiling salted water until tender but firm to the bite, about 20 seconds. Drain the cooked pasta in a colander, return to the pan, and toss with the remaining garlic butter.

Portion the pasta onto 8 warm soup/pasta plates. Place 1 skewer and 4 grilled pepper strips on each portion of pasta and serve immediately.

The Chef's Touch

The preparation of fresh snails is an arduous task, but fortunately one that a cook on this side of the Atlantic need not worry about, since fresh snails are rarely, if ever, available in the United States. The snails available are canned and usually come from France or Taiwan, although recently a delicious canned tiny snail from California has come on the market. For this recipe, I recommend that a 24-count (2 dozen per can) snail from France or Taiwan be used; the California snail is too tiny for skewering and grilling.

Smaller skewers of chicken and snails, basted with garlic butter, would make an excellent hot hors d'oeuvres.

A sauvignon blanc with just the right balance of fruit and acidity would be my wine selection. Try the 1985 Matanzas Creek.

Grilled Smoked Duck Breast with Country Ham, Melon, and Pistachio Dressing

Serves 4

1 whole duck
1 cup warm water
1/2 cup kosher salt
2 tablespoons granulated sugar
1 cup cool water
1 tablespoon vegetable oil
3/4 cup peanut oil
1/4 cup cider vinegar
2 ounces pistachios, shelled, skinned, and crushed

Salt and pepper to season
1 small cantaloupe, peeled, halved, and seeded
2 ounces country ham, sliced thin (about 6 slices) (see page 324)
1 medium head Bibb lettuce, washed and dried

EQUIPMENT: *Cutting board, boning knife, measuring spoons, measuring cup, two stainless-steel bowls, baking sheet, paper towels, ''Little Chief'' smoker, charcoal grill, tongs, French knife, whisk, film wrap, serrated slicer*

Remove the breasts from the duck (see page 316). Trim all fat and membrane from them.

Prepare the brine by combining the warm water, kosher salt, and sugar in a stainless-steel bowl. Add the cool water and stir to combine. Submerge the breasts in the brine for 2 minutes. Remove and pat dry with paper towels.

Lightly coat the bottom rack of a smoker (see page 320) with the vegetable oil. Place the duck breasts on the rack. Smoke for 2 1/2 hours.

Remove the breasts from the smoker and grill over a low charcoal or wood fire for 2 1/2 to 3 minutes on each side. (If grilling is not practical, roast the smoked duck breasts in a preheated 350-degree oven for 5 minutes.) Cool the breasts to room temperature, then refrigerate, uncovered, until thoroughly cool, about 1 hour.

Prepare the dressing by whisking together, in a stainless-steel bowl, the peanut oil and cider vinegar. Add the crushed pistachios, season with salt and pepper, and combine thoroughly. Cover with film wrap and refrigerate until needed.

Slice the breasts on an angle by tilting the cutting edge of a serrated slicer away from your hand and making the slices as thin (front to back) and as wide (top to bottom) as possible.

Cut the halved cantaloupe into ¼-inch slices.

Cut the slices of ham in half, to yield 12 semicircular slices.

Arrange equal portions of lettuce leaves on 4 chilled plates. Place 3 half slices of ham on top of the lettuce. Portion melon slices over the ham. Arrange the duck slices over the melon. Dress each plate with ¼ cup of the chilled dressing and serve.

The Chef's Touch

In this recipe, our variation on an old theme, we have the subtle smoke-flavored duck riding on the sweetness of the melon, countered by the saltiness of the country ham, which, in turn, is set off by the elegance of the pistachio dressing.

Although we have used pistachios in this recipe, other nuts, such as cashews or macadamia nuts, would also work well with the flavors of the duck, melon, and country ham.

The country ham used at The Trellis is a salt-cured and hickory-smoked product. The assertive flavor of this ham requires that it be used in judicious amounts. In this particular recipe, it is essential that the ham be sliced very thin. As you will only need a small amount (2 ounces), it will probably be more practical for you to purchase fully cooked salt-cured ham already sliced thin from your local delicatessen or fancy food store.

What to do with the duck legs, you are asking yourself? Marinate them in red wine for three days and grill. Or, if you have doubled or tripled the recipe and have several pairs on hand, you might want to cure them (see page 105).

We first served this appetizer at The Trellis in May 1981, for our premier Virginia vintners' barrel tasting. That evening, we paired the duck, melon, and ham with an openly fruity 1980 Ingelside Vineyards seyval blanc. It proved an agreeable match.

Asparagus with Brown Butter and Parmesan Cheese on Pistachio Fettuccine

Serves 4

³/₄ pound pistachios, shelled and skinned

1³/₄ cups all-purpose flour

2 eggs

1 egg yolk

1 tablespoon olive oil

1 teaspoon salt

¹/₄ cup cornmeal

³/₄ pound fresh asparagus

12 tablespoons unsalted butter, softened

1 tablespoon water

Salt and pepper to season

1 teaspoon fresh lemon juice

¹/₂ cup freshly grated Parmesan cheese

EQUIPMENT: *Cutting board, French knife, food processor, measuring cup, rubber spatula, fork, film wrap, pasta machine, baking sheet, parchment paper, vegetable peeler, two 5-quart saucepans, measuring spoons, two stainless-steel bowls, two non-stick sauté pans, colander, tongs*

Lightly crush and reserve a third of the pistachios. Process the remaining pistachios in a food processor fitted with a metal blade, adding 1¹/₂ cups flour, ¹/₂ cup at a time. Pulse until all the pistachios are ground and incorporated into the flour, about 4 minutes.

Prepare the pasta dough by placing the pistachio flour on a clean, dry cutting board or similar work surface. Make a well in the center and add the eggs, egg yolk, olive oil, and salt. Using a fork, combine the eggs, olive oil, and salt. When thoroughly mixed, begin to work the flour into the center, a small amount at a time. When enough flour has been added so that you can handle the dough, begin kneading by hand. Knead the dough by hand until all the flour has been incorporated, about 10 minutes. Cover the dough with film wrap and allow to relax at room temperature for 1 hour.

Cut the pasta dough into 4 equal portions. Roll and knead each portion of dough through a pasta machine, using the extra ¹/₄ cup flour as necessary to prevent the dough from becoming tacky. Cut the sheets of dough into fettuccine (see page 315). To prevent sticking, toss the cut pasta with the cornmeal, then place the pasta portions on a baking sheet lined with parchment paper. Cover the sheet tightly with film wrap and refrigerate until needed.

Snap the woody stem off each stalk of asparagus and peel the asparagus. Blanch the asparagus in 3 quarts boiling salted water until it is tender but still crisp, about 45 seconds. Transfer immediately to a bowl of ice water. When the asparagus is cool, drain and cut into 1¼-inch pieces. Cover with film wrap and refrigerate until needed.

Heat 2 tablespoons butter and 1 tablespoon water in a non-stick sauté pan over medium heat. When the butter is hot, add the asparagus, season with salt and pepper, and sauté for 5 minutes.

While the asparagus is cooking, place a non-stick sauté pan over medium high heat. When the pan is very hot, add 8 tablespoons butter and allow the butter to brown evenly.

While the butter is browning and the asparagus is heating, cook the pasta (see page 315) in boiling salted water for 30 to 45 seconds, depending on the thickness and the preferred degree of doneness. Drain the pasta in a colander, return to the pan, and toss with the remaining 2 tablespoons butter.

Place equal portions of the pasta on 4 warm plates. Divide the hot asparagus over the pasta. Add the lemon juice to the brown butter, shaking the pan vigorously so that the butter does not foam over the sides of the pan. Carefully pour equal amounts of the brown butter over each portion of pasta. Sprinkle Parmesan cheese and the reserved crushed pistachios over the top of each portion and serve immediately.

The Chef's Touch

The pistachios in this recipe can be replaced by a number of other nuts. Pecans, almonds, skinned hazelnuts, or walnuts would make excellent substitutes. Use 1½ cups of the type of nut you choose; crush and reserve one third for the topping and process the remainder in the food processor with the flour as described.

Although asparagus frustrates many food and wine pairing experts, I have no inhibitions about suggesting a 1985 Trefethen white riesling to enhance the specific flavors in this dish.

Marinated Soft-shell Crabs with Zucchini and Sweet Peppers

Serves 8

8 live jumbo soft-shell crabs
2 tablespoons fresh lemon juice
   Salt and pepper to season
3 medium red bell peppers,
   seeded and cut into thin,
   1¼-inch-long strips
1 cup olive oil
6 tablespoons white vinegar
6 tablespoons dry white wine
1 scallion, trimmed and minced

1 small jalapeño pepper, roasted,
   seeded, and minced (see
   page 314)
½ teaspoon chopped fresh basil
½ teaspoon chopped fresh dill
½ teaspoon chopped fresh
   tarragon
½ teaspoon chopped fresh thyme
1 teaspoon minced garlic
2 pounds zucchini, lightly peeled

EQUIPMENT: *Paring knife, cutting board, measuring spoons, baking sheet with sides, film wrap, tongs, French knife, two stainless-steel bowls, measuring cup, whisk, charcoal grill, flat plastic container*

Dress the crabs (see page 316). Sprinkle the lemon juice over the crabs and season with salt and pepper. Place the crabs on a sided baking sheet lined with film wrap. Cover the sheet tightly with film wrap and refrigerate until needed.

Mince enough of the red pepper strips to yield 1 tablespoon. Cover the remaining red pepper strips with film wrap and refrigerate until needed. Prepare the dressing by whisking together, in a stainless-steel bowl, the olive oil, vinegar, wine, minced red pepper, scallion, jalapeño, herbs, and garlic. Season with salt and pepper and combine thoroughly. Cover with film wrap and refrigerate until needed.

Season the crabs with salt and pepper. Grill the crabs over a medium hot charcoal or wood fire for 1½ minutes on each side, shell side first. Transfer the crabs to a flat plastic, ceramic, or stainless-steel container (do not use aluminum). Pour 1 cup of the dressing over the still-warm crabs. Cover with film wrap and marinate the crabs in the refrigerator for 3 hours.

Cut the zucchini into 2½-inch-long sections. Cut each section into ¼-inch-thick planks, cutting only the smooth-textured part of the squash and not the seeded center section (discard the center). Cut each plank into long, thin strips.

Combine the zucchini and red pepper strips in a stainless-steel bowl. Season with salt and pepper and combine thoroughly with the remaining dressing. Place equal portions of the dressed zucchini and pepper strips on 8 chilled luncheon plates. Place a crab in the center of each plate and serve immediately.

The Chef's Touch

The availability of fresh soft-shell crabs in early spring is very unpredictable. For that reason, we never list them on our printed spring menu, choosing instead to feature them as specials.

We purchase only live soft-shell crabs for use at The Trellis, as this ensures a high-quality product. Various agencies are heralding the virtues and availability of frozen soft-shell crabs, trying to overcome the handicap of the relatively short season in which soft-shell crabs are available. Blue crabs become soft-shell crabs periodically when they shed their hard shell. Since this only happens when the temperature of the water reaches about 70 degrees or more, their season is usually from May through August.

For this recipe any size soft-shell crab may be used. We prefer the larger, meatier "jumbos," which measure out at about 5 inches from point to point, rather than the smaller "mediums," "hotels," or "primes," which measure from 3½ to 5 inches.

This recipe is derived from *escabeche*, the Spanish method of cooking fish (sometimes poultry), then marinating it in wine or vinegar. This is not to be confused with *seviche*, which is the marination of raw foods to "cook" them. In both cases the foods are served chilled or at room temperature.

One small jalapeño pepper may not give the heat intensity some people yearn for; so if you dare, you can add one more pepper to the dressing.

The optimum marination time for the crabs is between three and five hours. Longer marination will over-"cook" them, resulting in a less than desirable texture as well as an overly "twangy" flavor.

The sleek, dry Shenandoah Vineyards 1984 vidal blanc paired with this dish works wonders in controlling the slightly sharp flavor of the marinated crabs.

Chilled Lump Backfin Crabmeat on Sun-dried Tomato Fettuccine and Chive Fettuccine

Serves 8

12 pieces sun-dried tomato, packed
  in olive oil
4 medium tomatoes, peeled,
  seeded, and cut into ³/₈-inch
  pieces (see page 316)
2 tablespoons water
2 cups Trellis Vinaigrette (see
  page 311)
  Salt and pepper to season

2³/₄ cups all-purpose flour
2 eggs
1 teaspoon salt
1 egg yolk
4 tablespons chopped fresh chives
1 teaspoon olive oil
¹/₂ cup cornmeal
1 pound lump backfin crabmeat,
  well picked of shell

EQUIPMENT: *Paper towels, cutting board, paring knife, french knife, 5-quart saucepan, tongs, 2¹/₂ quart saucepan, measuring cup, measuring spoons, food processor, medium-gauge strainer, rubber spatula, film wrap, two stainless-steel bowls, whisk, fork, pasta machine, two baking sheets, parchment paper, colander*

Drain 4 pieces sun-dried tomato on paper towels. Mince, cover with film wrap, and refrigerate until needed.

Heat the remaining sun-dried tomatoes with ³/₄ cup of the chopped tomatoes and 2 tablespoons water in a 2¹/₂ quart saucepan over medium heat. Cook slowly for 15 minutes, stirring occasionally. Remove the saucepan from the heat. Cool at room temperature for 15 minutes. Purée the cooled mixture in a food processor fitted with a metal blade. Using a rubber spatula, force the purée through a medium strainer (this should yield 6 tablespoons purée). Set aside.

In a stainless-steel bowl, whisk together the Trellis vinaigrette and 2 tablespoons of the puréed tomato mixture. Adjust the seasoning with salt and pepper and combine thoroughly. Cover with film wrap and refrigerate until needed.

Place 1¹/₄ cups of the flour on a clean, dry cutting board or similar work surface. Make a well in the center and add 1 egg, the remaining tomato purée, and ¹/₂ teaspoon salt. Using a fork, combine the egg, tomato, and salt. When thoroughly mixed, begin to work the flour into the center, a small amount at a time. When enough flour has been added that you can handle the dough, begin kneading by hand. Knead the dough by hand until all the flour has been incorporated, about 10 minutes. Cover the dough with film wrap and allow to relax at room temperature for 1 hour.

Using the above method, prepare the chive fettuccine. Make a well in the center of 1¼ cups flour. Add 1 egg, 1 egg yolk, 2 tablespoons chopped chives, 1 teaspoon olive oil, and ½ teaspoon salt. Proceed as above. Cover the dough with film wrap and allow to relax for 1 hour.

Cut each flavored pasta dough into 8 equal portions. Roll and knead each portion of dough through the pasta machine, using the extra ¼ cup flour as necessary to prevent the dough from becoming tacky. Be certain to roll the sheets of dough into equal thickness as they will be cooked together. Cut the sheets of dough into fettuccine (see page 315). To prevent sticking, toss the cut pasta with the cornmeal, then place the cut pasta portions on a baking sheet lined with parchment paper. Cover the sheet tightly with film wrap and refrigerate until needed.

Cook the pasta (see page 315) in 3 quarts boiling salted water for 30 to 45 seconds, depending on the thickness of the pasta and the desired degree of doneness. Drain the cooked pasta in a colander. Submerge the drained pasta in a large bowl of ice water for 30 to 45 seconds. When the pasta has cooled, drain thoroughly. Place in a large stainless-steel bowl and toss with 1 cup of the dressing. Cover the bowl with film wrap and refrigerate (up to 24 hours) until ready to serve.

Portion the dressed pasta onto 8 chilled 9- or 10-inch soup/pasta plates. Divide the remaining chopped tomatoes over the top and in the center of the pasta. Portion the crabmeat over the tomatoes. Sprinkle the minced sun-dried tomatoes and remaining chives over the crabmeat. Dress each portion with 2 tablespoons dressing and serve.

The Chef's Touch

Sun-dried tomatoes can be purchased in specialty food stores. They are usually packed in olive oil, and sold either by weight or by the piece. The intensity of their flavor, without acidity, makes them a special component of this recipe.

Cooked lump backfin crabmeat is available in the fresh seafood department of most good supermarkets on the Eastern seaboard. Although available year-round, the best quality crabmeat is found from April through late October.

As an accompaniment, a cool glass of 1983 Cakebread Cellars chardonnay would be difficult to surpass.

Blue Moon Gorgonzola
with Walnuts and Cream
on Roasted Corn Fettuccine

Serves 8

2 ears fresh corn, husks on
1¾ cups all-purpose flour
¾ cup masa harina (yellow corn flour)
2 eggs
1 egg yolk
1 tablespoon olive oil
1 teaspoon salt
½ cup cornmeal
2 cups heavy cream
1 cup walnut halves
2 tablespoons unsalted butter, softened
½ pound Blue Moon Gorgonzola, broken into ½-inch pieces

EQUIPMENT: *Two baking sheets (one with sides), measuring cup, cutting board, paring knife, French knife, food processor, measuring spoon, fork, pasta machine, parchment paper, film wrap, 2½-quart saucepan, ladle, medium-gauge strainer, double boiler, 5-quart saucepan, tongs, colander*

Preheat the oven to 400 degrees.

Pull away the corn husks without removing them from the cob. Remove the silk and discard. Rinse the corn and husks to dampen, then replace the husks. Place on a sided baking sheet with ¼ cup water. Roast in the preheated oven for 15 minutes. Remove from the oven and cool at room temperature for 15 minutes. Remove and discard the husks. Cut the kernels from the cob with a paring knife and finely chop by hand or in a food processor fitted with a metal blade.

Place 1½ cups all-purpose flour and the masa harina on a clean, dry cutting board or similar work surface. Make a well in the center, add the eggs, egg yolk, chopped corn, olive oil, and salt. Using a fork, combine the eggs, corn, olive oil, and salt. When thoroughly mixed, begin to work the flour into the center, a small amount at a time. When enough flour has been added that you can handle the dough, begin kneading by hand. Knead the dough by hand until all the flour has been incorporated, about 10 minutes. Cover the dough with film wrap and allow to relax at room temperature for 1 hour.

Cut the pasta dough into 8 equal portions. Roll and knead each portion of dough through a pasta machine, using the extra ¼ cup flour as necessary to prevent the dough from becoming tacky. Cut the sheets of dough into fettuccine (see page 315). To prevent sticking, toss the cut pasta with the cornmeal, then place the pasta portions on a baking sheet lined with parchment paper. Cover the sheet tightly with film wrap and refrigerate until needed.

Heat the cream in a 2½-quart saucepan over medium heat. When the cream begins to simmer, lower the heat so the cream will simmer slowly but not boil. Place a stainless-steel ladle in the saucepan and stir occasionally to keep the cream from foaming out of the pot. Simmer the cream until it is reduced by half, 45 to 50 minutes. Strain and keep warm in a double boiler.

Preheat the oven to 300 degrees.

While the cream is reducing, toast the walnut halves on a baking sheet in the preheated oven for 15 minutes. Set aside.

Cook the pasta (see page 315) in 3 quarts boiling salted water until tender but firm to the bite, 30 seconds to 1 minute. Pour the cooked pasta into a colander. Drain, return to the pan, and toss with the softened butter.

Place equal portions of pasta in eight 9- to 10-inch warm soup/pasta plates; divide the Gorgonzola over the pasta. Drizzle 2 tablespoons reduced cream over each portion and garnish with the toasted walnuts. Serve immediately.

The Chef's Touch

I do not use corn if fresh corn is not available. As a point of reference, however, the yield from 2 ears of fresh corn would be equivalent to ½ cup drained canned corn. The masa harina alone will give excellent corn flavor to the pasta.

The cheese is most easily broken into pieces when it is cold, but it should be at room temperature when it is placed on the pasta.

A crisp, dry 1986 Clos du Bois sauvignon blanc would go well with this style of pasta and cheese.

Smoked Catfish with Country Ham, Cucumbers, and Szechwan Peppercorn Vinaigrette

Serves

2 cups warm water
1 cup kosher salt
1/4 cup granulated sugar
2 cups cool water
8 skinless catfish fillets (4 ounces each)
1 tablespoon vegetable oil
1 cup peanut oil
2 tablespoons cider vinegar
1 teaspoon soy sauce

3/4 teaspoon brown Szechwan peppercorns, crushed
Salt and pepper to season
2 pounds cucumbers, peeled, halved lengthwise, and seeded
2 medium heads Bibb lettuce, washed and dried
1/2 pound country ham, cut into thin strips 1 1/4 inches by 1/8 inch

EQUIPMENT: *Two stainless-steel bowls, measuring spoons, measuring cup, baking sheet with sides, paper towels, "Little Chief" smoker, whisk, cutting board, vegetable peeler, French knife*

Prepare the brine for the catfish by placing 2 cups warm water in a stainless-steel bowl. Stir in the kosher salt and sugar until dissolved. Add 2 cups cool water and stir to combine. Submerge the fish fillets in the brine for 2 minutes. Remove from the brine and place on paper towels to drain.

Using a paper towel dipped in the vegetable oil, thoroughly wipe the smoker racks. Place the fish fillets on the racks and place the racks in the smoker. Smoke the fish for 3 hours, rotating the racks after 1 1/2 hours.

Preheat the oven to 250 degrees. Transfer the fish fillets from the smoker to a baking sheet. Place the baking sheet in the preheated oven for 6 minutes. Remove from the oven and refrigerate for 24 hours before serving.

In a stainless-steel bowl, whisk together the peanut oil, vinegar, soy sauce, and peppercorns. Adjust the seasoning with salt and pepper and combine thoroughly.

Slice each fish fillet at an angle, to obtain 4 to 6 slices.

Also at an angle, slice the cucumbers ⅛ inch thick.

Place 2 leaves of Bibb lettuce on each of 8 chilled plates. Divide the cucumber slices over the lettuce and sprinkle with 2 tablespoons of the dressing. Place a catfish fillet in the center of each plate, fanning out the slices. Sprinkle the ham strips over the catfish and serve.

The Chef's Touch

If catfish is not available, use another lean, delicate white fish, such as cod, flounder, or lake whitefish.

The smoking time may vary slightly from that stated in the recipe. In any case, the fish should be removed from the smoker when it has an attractive and uniform golden color. The fish will become unattractively brown if oversmoked.

The country ham of choice at The Trellis is purchased from the Edwards family in Surry, Virginia (see page 324). It is an excellent quality salt-cured ham which rivals the best of the so-called Smithfield-type hams. If desired, you may wish to use a cured ham local to your region or omit it entirely.

Brown Szechwan peppercorns may be purchased in gourmet food stores or Oriental markets. They have a wonderfully mild, spicy, and peppery flavor.

Consider an additional garnish of sliced scallions or whole chives placed directly over the sliced smoked fish.

The snappy finish of a 1984 Carneros Creek chardonnay would be the perfect foil for the smoky-flavored catfish and the spicy vinaigrette.

Shiitake Mushroom Pâté

Serves 8

2 pounds shiitake mushrooms	1 teaspoon chopped fresh
2 tablespoons clarified butter	tarragon (or 1/2 teaspoon dried)
(see page 312)	1 teaspoon minced garlic
1 medium onion, diced fine	1/2 pound cream cheese, softened
Salt and pepper to season	3 eggs
3 tablespoons brandy	1/4 cup chopped walnuts
1 cup dry white wine	Toasted Walnut Bread
1 10-ounce bag fresh spinach,	(see page 239)
washed, stemmed, and chopped	
(about 2 1/2 cups, tightly packed,	
after chopping)	

EQUIPMENT: *Cutting board, paring knife, French knife, food processor, measuring spoons, measuring cup, 5-quart saucepan, wooden spoon, stainless-steel bowl, rubber spatula, colander, pastry brush, 9 × 5 × 3-inch loaf pan, parchment paper, aluminum foil, 2 1/2-inch-deep roasting pan, instant-read test thermometer, baking sheet with sides, film wrap, serrated slicer*

Trim the dry, tough areas from the base of the mushroom stems. Remove the stems from the caps. Finely chop the caps and stems (this may be done in a food processor).

Heat 1 tablespoon clarified butter in a 5-quart saucepan over medium heat. When the butter is hot, add the diced onion. Season lightly with salt and pepper and sauté for 2 minutes. Add the chopped mushrooms and sauté for 3 to 4 minutes. Add the brandy and simmer for 2 minutes. Then add the white wine and simmer for 12 to 15 minutes, stirring frequently.

Add the spinach, tarragon, and garlic to the mushroom mixture and cook for an additional 3 minutes. Remove from the heat and transfer the mixture to a stainless-steel bowl. Cool at room temperature for 15 minutes, then refrigerate until the mixture is cold, about 30 to 40 minutes.

When the mixture is cold, transfer to a colander to drain off any excess liquid. Return the drained mushrooms to the stainless-steel bowl.

In a food processor fitted with a metal blade, process the cream cheese and eggs to a smooth paste.

Fold the cream cheese paste and chopped walnuts into the cold mushroom mixture. Adjust the seasoning with salt and pepper.

Preheat the oven to 350 degrees.

Lightly coat a 9-by-5-by-3-inch loaf pan with clarified butter, line the pan with parchment paper, and coat the parchment paper with clarified butter.

Add the mushroom mixture to the loaf pan and spread evenly with a spatula. Cover the top of the pan with aluminum foil. Place the loaf pan in a roasting pan half filled with hot water. Place in the preheated oven and bake until the internal temperature reaches 160 degrees, about 1½ hours.

Remove the loaf pan from the roasting pan. Allow the pâté to cool at room temperature for 30 minutes before removing the aluminum foil. Invert the pâté onto a baking sheet covered with film wrap. Remove the loaf pan and parchment paper. Cover the pâté with film wrap and refrigerate for 12 hours before serving.

Slice the chilled pâté and serve 1 to 2 slices per person with slices of warm Toasted Walnut Bread.

The Chef's Touch

The growing of shiitake mushrooms has become a thriving enterprise in Virginia. We are fortunate to have several growers that come directly to us to sell their harvests. The size and the quality vary from month to month, but availability is year-round. Among the best of these growers are Steve and Hiromi Turnage of Weaving Run Mushrooms in Hague, Virginia.

Shiitake mushrooms are also now available year-round throughout the country. If you are not able to find shiitakes you may replace all or a portion of the required 2 pounds shiitakes with domestic mushrooms. If you use domestic mushrooms, be certain to thoroughly drain any excess liquid from the cooked mushrooms.

Dried shiitake mushrooms or any other variety of dried wild mushrooms may be used singly or in combination for this recipe. To rehydrate 8 ounces dried wild mushrooms, soak them in 16 cups warm water for one hour. Remove the mushrooms from the water and drain thoroughly. If dried wild mushrooms are used, be certain to thoroughly drain any excess liquid from the cooked mushrooms.

The pâté must be baked to an internal temperature of 160 degrees. An instant-read test thermometer (see page 322) is a necessary piece of equipment to determine the proper temperature.

If you serve this appetizer in late November, I would suggest a slightly chilled beaujolais-nouveau. This wine, as both legend and fact state, must be consumed very soon after it is released in the middle of November. The 1986 Georges DuBoeuf nouveau was particularly good, and I enjoyed several glasses when the wine was at its peak.

Fresh Herb Tagliatelle with Oranges, Red Onions, and Black Pepper Butter

Serves 8

1 cup washed and dried fresh spinach leaves, tightly packed
¹/₄ cup fresh basil leaves, tightly packed
¹/₄ cup fresh dill, tightly packed
¹/₄ cup fresh tarragon leaves, tightly packed
¹/₄ cup fresh thyme leaves, tightly packed
3¹/₄ cups all-purpose flour
3 large eggs
1 tablespoon olive oil
1 teaspoon salt

¹/₂ pound unsalted butter, softened
6 tablespoons minced shallots
Salt and pepper to season
³/₄ cup dry white wine
1 tablespoon cracked black peppercorns
¹/₂ cup cornmeal
1 cup pecan halves
¹/₂ cup finely diced red onion
12 navel oranges, peeled and cut into sections
¹/₂ cup freshly grated Parmesan cheese

EQUIPMENT: *Cutting board, French knife, measuring cup, measuring spoons, fork, film wrap, pasta machine, two baking sheets with sides, parchment paper, non-stick sauté pan, stainless-steel bowl, serrated slicer, paring knife, 5-quart saucepan, tongs, colander*

Finely chop the spinach and herbs by hand or in a food processor fitted with a metal blade.

Place 3 cups flour on a clean, dry cutting board or similar work surface. Make a well in the center, add the eggs, olive oil, chopped spinach and herbs, and salt. Using a fork, combine the eggs, oil, spinach, herbs, and salt. When thoroughly mixed, begin to work the flour into the center, a small amount at a time. When enough flour has been added so that you can handle the dough, begin kneading by hand. Knead the dough by hand until all the flour has been incorporated, about 10 minutes. Cover the dough with film wrap and allow to relax at room temperature for 1 hour.

While the pasta dough is relaxing, prepare the black pepper butter. Heat 1 tablespoon butter in a non-stick sauté pan over medium heat.

When the butter is hot, add the minced shallots, season with salt and pepper, and sauté for 1 minute. Add the wine and bring to a simmer, lower the heat, and simmer until the pan is almost dry, about 15 minutes. Remove the pan from the heat, transfer the reduction to a stainless-steel bowl, and allow to cool. When the mixture is cool, combine with the remaining butter and cracked black peppercorns. Cover the black pepper butter with film wrap and hold at room temperature until ready to use.

Cut the dough into 8 equal portions. Roll and knead each portion of dough through the pasta machine, using the extra ¼ cup flour as necessary to prevent the dough from becoming tacky. Cut the dough into tagliatelle (see page 315). To prevent sticking, toss the cut pasta with cornmeal, then place the pasta portions on a baking sheet lined with parchment paper. Cover the sheet tightly with film wrap and refrigerate.

Preheat the oven to 300 degrees.

Toast the pecans on a baking sheet in the preheated oven for 15 minutes. Remove from the oven and keep at room temperature until needed.

Melt 6 tablespoons black pepper butter in a non-stick sauté pan over medium heat. When the butter is hot, add the red onion and sauté for 30 to 45 seconds. Adjust the heat to low and add the orange sections and an additional 6 tablespoons black pepper butter. Heat the mixture until it is just warm and adjust the seasoning with salt and pepper. Keep warm.

Cook the pasta (see page 315) in 3 quarts boiling salted water until tender but firm to the bite, 30 seconds to 1 minute. Drain the cooked pasta in a colander, return to the pan, and toss with the remaining black pepper butter.

Place equal portions of the pasta on each of 8 warm plates. Divide the orange and red onion mixture over the pasta. Sprinkle with the Parmesan cheese and toasted pecans. Serve immediately.

The Chef's Touch

A serrated slicer or a very sharp paring knife should be used to peel the oranges. Cut away the skin and the white membrane (pith) under the skin. Once the orange is peeled, use a paring knife to remove the sections by cutting along inside the membrane of each section down to the core.

As an excellent accompaniment to this pasta appetizer, I would choose a light-bodied and fruity zinfandel, such as the Joseph Phelps 1986 bottling.

Sautéed Duck Livers with Apples, Turnips, and Caramelized Onions

Serves 4

1 pound duck livers
1 cup whole milk
2 tablespoons clarified butter
  (see page 312)
2 medium onions, sliced thin
  Salt and pepper to season
³/₄ cup water

1 small turnip, cut into thin
  strips
¹/₂ tablepoon fresh lemon juice
1 Red Delicious apple
1 cup heavy cream
¹/₂ cup all-purpose flour

EQUIPMENT: *Stainless-steel bowl, film wrap, cutting board, paring knife, French knife, measuring spoons, measuring cup, two non-stick sauté pans, 2¹/₂-quart saucepan, medium-gauge strainer, tongs, rubber spatula, 9-inch pie pan*

Clean the duck livers, removing all fat and membrane. Place the livers in a stainless-steel bowl and cover with the milk. Cover the bowl with film wrap and refrigerate.

Heat 1 tablespoon clarified butter in a non-stick sauté pan over medium heat. When the butter is hot, add the onions and season with salt and pepper. Sauté the onions until they are evenly browned, adding 1 to 2 tablespoons water at a time to wash down the accumulated caramel. (This should be done 4 to 6 times during the cooking.) Stir frequently while the onions are browning. This process should take about 30 to 35 minutes. The caramelized onions may be cooled and refrigerated for later use, or kept warm while you complete the recipe.

Blanch the turnip strips in boiling salted water for 30 to 40 seconds. Transfer to ice water and let cool. Remove from the water and drain thoroughly.

Acidulate 2 cups water with 1¹/₂ teaspoons lemon juice. Core, quarter, and slice the unpeeled apple, placing the slices in the acidulated water as you go along.

Heat the cream in a non-stick sauté pan over medium heat. When the cream begins to simmer, lower the heat so the cream continues to simmer (do not boil!) for 10 minutes.

While the cream is simmering, remove the duck livers from the milk and drain well. Season with salt and pepper and dredge in all-purpose flour. Shake off any excess flour.

Heat the remaining tablespoon of clarified butter in a non-stick sauté pan over medium heat. When hot, add the livers. Sauté until golden brown, 5 minutes. Drain the apple slices in a colander, rinse under cold running water, and shake dry. Add the apple slices and turnip strips to the livers and adjust the seasoning. Add the cream and heat until the mixture is warm.

Divide the caramelized onions onto 4 warm plates. Spoon the warm duck liver mixture over the onions and serve immediately.

The Chef's Touch

Do not hesitate to substitute chicken livers in this recipe. Duck livers certainly are more interesting in flavor but can be difficult to locate. Given the choice, I would opt for fresh chicken livers over frozen duck livers.

For a color variation consider using half a Red Delicious apple and half a Granny Smith apple.

The sweet flavor of the caramelized onions and the slightly tart apple work well with the slight bitterness of the turnip and the subtle-flavored, silky-textured reduced cream. I have also served this taste experience as an entrée accompaniment, using grilled veal medallions or a grilled chicken paillard.

Consider serving the duck liver mixture in warm puff pastry rectangles. It could also be served in warm brioche (see page 229) or with Toasted Walnut Bread (see page 239).

A soft and mature California merlot complements the complexity of flavors in this recipe. I suggest a 1983 Clos Du Val.

Crispy Potato Cakes with Irish Smoked Salmon, Leeks, and Cream

Serves 6

1 large leek, white part only,
  cleaned and cut into thin strips
  1¹/₄ inches long
3 cups heavy cream
  Salt and pepper to season
6 5-ounce Crispy Potato Cakes
  (see page 233)

1 cup clarified butter (see
  page 312)
¹/₄ pound smoked salmon, cut into
  ¹/₄-inch cubes

EQUIPMENT: *5-quart saucepan, tongs or slotted spoon, two stainless-steel bowls, cutting board, French knife, two 2¹/₂-quart saucepans, medium-gauge strainer, paring knife, mandolin, whisk, two baking sheets with sides, film wrap, stainless-steel ladle, two non-stick sauté pans (one large), rubber spatula, metal spatula*

Blanch the leek strips in boiling salted water until tender but still slightly crunchy, 45 seconds to 1 minute. Pour the leeks into a strainer and place the strainer in ice water. When the leeks are cold, drain thoroughly, cover with film wrap, and refrigerate until needed.

Heat the cream in a 2¹/₂-quart saucepan over medium heat. Season lightly with salt and pepper. When the cream begins to simmer, lower the heat so the cream will continue to simmer slowly, but not boil. Place a stainless-steel ladle in the saucepan with the cream and occasionally stir the cream to keep it from foaming out of the saucepan. Simmer until it has reduced by half, about 45 to 50 minutes.

Preheat the oven to 350 degrees.

When the cream is almost ready, begin to fry the potato cakes. Heat ¹/₂ cup clarified butter in a large non-stick sauté pan over medium high heat. When the butter is hot, fry 3 potato cakes until evenly golden brown, 3¹/₂ to 4 minutes on each side. Transfer the fried cakes to a baking sheet and hold at room temperature. Discard any butter remaining in the pan, wipe dry, and repeat the cooking procedure with the remaining 3 cakes. When all the cakes have been fried, place the baking sheet in the preheated oven for 10 minutes.

Strain the reduced cream into a separate non-stick sauté pan. Add the leeks and smoked salmon and bring to a simmer. When the potato cakes are hot, ladle equal portions of the cream mixture onto each of 6 warm plates. Place a hot cake in the center of each and serve immediately.

The Chef's Touch

To clean the leek properly, split the trimmed leek in half lengthwise, from end to end. Hold each half of the leek under cold running water, spreading the sections apart and allowing the water to run through, thoroughly removing any dirt particles.

By themselves, the potato cakes are, quite simply, delicious. They are also excellent when served with sour cream and golden caviar; with apples, country ham, and Tillamook Cheddar; or with sautéed wild mushrooms and cream.

Serve with a 1985 Sonoma-Cutrer, Russian River, chardonnay.

SOUPS

Asparagus and Shiitake Mushroom Soup

Serves 8

1 pound fresh asparagus
1/2 pound shiitake mushrooms
1 tablespoon vegetable oil
1 tablespoon water
4 stalks celery, chopped
2 medium leeks, white part only, chopped

1 medium onion, chopped
    Salt and pepper to season
6 cups chicken stock (see page 305)
7 tablespoons unsalted butter
3/4 cup all-purpose flour
1 cup heavy cream

EQUIPMENT: *Paring knife, vegetable peeler, cutting board, French knife, film wrap, 5-quart saucepan, two 2¹/₂-quart saucepans, measuring cup, measuring spoons, wooden spoon, two whisks, medium-gauge strainer, rubber spatula, food processor, non-stick sauté pan*

Snap the woody stem off each stalk of asparagus, and lightly peel half the number of stalks. Chop the ends and the remaining unpeeled asparagus into ¹/₄-inch pieces. Cover with film wrap and refrigerate until needed. Blanch the peeled asparagus in 3 quarts boiling salted water. Do not overcook; the asparagus should be cooked yet remain crisp. Transfer the blanched asparagus to ice water. When cool, cut into ³/₄-inch pieces. Cover with film wrap and refrigerate until needed.

Remove and chop the mushroom stems. Slice and reserve the caps.

Heat the vegetable oil and water in a 2¹/₂-quart saucepan over medium heat. When hot, add the chopped asparagus, mushroom stems, celery, leeks, and onions. Season with salt and pepper and sauté until the onions are translucent, 5 to 7 minutes. Add the chicken stock and bring to a boil.

While the chicken stock is heating, melt the butter in a separate 2¹/₂-quart saucepan over low heat. Add the flour, to make a roux, and cook until the roux bubbles, 6 to 8 minutes. Stir constantly to prevent browning and scorching. Strain 4 cups boiling stock into the roux and whisk

29

vigorously until smooth. Add the remaining stock and vegetables. Whisk until well combined. Lower the heat and simmer for 10 minutes.

Remove the soup from the heat and purée in a food processor fitted with a metal blade. Strain into a 5-quart saucepan and return to low heat. Hold at a simmer for a few minutes while completing the recipe.

Heat the cream, sliced shiitakes, and asparagus pieces in a non-stick sauté pan over medium heat. When hot, add to the soup and adjust the seasoning. Serve immediately. (This soup may be held hot in a double boiler for up to one hour.)

The Chef's Touch

If the soup is prepared with young spring asparagus it is important that it not be cooked longer than the suggested time after thickening and puréeing; otherwise, the delicate flavor and color of the asparagus will be dissipated.

Cultivated white mushrooms can replace the shiitakes in this recipe. Use the same amount and prepare as directed for the shiitakes. For additional taste and texture, a cup of heated chopped, peeled, and seeded tomatoes may be added just before serving.

If not served within one hour, do not add the asparagus, shiitake mushrooms, and cream. Cool properly (see page 315), then cover and refrigerate for up to three days. To serve, reheat to a simmer over medium heat. Separately heat the asparagus and shiitake garnish with the cream in a non-stick pan. When hot, add to the simmering soup. Adjust the seasoning and serve immediately.

For a light spring meal consider a plate of mixed salad greens dressed with Trellis Vinaigrette (page 311), a bowl of Asparagus and Shiitake Mushroom Soup, toasted Black Pepper Brioche (page 228), and a glass of chardonnay.

Curried Apple and Onion Soup

Serves 8

5 tablespoons unsalted butter
1 large onion, sliced thin
   Salt and pepper to season
5¹/₂ cups chicken stock (see
   page 305)
¹/₂ cup dry white wine
1 tablespoon vegetable oil
1 tablespoon water
1 large onion, chopped
8 stalks celery, chopped

2 medium leeks, white part only,
   chopped
1 tablespoon chopped fresh thyme
   (or 1 teaspoon dried)
2 small bay leaves
1 tablespoon curry powder
6 tablespoons all-purpose flour
1 tablespoon fresh lemon juice
4 tart green apples
1 cup heavy cream

EQUIPMENT: *Paring knife, cutting board, French knife, measuring spoons, large non-stick sauté pan, 5-quart saucepan, 2¹/₂-quart saucepan, measuring cup, wooden spoon, cheesecloth, string, whisk, medium-gauge strainer, rubber spatula, food processor, colander*

Melt 1 tablespoon butter in a non-stick sauté pan over medium heat. Add the sliced onion, season with salt and pepper, and sauté until the onions are golden brown, 25 to 30 minutes. Add 2¹/₂ cups chicken stock and the wine. Bring to a boil. Lower the heat and simmer very slowly for 15 minutes.

Heat the vegetable oil and water in a 5-quart saucepan over medium heat. When hot, add the chopped onion, celery, and leeks. Season with salt and pepper and sauté for 5 minutes. Add the remaining 3 cups chicken stock. Tie thyme and bay leaves in a small piece of cheesecloth and add to the stock and vegetables. Bring to a boil, lower the heat, and simmer for 25 to 30 minutes.

Melt the remaining 4 tablespoons butter in a 2¹/₂-quart saucepan over low heat. Add the curry powder and whisk to blend. Add the flour, to make a roux, and cook until the roux bubbles, 6 to 8 minutes. Stir constantly to prevent browning and scorching. Strain 2 cups simmering stock from the 5-quart saucepan into the roux. Whisk vigorously until smooth, then add to the remaining stock and chopped vegetables. Whisk until well combined. Bring to a boil, then reduce the heat and allow to simmer for 10 minutes.

Remove from the heat. Remove and discard the tied herbs. Purée the soup in a food processor fitted with a metal blade. Strain. Return to low heat in a 5-quart saucepan. Add the sliced onion and stock mixture. Hold at a simmer.

Acidulate 4 cups water with 1 tablespoon lemon juice. Peel, core, quarter, and slice the apples widthwise. Place in the acidulated water as sliced, to prevent discoloration. Heat the cream in a non-stick sauté pan over medium heat. Drain the sliced apples in a colander. Rinse under cold running water and shake dry. When the cream is warm, add the apples and heat until the apples are hot, 3 to 4 minutes (do not boil). Add to the soup, adjust the seasoning with salt and pepper, and serve immediately. (This soup may be held hot in a double boiler for up to one hour.)

The Chef's Touch

As curry powders will vary in intensity, depending upon the brand, you may want to increase or decrease the amount suggested in the recipe.

Granny Smith apples have the perfect taste and texture for use in this soup. Other apples or a combination of apples may also be utilized with excellent results. Try Winesaps, Staymans, or Gravensteins—all tart and widely available.

This soup is enhanced if it is refrigerated for twenty-four hours before use, allowing the flavors to develop fully. If you decide to do this, cool the soup properly (see page 315) before adding the cream and apples. Cover and refrigerate for twenty-four to forty-eight hours. When ready to serve, heat the soup to a simmer, then add the separately heated cream and apples.

Atlantic Sea Scallop Soup with Spinach and Leeks

Serves 8

4 cups heavy cream
  Salt and pepper to season
4 cups fish stock (see page 307)
1 pound sea scallops, side muscle removed and sliced ¼ inch thick
2 small leeks, white part only, cut into thin strips

5 tablespoons unsalted butter
½ cup all-purpose flour
2 cups loosely packed spinach leaves (about 2 ounces), stemmed, washed, and cut into very fine strips

EQUIPMENT: *Cutting board, French knife, 5-quart saucepan, two 2½-quart saucepans, slotted spoon, measuring cup, measuring spoons, stainless-steel ladle, medium-gauge strainer, baking sheet with sides, film wrap, whisk, rubber spatula, non-stick sauté pan*

Heat the heavy cream in a 5-quart saucepan over medium heat. Lightly season with salt and pepper. Place a ladle in the saucepan and occasionally stir the cream so that it does not foam over the sides of the saucepan. Lower the heat if necessary so that the cream barely simmers. Simmer until reduced by half, about 1 hour.

While the cream is reducing, bring the fish stock to a boil in a 2½-quart saucepan over medium heat. Lower the heat to simmer and add the scallop slices. Poach for 30 seconds, remove the scallops from the stock, and place on a baking sheet covered with film wrap. Refrigerate to cool rapidly.

Return the stock to a simmer. Blanch the leek strips for 45 seconds in the simmering stock. Transfer the blanched leeks to ice water. When cool, remove the leeks from the water, drain, and refrigerate. Maintain the stock at a simmer.

Melt the butter in a 2½-quart saucepan over low heat. Add the flour to make a roux and cook until the roux bubbles, 6 to 8 minutes. Stir

33

constantly to prevent browning and scorching. Add the simmering stock and whisk vigorously until smooth. Simmer for an additional 10 minutes, whisking occasionally. Remove from the heat and strain.

Strain the reduced cream and combine with the thickened stock. Season with salt and pepper. Return to low heat and hold at a low simmer.

Heat the scallops and leeks in 1 tablespoon water in a non-stick sauté pan over medium heat. When warm, season with salt and pepper and add to the soup. Pour equal portions of the soup into each of 8 warm soup plates and sprinkle equal amounts of the raw spinach strips over each. Serve immediately.

The Chef's Touch

I developed this soup for a luncheon served to 350 members of the American Institute of Wine and Food for their first National Conference on Gastronomy, held in Santa Barbara early in 1985. I remember that I was very nervous as we ladled the soup, knowing that my wife, Connie, was seated at the same table as Julia Child!

At The Trellis, we use the bones from red snapper, grouper, or halibut to make a light but flavorful fish stock. Flounder bones can be used but produce a significantly less flavorful stock. You may wish to make stock when good bones are available from your fish dealer. If so, freeze the stock in 1- or 2-quart plastic containers filled only three-quarters full, as the stock will expand during freezing.

This recipe can be used as a basis for a variety of other seafoods. Lump crab, shrimp, bay scallops, or lobster meat would work well with the textures and flavor of the cream soup enhanced by leeks and spinach.

Roasted Corn and Smoked Tomato Soup

Serves 8

2 medium tomatoes
12 ears fresh corn, white or
   yellow, husks on
1 tablespoon vegetable oil
1 tablespoon water
4 stalks celery, chopped

1 medium onion, chopped
   Salt and pepper to season
6 cups chicken stock (see
   page 305)
7 tablespoons unsalted butter
3/4 cup all-purpose flour

EQUIPMENT: *5-quart saucepan, slotted spoon, paring knife, parchment paper, ''Little Chief'' smoker, charcoal grill, tongs, baking sheet with sides, cutting board, French knife, 2¹/₂-quart saucepan, measuring cup, measuring spoons, whisk, medium-gauge strainer, rubber spatula, food processor, non-stick sauté pan*

Line the wire shelves of a ''Little Chief'' smoker (see page 320) with parchment paper. Peel and seed the tomatoes (see page 316). Place the tomato halves in the smoker and smoke for 2 hours, turning them after the first hour. Remove the tomatoes from the smoker and cut into ¹/₄-inch cubes. Refrigerate until needed.

Preheat the oven to 250 degrees.

Peel away the corn husks but do not separate from the cobs. Remove and discard the corn silk, and replace the husk around the corn. Roast the corn in the husk over a low charcoal or wood fire for 20 to 25 minutes, turning corn frequently and sprinkling with water to prevent burning. Remove from the charcoal fire and place on a baking sheet in the preheated oven for 15 minutes. Remove from the oven. When the corn is cool enough to handle, remove and discard the husks. Cut the corn kernels off the cob and reserve for later use.

Heat the vegetable oil and water in a 5-quart saucepan over medium heat. When hot, add the chopped celery and onion. Season with salt and pepper and sauté 5 minutes. Add half the corn kernels (about 2 cups) and sauté an additional 5 minutes. Add the chicken stock. Bring to a boil, lower the heat, and simmer for 15 minutes.

While the stock is simmering, prepare a roux by melting the butter in a 2½-quart saucepan over low heat. Add the flour and stir. Cook until the roux bubbles, 6 to 8 minutes. Stir constantly to prevent browning and scorching. Strain 4 cups simmering stock into the roux, whisking vigorously until smooth. Add this mixture to the 5-quart saucepan with the remaining stock and vegetables and whisk until well combined. Simmer for an additional 15 minutes.

Remove from the heat. Purée the soup in a food processor fitted with a metal blade. Strain. Adjust the seasoning with salt and pepper. Return to low heat and hold at a simmer.

Heat the smoked tomatoes and remaining roasted corn in a non-stick sauté pan over medium heat. When hot, add to the soup. Serve immediately. (This soup may be held hot in a double boiler for up to two hours.)

The Chef's Touch

There is no substitute for smoked tomatoes. The procedure and the apparatus necessary for smoking are simple. "Little Chief" smokers are perfect for low-volume professional use or for home use. Anyone can learn how to use one in a matter of minutes.

A low fire is essential to ensure a properly roasted ear of corn. Be careful not to scorch the corn when roasting it over a charcoal fire. I leave the husks on the corn to prevent it from burning. If roasting the corn over charcoal is not practical or convenient, then roast in a pre-heated 400-degree oven for a total of 20 to 25 minutes.

For a richer and more elegant soup, reduce 1 cup heavy cream over low heat for ½ hour. Add to the hot soup just before serving.

If the soup is not to be served within two hours, do not add the smoked tomatoes and remaining corn. Cool the soup properly (see page 315), then cover and refrigerate for up to three days. When reheating the soup, slowly bring to a simmer before adding the separately heated tomatoes and corn.

Chilled Stilton and Pear Soup

Serves 8

1 tablespoon vegetable oil	6 tablespoons unsalted butter
1 tablespoon water	¹/₂ cup all-purpose flour
2 stalks celery, chopped	³/₄ pound Monterey Jack cheese,
1 medium onion, chopped	grated
1 medium leek, white part only,	1 tablespoon fresh lemon juice
chopped	2 small pears, unpeeled
Salt and pepper to season	¹/₂ cup half-and-half
6 cups chicken stock (see	6 ounces Stilton cheese, broken
page 305)	into ¹/₂-inch pieces

EQUIPMENT: *Paring knife, cutting board, French knife, 5-quart saucepan, 2¹/₂-quart saucepan, wooden spoon, measuring cup, measuring spoons, whisk, hand grater, stainless-steel bowl, rubber spatula, medium-gauge strainer, colander*

Heat the vegetable oil and water in a 5-quart saucepan over medium heat. When hot, add the chopped celery, onion, and leek. Season with salt and pepper and sauté until the onions are translucent, 5 to 7 minutes. Add the chicken stock, bring to a boil, lower the heat, and simmer for 15 minutes.

While the stock is simmering, melt the butter in a 2¹/₂-quart saucepan over low heat. Add the flour, to make a roux, and cook until the roux bubbles, 6 to 8 minutes. Stir constantly to prevent browning and scorching. Strain 4 cups simmering stock into the roux. Whisk vigorously until smooth. Add to the 5-quart saucepan with the remaining stock and vegetables. Whisk until well combined. Simmer an additional 15 minutes.

Remove from the heat and whisk in the grated Monterey Jack cheese, 1 cup at a time. Strain the soup, then cool properly (see page 315).

Acidulate 4 cups water with 1 tablespoon lemon juice. Core and cut into medium dice the unpeeled pears and immediately place in the acidulated water.

Pour the diced pears into a colander, rinse under cold running water, drain well, and add to the soup with the half-and-half and Stilton cheese. Adjust the seasoning with salt and pepper. Refrigerate for 2 hours before serving.

The Chef's Touch

Trellis co-owner John Curtis returned from a summer in England praising a chilled Stilton soup he had eaten at the well-known London restaurant Tante Claire. I immediately set about trying to re-create the flavor John described as so delicious.

After much experimentation, we added the Trellis version to the menu. The diced pear garnish is a Trellis twist, added to balance the assertiveness of the Stilton.

This soup is best eaten the day of preparation, or within twenty-four hours. The texture of the soup can be changed by the acidity of the cheese. Although I try to use American-produced cheeses whenever possible, I find Stilton gives the best results with this particular recipe. One American blue-veined cheese that has worked well is the Blue Moon Gorgonzola. On the other hand, the delicious Maytag blue cheese breaks down the texture of the soup, making it much thinner than desired.

If you do not serve this soup the same day you prepare it, omit adding the diced pear until shortly before serving. If pears are unavailable, you may substitute a good sweet apple.

Chesapeake Bay Clam Chowder

Serves 12

18 chowder clams
2 quarts plus 1 tablespoon cold
   water
1 tablespoon vegetable oil
4 stalks celery, diced
2 medium leeks, white part only,
   diced

1 medium onion, diced
   Salt and pepper to season
2 pounds potatoes, peeled, diced,
   and covered with cold water
2 bay leaves
2 tablespoons chopped fresh
   thyme (or 2 teaspoons dried)

EQUIPMENT: *Paring knife, cutting board, French knife, 5-quart saucepan, medium-gauge strainer, measuring cup, film wrap, measuring spoons, wooden spoon, cheesecloth, string, stainless-steel bowl*

Wash and scrub the clams under cold running water. Place in a 5-quart saucepan and cover with 2 quarts cold water. Place the saucepan over medium heat. Bring the water to a boil, lower the heat, and simmer until the clams begin to open, about 20 minutes. Remove the saucepan from the heat. Strain and reserve 6 cups clam stock. Shuck the clams, removing and discarding the tough side muscle. Slice the clams into thin strips. Cover with film wrap and refrigerate until needed.

Heat the vegetable oil with 1 tablespoon water in a 5-quart saucepan over medium heat. When hot, add the diced celery, leeks, and onion. Season with salt and pepper and sauté 5 minutes.

Add the reserved clam stock to the sautéed vegetables.

Drain and rinse the diced potatoes under cold running water. Add the potatoes to the stock and vegetables and bring to a simmer over medium heat. Tie the bay leaves and thyme in a small piece of cheesecloth and add to the simmering chowder.

Simmer until the potatoes are cooked, about 30 minutes. Add the clams and simmer for 2 minutes. Remove from the heat. Discard the tied herbs. Adjust the seasoning with salt and pepper.

Cool the chowder properly (see page 315), then cover and refrigerate for 24 hours before serving.

Heat the chowder slowly over low heat, stirring frequently so that the potatoes do not stick to the bottom of the pot. When hot, adjust the seasoning and serve immediately.

The Chef's Touch

As a New Englander, I come by my passion for clam chowder honestly. At home we often made a meal out of chowder and clam cakes.

The style of chowder which we now serve at The Trellis has evolved over the last six years. The only person who never seems to be 100 percent pleased is my mother, who insists on adding 2 tablespoons of cream to her bowl. Luckily, our chowder can handle this indulgent addition!

Chowder clams (large quahogs) produce the best chowder because of their assertive flavor and texture. Do not overcook the clams or they will be tough. Cook them only long enough to open the shells. Add the sliced clams only as directed.

Geography has a great influence on the flavor and salt content of clams. New England quahogs have more salt flavor than Carolina clams. Therefore, always taste your clam stock before adding salt.

The flavor of the chowder improves under refrigeration. I recommend that the chowder be refrigerated for at least twenty-four hours before serving. It can be kept under refrigeration for as long as three to four days.

Butternut Squash and Apple Soup

Serves 8

1 tablespoon vegetable oil
1 tablespoon water
4 stalks celery, chopped
2 medium leeks, white part only, chopped
1 medium onion, chopped
Salt and pepper to season
3 pounds butternut squash, peeled, seeded, and cut into 1-inch cubes, about 8 cups (see page 317)

6 cups chicken stock (see page 305)
7 tablespoons unsalted butter
³/₄ cup all-purpose flour
1 tablespoon fresh lemon juice
2 Red Delicious apples, unpeeled
¹/₂ cup grated Gruyère cheese
1 cup half-and-half

EQUIPMENT: *Paring knife, vegetable peeler, cutting board, French knife, hand grater, 5-quart saucepan, 2¹/₂-quart saucepan, measuring cup, measuring spoons, wooden spoon, whisk, stainless-steel bowl, film wrap, medium-gauge strainer, rubber spatula, food processor, non-stick sauté pan, colander*

Heat the vegetable oil and water in a 5-quart saucepan over medium heat. When hot, add the chopped celery, leeks, and onion. Season with salt and pepper and sauté until the onions are translucent, 5 to 6 minutes. Add the butternut squash cubes and sauté 8 minutes. Add the chicken stock. Bring to a boil, then lower the heat and simmer for 40 minutes.

When the soup has simmered for 30 minutes, prepare a roux by melting the butter in a 2¹/₂-quart saucepan over low heat. Add the flour and cook until the roux bubbles, 6 to 8 minutes. Stir constantly to prevent browning and scorching. Strain 4 cups simmering stock into the roux. Whisk vigorously until smooth. Add this mixture to the 5-quart saucepan with the remaining stock and vegetables and whisk until well combined. Simmer over low heat for an additional 10 minutes.

While the soup is simmering, acidulate 1 quart cold water with 1 tablespoon lemon juice. Core, quarter, and slice the unpeeled apples widthwise into the acidulated water. Cover with film wrap and set aside until needed.

Remove the soup from the heat. Purée in a food processor fitted with a metal blade. Strain. Return the soup to medium heat. Bring to a simmer, then reduce heat to low. Whisk in the grated Gruyère cheese.

Drain the sliced apples in a colander, then rinse under cold running water. Shake dry. Heat the half-and-half in a non-stick sauté pan; when warm, add the sliced apples. Bring to a simmer, then add to the hot soup. Adjust the seasoning with salt and pepper and serve immediately. (This soup may be held hot in a double boiler for up to one hour.)

The Chef's Touch

The aroma, flavor, and texture contained in a bowl of this squash and apple soup should warm the coldest winter night. The Gruyère cheese gives the soup an additional flavor dimension as well as adding protein.

For variations on taste and color, several other varieties of winter squash are adaptable to this recipe. A total of 2½ pounds peeled and seeded squash is necessary to achieve the desired consistency. With butternut squash, 3 pounds unpeeled squash will yield 2½ pounds usable squash meat. If acorn squash is used, it will take about 6 pounds unpeeled squash to yield the necessary 2½ pounds usable squash meat. Pumpkin, hubbard, banana, and sweet dumpling squash are also excellent in this soup, used singly or in combination.

Gruyère cheese gives this soup an interesting taste. However, grated Swiss cheese may be easily substituted, or the cheese may be left out of the recipe altogether.

The apples are left unpeeled to add color and texture to the finished soup; a combination of apples such as Golden Delicious, Empire, and McIntosh would be a colorful and tasteful addition.

If the soup is not to be served within one hour, do not add the cheese, half-and-half, and sliced apples. Cool the soup properly (see page 315), then cover and refrigerate for up to three days. Reheat the soup to a simmer before whisking in the cheese and adding the separately heated cream and apples.

I would serve several slices of Toasted Walnut Bread (see page 239) with this soup. Two other excellent accompaniments are a thick slice of Gruyère cheese and a glass of fumé blanc—a meal designed to put winter-weary cooks in a positive frame of mind!

Wild Mushroom Soup

Serves 8

1 pound shiitake mushrooms or
   other available fresh wild
   mushrooms
6 cups chicken stock (see
   page 305)
1 tablespoon vegetable oil
1 tablespoon water
2 stalks celery, chopped
1 medium onion, chopped
1 medium carrot, chopped
1 medium leek, white part only,
   chopped

1 clove garlic, peeled and crushed
   Salt and pepper to season
6 tablespoons unsalted butter
1/2 cup all-purpose flour
1 tablespoon clarified butter
   (see page 312)
2 medium tomatoes, peeled,
   seeded, and chopped (see
   page 316)
1 cup heavy cream

EQUIPMENT: *Paring knife, vegetable peeler, cutting board, French knife, 5-quart saucepan, two 2¹/₂-quart saucepans, wooden spoon, measuring cup, measuring spoons, whisk, medium-gauge strainer, rubber spatula, food processor, large non-stick sauté pan*

Remove the stems from the mushrooms. Slice enough mushroom caps to make 3 cups. Reserve. Place the remaining caps and stems in a 2¹/₂-quart saucepan with the chicken stock. Bring to a boil, then lower the heat and simmer for 30 minutes.

While the stock is simmering, heat the vegetable oil and water in a 5-quart saucepan over medium heat. When hot, add the chopped celery, onion, carrot, and leek, along with the garlic. Season with salt and pepper and sauté until the onions are translucent, 5 to 8 minutes. Add the chicken and mushroom stock to the sautéed vegetables. Bring to a simmer.

In a 2¹/₂-quart saucepan, melt the butter on low heat. Add the flour, to make a roux, and cook until the roux bubbles, 6 to 8 minutes. Stir constantly to prevent browning and scorching. Strain 4 cups simmering stock into the roux. Whisk vigorously until smooth, then add to the large pot with the remaining stock and vegetables. Whisk until well combined. Simmer over low heat for 20 minutes.

Remove from the heat and purée in a food processor fitted with a metal blade. (Pass the soup through a strainer if a smoother texture is desired.)

Heat the clarified butter in a large non-stick sauté pan over medium heat. When hot, add the reserved 3 cups sliced mushrooms and sauté for 4 minutes. Add the tomatoes and cook for an additional 4 minutes. Season with salt and pepper. Add the cream. As soon as this mixture is hot (do not boil), add to the puréed soup. Adjust the seasoning with salt and pepper. Serve immediately. (This soup may be held hot in a double boiler for up to two hours.)

The Chef's Touch

Because of their wide availability on a year-round basis, shiitake mushrooms have become the fresh wild mushroom of choice at The Trellis. Many other varieties of fresh wild mushrooms are also available seasonally. Some of our favorites include: oyster tree, black trumpet, white trumpet, chicken-of-the-woods, morel, porcini, and chanterelle. When fresh varieties are not available, do not hesitate to use the dried variety, especially for a soup or stew. For this recipe, rehydrate 4 ounces dried wild mushrooms in 2 quarts warm water for one hour; drain well before using. If for some reason wild mushrooms, fresh or dried, are not available, an acceptable soup can be prepared by using 1 pound cultivated white mushrooms.

If the soup is not to be served within two hours, omit adding the sliced mushrooms, tomatoes, and cream. Cool the soup properly (see page 315), then cover and refrigerate for up to three days. When reheating the soup, bring to a simmer before adding the separately heated garnish of mushrooms, tomatoes, and cream.

Wild Rice and Smoked Sausage Soup

Serves 8

¹/₄ pound Minnesota wild rice
8 cups chicken stock (see
page 305)
¹/₂ pound smoked sausage, cut into
thin strips
1 tablespoon vegetable oil
3 tablespoons water

2 stalks celery, chopped
1 medium onion, chopped
Salt and pepper to season
6 tablespoons unsalted butter
¹/₂ cup all-purpose flour
2 scallions, trimmed and sliced

EQUIPMENT: *Paring knife, cutting board, French knife, three 2¹/₂-quart saucepans (one with lid), medium-gauge strainer, two stainless-steel bowls, measuring cup, measuring spoons, wooden spoon, whisk, rubber spatula, non-stick sauté pan*

In a covered 2¹/₂-quart saucepan, bring the wild rice and chicken stock to a simmer over medium high heat. Lower the heat and simmer for 30 minutes. Strain the stock and refrigerate the rice.

Reheat the stock to a simmer, then poach the sausage strips in the simmering stock for 5 minutes. Strain the stock and refrigerate the sausage. If necessary, add water to the stock to make 6 cups and reheat the stock to a boil.

Heat the vegetable oil and 1 tablespoon water in another saucepan over medium heat. When hot, add the chopped celery and onion and season with salt and pepper. Sauté for 5 minutes over medium heat. Add the boiling stock to the vegetables and keep at a simmer while preparing a roux.

Melt the butter in a 2¹/₂-quart saucepan over low heat, then add the flour to make the roux. Cook until the roux bubbles, 6 to 8 minutes. Stir constantly to prevent browning and scorching. Add the boiling stock and whisk vigorously until well combined. Simmer for 10 minutes. Strain. Return to low heat and hold at a simmer.

Heat the wild rice, sausage, and sliced scallions in a non-stick pan with 2 tablespoons water over medium high heat. When hot, add to the soup. Adjust the seasoning with salt and pepper. Serve immediately. (This soup may be held hot in a double boiler for up to one hour.)

The Chef's Touch

I use a smoked sausage from the Edwards family in Surry, Virginia (see page 324). It is an excellent smoked sausage, mild and fully cooked. Any high-quality *smoked* sausage may be used, giving your own regional flair to this soup.

The textural quality of this soup calls for Minnesota wild rice, not a mixture of converted rice and wild rice. Preparing wild rice according to our suggested cooking time will result in crunchy and nutty-tasting rice. If you prefer the rice with less texture, cook for 40 to 45 minutes rather than 30 minutes. By cooking the rice in the stock, the flavors of both rice and stock are reinforced.

If the soup is not to be served within one hour, do not add the rice, sausage, and scallions. Cool the soup properly (see page 315), then cover and refrigerate for up to three days. To reheat the soup, bring to a simmer before adding the separately heated wild rice, sausage, and scallions. Adjust the thickness of the soup with hot chicken stock if necessary.

Cheddar Cheese Soup

Serves 8

1 tablespoon vegetable oil
1 tablespoon water
4 stalks celery, sliced thin
2 medium carrots, sliced thin
1 medium onion, sliced thin
  Salt and pepper to season

6 cups chicken stock (see
  page 305)
7 tablespoons unsalted butter
$^3/_4$ cup all-purpose flour
$^3/_4$ pound Oregon Tillamook
  Cheddar cheese, grated

EQUIPMENT: *Paring knife, vegetable peeler, cutting board, French knife, 5-quart saucepan, two 2$^1/_2$-quart saucepans, measuring cup, measuring spoons, whisk, slotted spoon, rubber spatula*

Heat the vegetable oil and water in 5-quart saucepan over low heat. Add the sliced celery, carrots, and onion. Season with salt and pepper and sauté until the onions are translucent, 8 to 10 minutes. Remove the pot from the heat and hold at kitchen temperature.

Heat the chicken stock to a boil in a 2$^1/_2$-quart saucepan.

Melt the butter in another 2$^1/_2$-quart saucepan over low heat. Add the flour, to make a roux, and cook until the roux bubbles, 6 to 8 minutes. Stir constantly to prevent browning and scorching. Add the boiling stock and whisk vigorously until smooth. Bring to a boil, then lower the heat and allow to simmer for 15 minutes.

Remove the soup from the heat. Whisk in the grated cheese, 1 cup at a time. Add the sautéed vegetables, adjust the seasoning with salt and pepper, and serve immediately. (If desired, you may hold the soup in a double boiler for up to one hour before serving.)

The Chef's Touch

Cheese soups have always been among my favorites. Most of the variations I have encountered over the years combine a smooth Cheddar cheese with a crisp bacon garnish. The Trellis version is very textural, with lots of vegetables and a very distinctive flavor derived from using Oregon Tillamook Cheddar. It is firm, medium sharp, and almost orange in color. It is unequivocally the secret to this terrific soup. Other distinctive Cheddars could be used; however, our experience proves that the results will be less satisfactory.

When sautéing the sliced vegetables in this recipe, it is important not to overcook them or they will fall apart. However, they should be sufficiently cooked—slightly crisp, yet not hard to the bite.

This soup is at its best when served shortly after preparation. Cooking and reheating result in a grainy and unattractive texture.

Lentil and Smoked Sausage Soup

Serves 8

1 tablespoon vegetable oil
1 tablespoon water
2 stalks celery, diced
1 medium onion, diced
1 large carrot, diced
    Salt and pepper to season
8 cups chicken stock (see
    page 305)
1 pound dried brown lentils,
    washed and drained

1 tablespoon chopped fresh
    oregano (or 1 teaspoon dried)
1 tablespoon cracked black
    peppercorns
2 small bay leaves
1/2 pound smoked sausage, cut into
    small strips

EQUIPMENT: *Paring knife, vegetable peeler, cutting board, French knife, 5-quart saucepan, measuring cup, measuring spoons, cheesecloth, string, wooden spoon, food processor, rubber spatula, non-stick sauté pan*

Heat the vegetable oil and water in a 5-quart saucepan over medium heat. Add the diced vegetables, season with salt and pepper, and sauté until the onions are translucent, 4 to 5 minutes.

Add the chicken stock and lentils. Tie the oregano, peppercorns, and bay leaves in a small piece of cheesecloth and add to the stock and lentils. Bring to a boil. Lower the heat and simmer for 30 minutes. Stir the soup frequently while cooking to prevent sticking.

Remove the cheesecloth bundle and discard. Remove 2 cups lentils from the saucepan and purée in a food processor fitted with a metal blade. Return the purée to the saucepan with the soup. Add the sausage strips and simmer an additional 5 minutes.

Adjust the seasoning with salt and pepper and serve immediately. (If desired, the soup may be held in a double boiler for up to one hour.)

The Chef's Touch

Many dried beans and peas could easily be used in place of the brown lentils called for in this recipe. Additional cooking time may be necessary, and larger beans such as black turtle beans will need several hours of soaking before cooking.

As with most Trellis-style soups, the composition is very definite in this lentil soup. Both the beans and vegetables are obvious in appearance and texture. A more traditional preparation would be to purée the entire quantity of the soup. Prepared either way, this is a very hearty soup, one which will warm and nourish.

The smoked sausage used at The Trellis for this recipe is a fully cooked sausage from Surry County, Virginia. If a similar smoked sausage is not available, other varieties of sausage such as bratwurst or even frankfurters could be used.

If the soup is not to be served within one hour, do not add the sausage. Cool the soup properly (see page 315), then cover and refrigerate for up to three days. When reheating the soup, slowly bring to a simmer while separately heating the sausage strips in a non-stick pan with a very small amount of stock or water. When the sausage is hot, add to the simmering soup. Adjust the seasoning and serve.

Roasted Shallot and Bacon Soup

Serves 8

³/₄ *pound hickory-smoked slab*
   bacon
1 *pound shallots*
¹/₄ *cup olive oil*
   Salt and pepper to season
1 *tablespoon water*

2 *stalks celery, chopped*
1 *medium onion, chopped*
6 *cups chicken stock (see*
   page 305)
7 *tablespoons unsalted butter*
³/₄ *cup all-purpose flour*

EQUIPMENT: *Paring knife, cutting board, French knife, serrated slicer, two baking sheets with sides, paper towels, film wrap, slotted spoon, measuring cup, measuring spoons, two 2¹/₂-quart saucepans, wooden spoon, whisk, rubber spatula, food processor, medium-gauge strainer, non-stick sauté pan*

Preheat the oven to 325 degrees.

Trim the rind and excess fat from the bacon. Slice the bacon into strips, then cut the strips into ³/₈-inch dice. Place the diced bacon on a baking sheet and cook in the preheated oven until well browned, about 30 minutes. Transfer the bacon from the baking sheet with a slotted spoon onto paper towels to drain. Reserve 2 tablespoons bacon fat. Lower the oven temperature to 275 degrees.

Cut the whole shallots into quarters (do not peel). Place the shallots on a baking sheet. Sprinkle with the olive oil and season with salt and pepper. Place the baking sheet in the 275-degree oven and roast the shallots for 20 minutes. Remove the pan from the oven and cool for a few moments. Trim and then peel the shallots. Cut half the shallots into ¹/₄-inch dice.

Heat the reserved bacon fat with 1 tablespoon water in a 2¹/₂-quart saucepan over medium heat. When hot, add the peeled and quartered shallots with the chopped celery and onion. Season with salt and pepper. Sauté for 5 minutes, then add the chicken stock and bring to a boil.

In a separate 2¹/₂-quart saucepan, melt the butter over low heat and add the flour to make a roux. Cook until the roux bubbles, 6 to 8 minutes. Stir constantly to prevent browning and scorching. Strain 4 cups boiling chicken broth into the roux. Whisk vigorously until smooth. Add the remaining stock and vegetables and whisk until well combined. Bring to a boil, then lower the heat and simmer for 15 minutes.

Remove the soup from the heat. Purée in a food processor fitted with a metal blade. Strain. Return to medium heat and bring to a simmer.

Warm the bacon and diced shallots in a non-stick pan over medium high heat. Add to the hot soup, adjust the seasoning with salt and pepper, and serve immediately. (If desired, the soup may be held for up to one hour in a double boiler.)

The Chef's Touch

It is essential that a high-quality slab bacon be used, both for flavor and so that the bacon may be cut into a properly sized cube that will maintain its texture when cooked. At The Trellis, our slab bacon is a hickory-smoked product which we purchase from the Edwards family in Surry, Virginia (see page 324).

This is a hearty and comforting soup. If a bit of elegance is desired, consider the addition of ½ pound lump backfin crabmeat warmed in ¼ cup heavy cream.

If the soup is not to be served within one hour, do not add the diced bacon and shallots. Cool the soup properly (see page 315), then cover and refrigerate for up to three days. When reheating, bring to a simmer and adjust the consistency with a bit of chicken stock if necessary. Warm the diced bacon and diced shallots in a non-stick sauté pan and add to the soup just before serving.

Fennel, Red Pepper, and Country Ham Soup

Serves 8

1 tablespoon vegetable oil
1 tablespoon water
2 stalks celery, sliced thin
1 medium onion, sliced thin
1 small fennel bulb, cored and
cut into long, thin strips
Salt and pepper to season
1 large red bell pepper, seeded
and cut into long, thin strips

6 cups chicken stock (see
page 305)
7 tablespoons unsalted butter
3/4 cup all-purpose flour
3/4 pound Monterey Jack cheese,
grated
1/4 pound country ham, cut into
long, thin strips

EQUIPMENT: *Paring knife, cutting board, French knife, 5-quart saucepan, two 2 1/2-quart saucepans, measuring cup, measuring spoons, wooden spoon, whisk, rubber spatula*

Heat the vegetable oil and water in a 5-quart saucepan over medium heat. When hot add the celery, onion, and fennel. Season the vegetables very lightly with salt and pepper and sauté for 5 minutes. Add the red pepper and sauté for an additional 3 minutes. Remove from the heat and hold at room temperature.

Heat the chicken stock to a boil in a 2 1/2-quart saucepan.

In a separate 2 1/2-quart saucepan, melt the butter over low heat. Add the flour to make a roux. Cook until the roux bubbles, 6 to 8 minutes. Stir constantly to prevent browning and scorching. Add the boiling stock and whisk vigorously until smooth. Simmer for 15 minutes.

Remove from the heat and whisk in the grated cheese, 1 cup at a time. Add the sautéed vegetables and country ham. Adjust the seasoning with salt and pepper. Serve immediately. (If desired, you may hold the soup in a double boiler for up to one hour before serving.)

The Chef's Touch

In January 1985, I faced the challenge of creating a menu for a Trellis-style meal to be served at the famous Ahwahnee Hotel in Yosemite National Park. I had been asked to participate in a new program called The Chef's Holiday. Invited chefs were asked to develop a menu that would reflect both the region of the country they were from and the style of cooking in their restaurants.

This fennel, red pepper, and country ham soup was the first course for our dinner. The crisp licorice flavor of the fennel paired with the sweetness of the red pepper proved to be a perfect counterbalance to the saltiness of the ham and the rich texture of the cheese. This soup creates a wonderful flavor on the palate, not unlike the flavor created by eating pizza!

Season the vegetables and the finished soup very lightly since the addition of country ham will dramatically increase the flavor of the soup. Also, note that the vegetables should be gently sautéed and kept crisp, both for texture and color.

Be careful not to boil the soup after the Monterey Jack has been added. Boiling will cause the soup and cheese to separate, resulting in an unattractive appearance.

A salt-cured Virginia ham imparts a distinctive flavor to this soup. If you are unable to procure this product, you may substitute any other type of cured ham.

This particular soup should be served shortly after it has been prepared. I do not recommend that you cool and refrigerate this soup: successful reheating is difficult because of its texture.

SALADS

Dandelion, Bibb Lettuce, Red Radishes, and Mushrooms with Sherry Wine Vinegar Dressing

Serves 8

¾ cup walnut oil
¼ cup sherry wine vinegar
  Salt and pepper to season
1½ pounds red radishes, washed
  and trimmed
1 medium head Bibb lettuce,
  washed and dried

8 cups loosely packed dandelion
  greens, washed and dried
16 large mushrooms, cleaned,
  stems trimmed, and sliced
  (about 4 center-cut slices per
  mushroom)

EQUIPMENT: *Measuring cup, stainless-steel bowl, whisk, film wrap, cutting board, paring knife, food processor, colander, measuring spoons*

In a stainless-steel bowl, whisk together the walnut oil and sherry wine vinegar. Adjust the seasoning with salt and pepper and combine thoroughly. Cover with film wrap and refrigerate until needed.

Using a food processor fitted with a grating disk, shred the radishes. Arrange equal portions of grated radish around the borders of each of 8 chilled luncheon plates, forming them into a ring 1½ inches wide.

Form the Bibb lettuce leaves into 8 "cups" and place one in the center of each of the radish rings.

Divide the dandelion greens among the Bibb lettuce cups.

Arrange 8 mushroom slices in the center of each salad, on top of the dandelion, stem ends toward the center. Salads may now be covered with film wrap and refrigerated for 2 to 3 hours before use if desired.

Whisk the dressing vigorously and spoon 2 tablespoons over each salad. Serve immediately.

The Chef's Touch

This salad is a favorite of our French-born pantry supervisor, Gisele Hicks, who says that it reminds her of a favorite childhood snack: freshly picked dandelion and shredded radishes in a well-buttered, crusty baguette.

The combination of walnut oil and sherry wine vinegar gives this salad a very specific and delightful flavor. Other oils as well as other vinegars could be used, although the unique flavor would be sacrificed.

In spring, dandelion greens can be found in most backyards or at roadside produce stands. If unavailable, substitute other peppery greens; curly endive, frisée, or arugula would work well. The quality and yield of the dandelion greens will vary tremendously—a 50 percent loss is not unusual.

After washing the lettuce and greens for this salad, shake dry in a colander or pat dry with paper towels. At The Trellis we use a large electric-powered lettuce spinner called the "Greens Machine." Smaller non-electric spinners are available for home use and are the most desirable way of drying greens. To ensure crispness after drying, I recommend refrigerating lettuce and greens for one to two hours before using.

A light sprinkling of salt directly over the radishes just before serving will accentuate their flavor.

Cucumbers, Watercress, and Romaine Lettuce with Maytag Blue Cheese Dressing

Serves 8

2 large cloves garlic, unpeeled
¼ teaspoon olive oil
  Salt and pepper to season
2 egg yolks
3 tablespoons cider vinegar
½ cup vegetable oil
½ cup virgin olive oil
¼ cup water
4½ pounds cucumbers, peeled, cut in half lengthwise, seeded, and cut into long, thin strips the length of the cucumber

1 large bunch watercress, stems trimmed, washed, and dried
1 small head romaine, washed, dried, and cut into ½-inch pieces
¼ pound Maytag blue cheese, broken into small pieces

EQUIPMENT: *9-inch pie pan, measuring spoons, cutting board, French knife, two stainless-steel bowls, whisk, measuring cup, film wrap, vegetable peeler, mandolin, colander*

Preheat the oven to 325 degrees.

Place the unpeeled garlic cloves on a pie pan, coat with ¼ teaspoon olive oil, and season with salt and pepper. Roast the garlic for 20 minutes in the preheated oven. When done, remove the skins from the roasted garlic. Purée the garlic cloves by mashing them with the side of the blade of a French knife. Reserve for later use.

In a stainless-steel bowl, vigorously whisk together the egg yolks and vinegar until frothy and slightly thickened. Combine the vegetable oil and olive oil. Slowly add the combined oils to the egg yolk and vinegar mixture, whisking continuously until the oil has all been incorporated. Add the garlic purée and water. Adjust the seasoning with salt and pepper and combine thoroughly.

Arrange equal portions of cucumber in a 1½-inch-wide ring along the outside border of each of 8 chilled luncheon plates. Arrange the water-cress inside the cucumber rings, with the stems facing toward the center of the plate. Place equal portions of the romaine lettuce on top of the watercress. Sprinkle with the blue cheese. Spoon 2 to 3 tablespoons of dressing over each salad and serve immediately.

The Chef's Touch

The 2 large cloves of garlic suggested in this recipe will create a mild, but flavorful, dressing. If you are a garlic lover, you may increase the amount to 3 or even 4 large cloves. The garlic flavor becomes very mellow when roasted, so do not be timid.

Substitute pure olive oil if virgin olive oil is not available. Taste the oil before using to ascertain quality and flavor (a previously opened container of oil may be stale or rancid). If the olive oil is not top quality, then it is better to use all vegetable oil in the dressing.

The prepared dressing may be covered with film wrap and refrigerated for up to two days before using.

To cut the cucumber strips, use a mandolin (see page 320). This handy piece of equipment will permit you to cut very uniform, long, thin spaghetti-like strands quickly and easily. If you do not have a mandolin in your tool kit, try using a very sharp French knife to cut the peeled and seeded cucumber halves into long, thin strips the length of the cucumber.

After washing the watercress for this salad, shake it dry in a colander or, preferably, spin it dry in a lettuce spinner. The washed romaine can be patted dry with paper towels, shaken dry, or spun dry. For crisper greens, refrigerate for one to two hours before serving.

Maytag blue cheese from Iowa is available in specialty cheese stores, along with other fabulous American-made blue cheeses such as Nauvoo Blue from Illinois and Blue Moon Gorgonzola. Of course, there is always imported Stilton or Roquefort. Whichever you choose will work well in this salad while lending its own personality to complement the overall taste experience.

Asparagus, Spring Onions, and Red Peppers with Lemon and Dill Vinaigrette

Serves 8

1 pound fresh asparagus
¾ cup virgin olive oil
2 lemons, 1 zested and both
   juiced (see page 314)
1 tablespoon chopped fresh dill
   Salt and pepper to season
1 medium head Bibb lettuce,
   washed and dried
1 medium bunch watercress,
   stems trimmed, washed, and
   dried

8 scallions, white part only,
   trimmed and cut into 3-inch-
   long strips
2 small red bell peppers, seeded,
   membrane removed, and cut
   into thin strips the length of the
   pepper

EQUIPMENT: *Vegetable peeler, cutting board, French knife, 5-quart sauce-pan, tongs, film wrap, zester, measuring cup, measuring spoons, stainless-steel bowl, whisk, colander*

Snap the woody stem from and peel each stalk of asparagus. Blanch the asparagus in 3 quarts boiling salted water for about 45 seconds or slightly longer, depending upon the thickness. The asparagus should remain very crisp. Immediately transfer the blanched asparagus to ice water. When cold, drain thoroughly, then trim the base of each stalk to make it 6 inches long.

In a stainless-steel bowl, whisk together the olive oil, lemon juice, lemon zest, and chopped dill. Adjust the seasoning with salt and pepper and combine thoroughly.

Arrange a small "cup" of Bibb lettuce on one side of each of 8 chilled luncheon plates. Place a small spray of watercress in each lettuce cup. Portion the asparagus in front of the lettuce cup on each plate, all the tips pointing in the same direction and formed into a neat stack. Garnish the asparagus with the scallion and red pepper strips. Whisk the dressing vigorously and spoon 2 tablespoons over each salad. Serve immediately.

The Chef's Touch

There is an excellent reason for the absence of vinegar from the dressing for this salad. There is no need to mask the flavors of the very fresh ingredients: long, delicate, pencil-thin stalks of spring asparagus, lively-flavored young onion shoots, and soft, feathery sprigs of dill, all accented by the brightly colored red pepper strips and just a splash of the clear-flavored olive oil and lemon dressing.

I prefer peeled asparagus no matter how thin it is. I like the pale green color and also the fact that, when peeled, the asparagus will absorb the dressing or sauce that accompanies it. Most professionals will tell you to peel asparagus if it is more than 1/4 inch in diameter. Whatever you decide, be certain not to overcook the asparagus, because it will lose its delicate flavor and texture very quickly.

The quality of the oil is very important in this recipe as there is no assertive vinegar to mask the flavor of a mediocre oil. Also, the delicate flavors of the salad's components demand a very high-quality virgin olive oil. If not available, use a very good-quality pure olive oil.

After washing the Bibb lettuce for this salad, dry with paper towels, shake dry in a colander, or, preferably, spin dry in a lettuce spinner. For the more delicate watercress, shake or spin dry. For crisper greens, refrigerate for one to two hours before serving.

Curly Endive, Spinach, Fresh Corn, and Roasted Peppers with Smoked Bacon Dressing

Serves 8

1 pound hickory-smoked slab
   bacon
2 medium ears fresh yellow corn,
   husk and silk removed
¾ cup peanut oil
¼ cup cider vinegar
   Salt and pepper to season
1 large head curly endive,
   washed, dried, and cut into
   ¾-inch pieces

¾ pound flat leaf spinach, or 5
   ounces curly spinach, stemmed,
   washed, and dried
3 medium bell peppers (assorted
   colors), roasted, seeded, and cut
   into thin strips (see page 315)

EQUIPMENT: *Tongs, paring knife, cutting board, French knife, baking sheet with sides, metal spatula, paper towels, 5-quart saucepan, measuring cup, stainless-steel bowl, whisk, colander, measuring spoons*

Preheat the oven to 325 degrees.

Trim the rind and excess fat from the bacon, slice into strips, then cut into ⅜-inch cubes. Cook the cubes on a baking sheet for 30 minutes in the preheated oven. Transfer the cooked bacon to paper towels and drain. Keep the drained bacon at kitchen temperature until needed.

Blanch the corn for 1 minute in 3 quarts boiling salted water. Drain, then cool under cold running water. When the corn is cool enough to handle, cut away the kernels. Cover with film wrap and refrigerate until needed.

In a stainless-steel bowl, whisk together the peanut oil and cider vinegar. Adjust the seasoning with salt and pepper and combine thoroughly.

Portion the curly endive onto each of 8 chilled luncheon plates. Place equal portions of the spinach leaves on top of the curly endive. Sprinkle the corn kernels over the spinach and endive. Arrange the pepper strips around the edge of the spinach leaves and place the bacon cubes in the center of each salad. Whisk the dressing vigorously and spoon 2 tablespoons over each salad. Serve immediately.

The Chef's Touch

Hickory-smoked slab bacon is best for this salad, both for taste and because it can be cut into the desired-size cube. Presliced bacon may be used; however, the texture will not be quite the same.

The eye appeal of this salad is enhanced by using a variety of colored peppers. During the summer months, there is a wide availability of green, red, and yellow peppers. If only green peppers can be located, this salad will still be delicious, although not so colorful.

"Super sweet," "bright yellow," and "very fresh" are the adjectives to describe corn suited to this salad. Cooked very quickly for only a minute, the corn will retain its bright yellow color and sweet taste.

If peanut oil is not available, substitute another good vegetable oil such as corn or safflower.

After washing the curly endive and spinach for this salad, pat dry with paper towels, shake dry in a colander, or, preferably, spin dry in a lettuce spinner. For crisper greens, refrigerate for one to two hours before serving.

Yellow Squash, Green Beans, and Scallions with Herb Vinaigrette

Serves 8

1 pound tiny green beans, trimmed

³/₄ cup olive oil

6 tablespoons vegetable oil

¹/₄ cup red raspberry vinegar

¹/₂ tablespoon chopped fresh chervil

¹/₂ tablespoon chopped fresh dill

¹/₂ tablespoon chopped fresh parsley

¹/₂ tablespoon chopped fresh tarragon

Salt and pepper to season

5 medium zucchini, lightly peeled and cut into strips 2¹/₂ inches long, ³/₈ inch wide, and ¹/₈ inch thick

1 small red bell pepper, seeded and cut into ¹/₄-inch pieces

3 small yellow squash, washed, dried, and cut into ¹/₈-inch-thick round slices

1 medium head Bibb lettuce, washed and dried

2 scallions, trimmed and sliced thin

EQUIPMENT: *Paring knife, 5-quart saucepan, medium-gauge strainer, vegetable peeler, cutting board, French knife, measuring cup, measuring spoons, stainless-steel bowl, whisk, colander*

Blanch the tiny green beans in 3 quarts boiling salted water until tender but still crunchy, about 2 minutes. Drain the beans, then plunge into ice water. When the beans are thoroughly cooled, remove from the ice water and drain well.

In a stainless-steel bowl, whisk together the olive oil, vegetable oil, raspberry vinegar, and chopped fresh herbs. Adjust the seasoning with salt and pepper and combine thoroughly.

Arrange equal portions of the zucchini in a ring near the outside edge of each of 8 chilled luncheon plates. The ring should be about 2 inches wide, leaving a 3-inch hole in the center. Sprinkle the red pepper pieces over each ring of zucchini. Arrange a circle of yellow squash slices around the inside edge of the zucchini ring; each squash slice should slightly overlap the previous slice. Arrange a small "cup" of Bibb lettuce in the center of each plate on top of, but not completely covering, the yellow squash slices. Divide and arrange the tiny green beans in a small stack on top of each Bibb lettuce cup. The beans should be arranged parallel to each other. Whisk the vinaigrette and spoon 3 tablespoons over each salad. Finish by sprinkling the scallions directly over the beans on each salad and serve immediately.

The Chef's Touch

This salad, with its variety of shapes, textures, colors, and flavors, is a delightful summertime dish. It exemplifies the Trellis philosophy of highlighting fresh ingredients at their peak.

The tiny green beans used at The Trellis are the very fine thin beans known to the French as *haricots verts*. We are able to purchase them year-round. If you are unable to locate them, purchase the thinnest snap beans you can find and trim them to a length of $2^{1}/_{2}$ to $2^{3}/_{4}$ inches.

Almost every supermarket now carries fresh herbs. If the variety is not vast, consider using only one herb, such as dill or tarragon, rather than the suggested assortment. The important thing is that the herbs be fresh and of good quality.

Although the recipe calls for lightly peeled zucchini, unpeeled zucchini may be used if unblemished and thoroughly washed.

It is best to use very young and small yellow squash because their less-developed seeds make them much more palatable.

After washing the Bibb lettuce for this salad, shake dry in a colander, pat dry with paper towels, or spin dry in a lettuce spinner. For crisper greens, refrigerate for one to two hours before serving.

Sweet Peppers, Goat Cheese, and Red Leaf Lettuce with Fresh Basil Dressing

Serves 8

1/2 cup chopped fresh basil leaves
8 ounces log-shaped goat cheese
3/4 cup olive oil
3/4 cup vegetable oil
6 tablespoons cider vinegar
1 1/2 tablespoons Dijon-style mustard
Salt and pepper to season

2 medium heads red leaf lettuce, washed and dried
4 small bell peppers (assorted colors), seeded and cut into thin strips 1 1/4 inches long

EQUIPMENT: *Measuring cup, cutting board, French knife, serrated slicer, baking sheet, film wrap, measuring spoons, stainless-steel bowl, whisk, colander*

Reserve 2 tablespoons chopped basil for the vinaigrette. Sprinkle the remaining basil on a clean, dry surface. Roll the piece of goat cheese in the basil, pressing gently but firmly so that the basil will adhere to, and completely cover, the cheese. Cut the goat cheese into 8 equal slices. Transfer them to a baking sheet lined with film wrap and refrigerate until needed.

In a stainless-steel bowl, whisk together the olive oil, vegetable oil, cider vinegar, mustard, and reserved chopped basil. Adjust the seasoning with salt and pepper and combine thoroughly.

Arrange an equal number of leaves of red leaf lettuce on each of 8 chilled luncheon plates. Place a slice of herbed goat cheese in the center of each plate. Randomly sprinkle the assorted pepper strips on the lettuce, but not on top of the goat cheese. Whisk the dressing and spoon 4 tablespoons over each salad. Serve immediately.

The Chef's Touch

Summertime brings a bounty of peppers. Create a lavish landscape of pepper strips on this salad with red, yellow, white, purple, and, perhaps, even a few strips of jalapeño.

To yield ½ cup chopped basil, start with ½ cup *tightly* packed stemmed, washed, and dried basil leaves. Fresh spinach leaves are a good substitute for fresh basil; their vibrant color, subtle but distinct flavor, and easy availability make them preferable to using dried basil if fresh is not available.

Aromatic goat cheese logs are available in a variety of sizes. If you must purchase more than an 8-ounce log, be certain to have some crusty French bread on hand so that you can enjoy the excess goat cheese while preparing the salad.

After washing the red leaf lettuce for this salad, shake dry in a colander and pat dry with paper towels, or, preferably, spin dry in a lettuce spinner. For crisper greens, refrigerate for one to two hours before serving.

Romaine, Apples, and Oregon Tillamook Cheddar with Walnut Oil Dressing

Serves 8

1 cup hazelnuts
1¹/₄ cups walnut oil
¹/₂ cup red raspberry vinegar
   Salt and pepper to season
1 tablespoon fresh lemon juice
1 Granny Smith apple, unpeeled
1 Red Delicious apple, unpeeled
1 large bunch watercress, stems
   trimmed, washed, and dried

1 large head romaine lettuce,
   washed, dried, and cut into
   ³/₄-inch pieces
¹/₄ pound Oregon Tillamook
   Cheddar cheese, cut into
   ¹/₄-inch cubes

EQUIPMENT: *Two baking sheets with sides, 100% cotton kitchen towel, film wrap, stainless-steel bowl, measuring cup, whisk, paring knife, cutting board, serrated slicer*

Preheat the oven to 450 degrees.

Toast the hazelnuts on a baking sheet in the preheated oven for 5 to 6 minutes. Remove from the oven and immediately cover with a damp cotton towel. Invert another baking sheet over the first one to hold in the steam (this makes the nuts easier to skin). After 5 minutes, remove the skins from the nuts by placing small quantities inside a folded kitchen towel and rubbing vigorously. Split the skinned nuts in half, cover with film wrap, and keep at kitchen temperature until needed.

In a stainless-steel bowl, whisk together the walnut oil and raspberry vinegar. Adjust the seasoning with salt and pepper and combine thoroughly. Cover with film wrap and refrigerate until needed.

Acidulate 2 cups water with 1 tablespoon lemon juice. Core and quarter the apples. Slice each quarter lengthwise into eight ¹/₈-inch-thick slices and immediately place in the acidulated water.

Portion the watercress onto each of 8 chilled luncheon plates. Arrange the watercress to cover the base of the plate, with the stem ends toward the center. Neatly arrange the romaine pieces on top and in the center of the watercress; the watercress leaves should still be visible around the edge of the romaine. Drain the apples in a colander, rinse under cold running water, and shake dry. Arrange the apple slices, alternating the green and the red, around the edge of each plate, with each slice pointing in the same direction and the tips just underneath the romaine leaves. Sprinkle Tillamook pieces and hazelnut halves over each salad. Whisk the dressing vigorously and spoon 3 to 4 tablespoons over each salad. Serve immediately.

The Chef's Touch

Chefs are often asked about their favorite foods. When I am asked this question I include this salad on my list.

Walnuts used in place of the hazelnuts are also excellent in this salad. Toast 1 cup walnut halves on a baking sheet in a preheated 300-degree oven for fifteen minutes. Remove from the oven and keep at kitchen temperature until needed.

After washing the watercress for this salad, shake dry in a colander or, preferably, spin dry in a lettuce spinner. The washed romaine may be patted dry with paper towels, shaken dry, or spun dry. For crisper greens, refrigerate for one to two hours before serving.

Good to excellent Red Delicious apples are available year-round. Granny Smith apples are also usually available year-round, especially if you are willing to pay the higher price when only the South African apples are available. In any case, do not hesitate to use your favorite varieties for this salad; almost any eating apple will work well.

At The Trellis, we usually purchase Tillamook Cheddar in 44-pound blocks direct from the Tillamook County Oregon Co-op. Tillamook Cheddar is medium sharp in flavor, firm in texture, and almost orange in color. Found in most specialty cheese stores, Tillamook can certainly be purchased in much smaller quantities than the large blocks we buy for The Trellis.

Curly Endive, Country Ham, Virginia Peanuts, and Black-eyed Peas with Peanut Oil Dressing

Serves 8

2/3 cup dried black-eyed peas, washed and picked over

1/2 teaspoon salt

1 1/2 cups peanut oil

3 tablespoons cider vinegar

2 1/4 teaspoons peanut butter
Salt and pepper to season

2 egg yolks

3/4 cup unsalted shelled Virginia peanuts

1 medium head red leaf lettuce, washed and dried

1 large head curly endive, washed, dried, and cut into 3/4-inch pieces

6 ounces country ham, cut into strips 1/8 inch wide and 1 1/4 inches long

EQUIPMENT: *Measuring cup, 2 1/2-quart saucepan, measuring spoon, medium-gauge strainer, two stainless-steel bowls, film wrap, whisk, baking sheet with sides, colander, cutting board, French knife*

Place the peas in a 2 1/2-quart saucepan with 3 cups water and 1/2 teaspoon salt. Cook the peas over medium high heat until fully cooked but not mushy, 25 to 30 minutes. While the peas are cooking, prepare the marinade by whisking together in a stainless-steel bowl 2 table-spoons peanut oil, 1 tablespoon vinegar, and 1/4 teaspoon peanut butter. Adjust the seasoning with salt and pepper and combine thoroughly. Set the marinade aside until the peas are cooked. When the peas are cooked, drain thoroughly, then rinse under cold water. When the peas are cool, shake dry, season with salt and pepper, and combine with the marinade. Cover with film wrap and allow to marinate for 2 hours in the refrigerator.

Preheat the oven to 300 degrees.

In a stainless-steel bowl, combine the egg yolks and the remaining 2 tablespoons vinegar and 2 teaspoons peanut butter, whisking vigor-ously for 2 minutes. Continue to whisk while adding the remaining peanut oil in a slow and steady stream. When all the oil has been incorporated, adjust the consistency with 1 tablespoon water, if necessary. Adjust the seasoning with salt and pepper and combine thoroughly. Cover with film wrap and refrigerate until needed.

Toast the peanuts on a baking sheet in the preheated oven for 20 to 25 minutes. Remove from the oven and hold at room temperature.

Arrange 2 or 3 leaves of red leaf lettuce on each of 8 chilled luncheon plates. Divide and place the curly endive pieces on top of the red leaf lettuce. Sprinkle the black-eyed peas and country ham over the curly endive on each plate. Dress each salad with 3 to 4 tablespoons dressing. Finish by sprinkling the toasted peanuts over each salad and serve immediately.

The Chef's Touch

Black-eyed peas are always available dried. Depending upon the time of the year and the geographic location, they also can be found fresh in supermarkets and at produce stands. Dried black-eyed peas do not have to be soaked before cooking, although soaking usually helps ensure evenly cooked peas. If you always prefer to soak dried beans, then cover the ⅔ cup black-eyed peas with 2 cups cold water and allow to soak for 2 hours at room temperature. Rinse soaked beans thoroughly, then cook as directed. It is better to do without these delicious peas than to purchase them canned.

The use of peanut oil not only lends character to the dressing, it also reinforces the peanut flavor of the garnish. If peanut oil is not available use another good vegetable oil, such as safflower or sunflower oil.

Most supermarkets carry various brand-name unsalted shelled peanuts. These are acceptable if you cannot buy locally the special Virginia shelled unsalted nuts. (If you wish to order the Virginia nuts, see the address on page 324.)

After washing the red leaf lettuce and curly endive for this salad, pat dry with paper towels, shake dry in a colander, or, preferably, spin dry in a lettuce spinner. For crisper greens, refrigerate for one to two hours before serving.

We use a country-style salt-cured ham from Surry, Virginia, at The Trellis. Many other good salt-cured hams are available from other areas of Virginia, as well as from other states such as Kentucky and Arkansas.

Chicory, Beets, and Walnuts
with Mustard Vinaigrette

Serves 8

8 small beets, trimmed (about
   1¹/₂ pounds)
6 tablespoons cider vinegar
3 tablespoons fresh lemon juice
2 tablespoons coarse-grained
   mustard
4 teaspoons Dijon-style mustard
¹/₂ teaspoon salt

¹/₄ teaspoon ground black pepper
1¹/₂ cups vegetable oil
   Salt and pepper to season
1 cup walnut halves
1 large head chicory, cut into
   ³/₄-inch pieces, washed and
   dried

EQUIPMENT: *2¹/₂-quart saucepan, paring knife, two stainless-steel bowls, mandolin, film wrap, measuring spoons, measuring cup, whisk, baking sheet, serrated slicer or French knife, cutting board, colander*

Cook the beets in 2 quarts boiling salted water for 20 minutes; the texture of the cooked beets should be very firm. Transfer the cooked beets to ice water and allow to cool for 15 minutes.

Peel the beets and slice ¹/₈ inch thick on the wavy-edged cutter of the mandolin. Cover with film wrap and refrigerate until needed.

Preheat the oven to 300 degrees.

In a stainless-steel bowl, whisk together the vinegar, lemon juice, both mustards, ¹/₂ teaspoon salt, and ¹/₄ teaspoon black pepper. Continue to whisk the mixture while pouring in a steady and slow stream of vegetable oil. When all the oil has been added, adjust the seasoning with salt and pepper and combine thoroughly. Cover with film wrap and refrigerate until needed.

Toast the walnuts on a baking sheet in the preheated oven for 15 minutes. Remove from the oven and hold at kitchen temperature.

Arrange enough beet slices to form a ring around the outside edge of each of 8 chilled luncheon plates; the slices should slightly overlap each other. Portion the chicory pieces in the center of each plate but do not

73

cover the beets. Place 4 beet slices on top and in the center of each salad, slices touching in the center but pointing in opposite directions. Whisk the vinaigrette and spoon 4 tablespoons over each salad. Finish by sprinkling the toasted walnuts on each salad and serve immediately.

The Chef's Touch

Textures play an important role in how the palate perceives certain flavors. In this case, the texture of a waffle-cut beet creates a different flavor perception than flat-sliced beets. In order to slice a beet into a waffle cut on the mandolin (see page 320), cut the beet on the wavy-edged cutting blade. Slice the beet from flat end to flat end, not from side to side. Discard the first slice, then turn the beet 90 degrees after each slice (this will create the waffle effect). If you do not have a mandolin, slice the beets with a crinkle-cut knife.

There are countless mustards available these days (for an excellent list see *Tastings,* by Jenifer Harvey Lang). My favorite coarse-grained mustard is Pommery Meaux. It is available in most specialty food stores.

After washing the chicory for this salad, shake dry in a colander, pat dry with paper towels, or, preferably, spin dry in a lettuce spinner. For crisper greens, refrigerate for one to two hours before serving.

Romaine, Grapefruit, and Walnuts with Stilton Cheese and Port Wine Vinaigrette

Serves 8

1 cup walnut halves

6 tablespoons fresh grapefruit juice

6 tablespoons port wine

6 tablespoons olive oil

6 tablespoons vegetable oil

1¹/₂ tablespoons red raspberry vinegar

1¹/₂ tablespoons cider vinegar

Salt and pepper to season

8 large ruby grapefruit, peeled and sectioned

1 large head romaine, washed, dried, and cut into ¹/₂-inch pieces

¹/₄ pound Stilton cheese, broken into small pieces

EQUIPMENT: *Baking sheet, measuring cup, measuring spoons, stainless-steel bowl, whisk, film wrap, cutting board, serrated slicer, paring knife*

Preheat the oven to 300 degrees.

Toast the walnut halves on a baking sheet in the preheated oven for 12 to 15 minutes. Remove from the oven and keep at room temperature until needed.

In a stainless-steel bowl, whisk together the grapefruit juice, port wine, olive oil, vegetable oil, raspberry vinegar, and cider vinegar. Adjust the seasoning with salt and pepper and combine thoroughly.

Arrange equal portions of the grapefruit sections in a circle (curved side facing out) around the outside edge of each of 8 chilled luncheon plates. The natural curve of the sections should follow the curve of the plate. Divide and place the romaine in the center of each plate, touching but not covering the grapefruit sections. Sprinkle the Stilton pieces over the romaine. Whisk the vinaigrette vigorously and spoon 2 to 3 tablespoons over each salad. Top with the walnut halves and serve immediately.

The Chef's Touch

This salad would make a perfect first course for a meal with no appetizer. Although this salad invigorates the palate, its lightness still allows for the main course to be substantial—exactly what one might serve on a cold and damp February evening.

The fresh grapefruit juice needed for the vinaigrette may be obtained by squeezing the center pulp of the fruit after it has been peeled and sectioned.

Although it is not necessary to use a Warre 1977 vintage port, as we do, for the vinaigrette, a good, drinkable port should be used.

The pink flesh of the ruby grapefruit makes a very attractive salad. Do not hesitate, however, to use white grapefruit (yellowish flesh). For a really striking effect, alternate sections of both pink and white.

Use a serrated slicer or a very sharp paring knife to peel the grapefruit. Cut away the skin and the white membrane (pith) under the skin. Once the grapefruit is peeled use a paring knife to remove the sections by cutting along inside the membrane of each section down to the core.

After washing the romaine for this salad, pat dry with paper towels, shake dry in a colander, or, preferably, spin dry in a lettuce spinner. For crisper greens, refrigerate for one to two hours before serving.

Leaf Spinach and Curly Endive with Sautéed Shiitake Mushrooms and Sherry Wine Vinegar Dressing

Serves 8

¼ cup vegetable oil
¼ cup peanut oil
¼ cup olive oil
¼ cup sherry wine vinegar
 Salt and pepper to season
1 cup pecan halves
4 pieces sun-dried tomatoes
 packed in olive oil
1 large bunch flat leaf spinach,
 stemmed, washed, and dried

1 medium head curly endive, cut
 into ¾-inch pieces, washed,
 and dried
1 tablespoon clarified butter (see
 page 312) or olive oil
1 tablespoon minced shallots
1 pound shiitake mushrooms,
 stemmed and sliced

EQUIPMENT: *Measuring cup, measuring spoons, stainless-steel bowl, whisk, film wrap, baking sheet, paper towels, French knife, cutting board, paring knife, colander, large non-stick sauté pan, wooden spoon*

Preheat the oven to 300 degrees.

In a stainless-steel bowl, whisk together the vegetable oil, peanut oil, olive oil, and vinegar. Adjust the seasoning with salt and pepper and combine thoroughly. Cover with film wrap and hold at room temperature until needed.

Toast the pecan halves on a baking sheet in the preheated oven for 15 minutes. Hold at room temperature until needed.

Drain the sun-dried tomato pieces on paper towels. When well drained, cut into thin strips.

Arrange 7 to 8 leaves of the flat leaf spinach on each of 8 chilled luncheon plates. Portion the curly endive on top of the spinach. (At this point, the plates may be individually covered with film wrap and refrigerated for 2 to 3 hours.)

Heat 1 tablespoon clarified butter or olive oil in a large non-stick sauté pan over medium high heat. When the butter or oil is hot, add the shallots and sauté for 1 minute. Add the shiitake mushrooms and the sun-dried tomato strips, adjust the seasoning with salt and pepper, and sauté until the mixture is warm. Portion the warm mushroom mixture over the greens. Whisk the dressing vigorously and spoon 2 tablespoons over each salad. Sprinkle the pecan halves over the salads and serve immediately.

The Chef's Touch

I have always disliked the term "wilted," which usually refers to salads that are bathed in an overly heated dressing. This does, in fact, wilt the greens, resulting in the loss of much of their good eating qualities. The appeal of this salad is that the flavors of the greens are highlighted by the warm mushrooms and all of the textures are preserved.

Sherry wine vinegar can usually be found in specialty food stores. If it is not available, a very good dressing can be made by substituting 3 tablespoons cider vinegar and 2 tablespoons dry sherry for the 1/4 cup sherry wine vinegar specified in the recipe.

When sun-dried tomatoes are not available, consider using oven-dried cherry tomatoes. Place cherry tomato halves, cut side up, on a baking sheet covered with parchment paper. Season the tomato halves generously with salt and bake in a preheated 200-degree oven for three to four hours. Allow to cool (cooled oven-dried tomatoes may be placed in a covered container and kept in the refrigerator for several days), then add to the hot mushrooms, rather than sautéing them with the mushrooms as directed for the sun-dried tomatoes.

If flat leaf spinach is not available, use curly spinach leaves. Combine the curly spinach with the pieces of curly endive. You may also serve this salad using only spinach; if so, use a combination of flat leaf and curly spinach or use only curly leaf spinach.

Many other mushrooms would work well used singly or in combination in this recipe. Oyster tree mushrooms, chanterelles, and porcini mushrooms are also particularly good sautéed and served over chilled greens. Whatever the variety, be careful not to get the mixture too hot. This is not a "wilted" salad.

After washing the spinach and curly endive for this salad, shake dry in a colander, pat dry with paper towels, or, preferably, spin dry in a lettuce spinner. For crisper greens, refrigerate for one to two hours before serving.

Bibb Lettuce, Romaine, Watercress, and Gruyère Cheese Salad with Walnut Oil and Raspberry Vinaigrette

Serves 8

2 cups walnut halves
1¼ cups walnut oil
½ cup red raspberry vinegar
　Salt and pepper to season
1 medium head romaine, washed
　and dried
1 medium head Bibb lettuce,
　washed and dried

1 large bunch watercress, stems
　trimmed, washed, and dried
6 ounces Gruyère cheese (brown
　rind removed), cut into strips 3
　inches long and ⅛ inch wide

EQUIPMENT: *Baking sheet, measuring cup, stainless-steel bowl, whisk, film wrap, colander, cutting board, French knife*

Preheat the oven to 300 degrees.

Toast the walnut halves on a baking sheet in the preheated oven for 15 minutes. Remove from the oven and keep at kitchen temperature.

In a stainless-steel bowl, whisk together the walnut oil and raspberry vinegar. Adjust the seasoning with salt and pepper and combine thoroughly.

Arrange 3 romaine leaves side by side and slightly overlapping to cover three quarters of the surface of each of 8 chilled luncheon plates. In the remaining space, arrange a small "cup" of Bibb lettuce. Place the watercress in a small fan on top of the romaine so that the stems are touching the Bibb lettuce cup. Divide and arrange the Gruyère strips over and parallel to the watercress. Divide the walnut halves over the Bibb lettuce cups. Whisk the dressing vigorously and spoon 3 tablespoons over each salad. Serve immediately.

The Chef's Touch

This is perhaps the quintessential Trellis salad: a combination of distinctive greens with a flavorful cheese and a nut flavor and texture, bound together by a superb but simple vinaigrette. This represents not only the style of Trellis salad making, but a traditional approach to the use of the best of available seasonal products as well. A good olive oil and red wine vinegar dressing would also be excellent with the other flavor components in this salad.

After washing the romaine and Bibb lettuce for this salad, pat dry with paper towels, shake dry in a colander, or, preferably, spin dry in a lettuce spinner. Shake or spin dry the washed watercress. For crisper greens, refrigerate for one to two hours before serving.

Very good Swiss Gruyère is easily found these days. Buy it in ½-pound or 1-pound blocks.

The flavor and texture of the thin strips of Gruyère and the toasted walnut halves on this salad create a palate-pleasing experience. Do not hesitate, however, to experiment with other nut and cheese combinations.

A TRELLIS SOUP SELECTION

THE TRELLIS BREAD BASKET

TRELLIS DESSERT TABLE

FRONT LEFT TO RIGHT *Pear Fritters with Toasted Pecan Ice Cream and Pear Custard Sauce* (PAGE 290), *Chocolate Damnation* (PAGE 296), *Chocolate Cashew Dacquoise* (PAGE 273)

BACK ROW LEFT TO RIGHT *Cranberry Walnut Cake* (PAGE 293), *Chocolate Praline Ice Cream Terrine* (PAGE 287)

A TRELLIS DINNER

FRONT *Sautéed Pheasant with Shiitake Mushrooms, Seasonal Squash, and Cashew Butter* (PAGE 154), *Tiny Green Beans*

LEFT *Chocolate Temptation* (PAGE 277)

RIGHT *Romaine, Grapefruit, and Walnuts with Stilton Cheese and Port Wine Vinaigrette* (PAGE 75)

RIGHT REAR *Roasted Garlic Breadsticks* (PAGE 203), *Apricot Almond Bread* (PAGE 224), *Irish Soda Bread with Herbs* (PAGE 201)

SPRING

*Asparagus and Shiitake
Mushroom Soup*
(PAGE 29)

SPRING

FRONT *Asparagus, Spring Onions, and Red Peppers with Lemon and Dill Vinaigrette*
(PAGE 61)
REAR *Grilled Smoked Duck Breast with Country Ham, Melon, and Pistachio Dressing*
(PAGE 6)

SPRING

Strawberry and Papaya Sorbet (PAGE 247)

SPRING

Grilled Calves' Liver with Avocado, Red Onion, and Brown Butter (PAGE 100)

SPRING

*Caramel Macadamia Nut
Ice Cream Cake*
(PAGE 249)

SPRING

Chocolate Pecan Cake
(PAGE 257)

ENTRÉES

Shad Roe with Lump Backfin Crabmeat

Serves 8

1½ pounds hickory-smoked slab
   bacon
8 pairs shad roe
3 tablespoons clarified butter
   (see page 312)
Salt and pepper to season

¼ cup water
10 tablespoons unsalted butter
1 pound lump backfin crabmeat,
   well picked of shell
1 teaspoon fresh lemon juice
1 teaspoon chopped fresh parsley

EQUIPMENT: *Cutting board, serrated slicer, two baking sheets with sides, paper towels, parchment paper, pastry brush, measuring spoons, two non-stick sauté pans, tongs*

Preheat the oven to 325 degrees.

Remove the rind from the slab bacon and slice into sixteen ⅛-inch-thick slices. Lay out the bacon slices on a baking sheet and bake in the preheated oven for 25 minutes. When done, transfer to paper towels and drain. Keep at room temperature until needed. Raise the oven temperature to 350 degrees.

Handling them carefully, rinse each pair of shad roe under cold running water. Separate each pair, removing the connective tissue. Pat dry with paper towels. Cut eight 8-by-12-inch pieces of parchment paper. Lightly brush one side of the parchment paper with the clarified butter. Place a pair (2 pieces) of roe on each piece of parchment paper so that the length of the roe is within the length of the paper. Season the roe with salt and pepper. Fold the parchment paper over and crimp the edges.

Pour ¼ cup water into a sided baking sheet and place the parchment-wrapped shad roe on it. Bake the roe at 350 degrees for 10 minutes. Lower the heat to 200 degrees and keep the shad roe in the oven while completing the recipe.

Melt 2 tablespoons butter in a non-stick sauté pan over medium heat.

When hot, add the crabmeat. Season with salt and pepper and sauté until just warm, 4 to 5 minutes. While the crabmeat is warming, heat the bacon in the 200-degree oven.

While the crabmeat and bacon are heating, place a non-stick sauté pan over high heat. When the pan is very hot, add the remaining 8 tablespoons butter and allow to brown evenly. Place 2 bacon slices in the form of an **X** in the center of each of 8 warm plates. Carefully remove each pair of shad roe from the parchment paper and place on top of the bacon on each plate. Portion the crabmeat over each set of roe. Add the lemon juice to the brown butter, shaking the pan vigorously so that the butter does not foam over the sides. Carefully pour equal amounts of brown butter over each portion. Garnish with the chopped parsley and serve immediately.

The Chef's Touch

I have tried several methods for cooking shad roe over the years. Until recently I had found the following to be the best method: Poach the roe in gently simmering water for 90 seconds to firm the texture, remove the roe from the water and pat dry with paper towels, season with salt and pepper, and sauté the roe in clarified butter until brown on both sides. Although this is an excellent method, the roe, as it does in other preparations, has a tendency to rupture and look unattractive. The method described in this recipe, although not foolproof, is the easiest and gives the best results encountered to date. This method was suggested to me by one of our first-year apprentice cooks who is an avid shad fisherman.

Because of my partiality to hickory-smoked slab bacon, I recommend it for this recipe. If not available, buy the best-quality sliced bacon you can find. Bake it until crisp, which will take a few minutes less than the thicker-sliced slab bacon.

A well-chilled glass of Chateau St. Jean fumé blanc would be the perfect counterpoint to the richness of this dish.

Sautéed Soft-shell Crabs with Sugar Snap Peas and Toasted Almonds

Serves 8

16 live jumbo soft-shell crabs
4¹/₂ tablespoons fresh lemon juice
   Salt and pepper to season
1 cup sliced almonds
2 pounds sugar snap peas, ends trimmed and strings removed

3 tablespoons clarified butter (see page 312)
¹/₄ pound unsalted butter, softened

EQUIPMENT: *Cutting board, paring knife, measuring spoons, two baking sheets (one with sides), film wrap, measuring cup, 2¹/₂-quart saucepan, colander, stainless-steel bowl, paper towels, three non-stick sauté pans (two large), tongs, slotted spoon*

Preheat the oven to 350 degrees.

Dress the crabs (see page 316) and sprinkle with 4 tablespoons lemon juice. Season with salt and pepper. Place the crabs on a baking sheet lined with film wrap. Cover tightly with film wrap and refrigerate until needed.

Toast the almonds on a baking sheet in the preheated oven until golden brown, 12 to 15 minutes. Keep at room temperature. Do not turn off the oven.

Blanch the sugar snap peas in 2 quarts boiling salted water for 45 seconds. Drain, then immediately transfer to ice water. When the peas are cold, drain thoroughly.

Pat the crabs dry with paper towels. Season with salt and pepper. Heat 1 tablespoon clarified butter in each of two large non-stick sauté pans over medium high heat. When hot, add 8 crabs, shell side down, to each pan. Sauté for 1¹/₂ minutes. Turn the crabs over and sauté for an additional 1¹/₂ minutes. Transfer the crabs to a baking sheet and hold in the 350-degree oven while completing the recipe.

Heat the remaining 1 tablespoon clarified butter in a clean large non-stick sauté pan over high heat. When hot, add the sugar snap peas, season with salt and pepper, and sauté until hot, but still bright green and crisp, 5 to 6 minutes.

Place a non-stick sauté pan over high heat. When hot, add the unsalted butter and allow to brown evenly. While the butter is browning, place equal portions of sugar snap peas onto each of 8 warm 10-inch plates. Place 2 crabs on top of the peas on each plate. Add the remaining ½ tablespoon lemon juice to the brown butter, shaking the pan vigorously so that the butter does not foam over the sides of the pan. Carefully pour equal amounts of the brown butter over each portion and sprinkle with the toasted almonds. Serve immediately.

The Chef's Touch

Upon reading William W. Warner's *Beautiful Swimmer*, a delightful and informative book about watermen, crabs, and the Chesapeake Bay, I learned that the scientific name for blue crabs is *Callinectes sapidus*. *Callinectes* is Greek for beautiful swimmer and *sapidus* is Latin for savory. The primary definition of crab is that of a number of crustaceans, with blue crabs being truly incredible specimens. They become even more wondrous when they shed their hard shells and are transformed into soft-shell crabs.

Purchase live jumbo soft-shell crabs from your fishmonger. The only way to ensure top-quality soft crabs is to buy live ones. All too often dealers try to disguise a poor-quality product by dressing or freezing crabs that have met an untimely end. If you are a bit squeamish about dressing live crabs, ask your fishmonger to dress the crabs for you, but insist that these be live crabs. Jumbo crabs measure about 5 inches from point to point. We prefer this size live crab because it is meatier, although no more succulent, than the smaller graded ''mediums,'' ''hotels,'' or ''primes.''

The primary reason that so many soft crabs are frozen is to make them available on a year-round basis. I insist that we purchase only live crabs for The Trellis; therefore, we serve soft-shell crabs only during the primary molting season (when the crabs shed their hard shell) in the Chesapeake Bay, which is usually from May through August.

Until the last few years, sugar snap peas were eaten only by the ambitious gardeners who grew them. Happily, they are now more widely available. These edible podded peas are deliciously sweet and, like snow peas, totally edible save for the very fibrous string, which should be removed. Soft crabs are also excellent served with tiny green beans, snow peas, or snap beans.

For a recipe lower in saturated fat, sauté the crabs and peas in peanut oil rather than clarified butter and eliminate the brown butter. Serve a half lemon with each portion.

Sauvignon blanc wines run the gamut from powerfully herbaceous to assertively fruity. With this dish, my personal preference is a sauvignon with a pleasant touch of fruit and a slight nuance of grass, backed by an obvious contact with oak. The Groth Vineyards 1985 sauvignon blanc is such a wine.

Grilled Sea Scallops with Shallots, Garlic, and Citrus Ricciarelle

Serves 8

1 tablespoon fresh grapefruit juice
1 tablespoon fresh lemon juice
1 tablespoon fresh lime juice
1 tablespoon fresh orange juice
4¹/₂ cups all-purpose flour
5 eggs
3 tablespoons olive oil
¹/₂ tablespoon finely chopped grapefruit zest (see page 314)
¹/₂ tablespoon finely chopped lemon zest
¹/₂ tablespoon finely chopped lime zest

¹/₂ tablespoon finely chopped orange zest
1 teaspoon salt
³/₄ pound shallots, unpeeled
¹/₂ pound unsalted butter, softened
Salt and pepper to season
³/₄ cup dry white wine
2 tablespoons chopped fresh parsley
1 tablespoon minced garlic
¹/₂ cup cornmeal
3 pounds sea scallops, side muscle removed
6 tablespoons vegetable oil

EQUIPMENT: *Zester or vegetable peeler, cutting board, French knife, medium-gauge strainer, two small non-stick sauté pans, rubber spatula, measuring cup, measuring spoons, fork, film wrap, pasta machine, two baking sheets with sides, parchment paper, stainless-steel bowl, eight 9-inch bamboo or metal skewers, charcoal grill, tongs, 5-quart saucepan, colander*

Heat the citrus juices to a simmer in a non-stick sauté pan over low heat. Simmer until reduced to about 1 teaspoon, 8 to 10 minutes. Remove from the heat and allow to cool.

Place 4 cups flour on a clean, dry cutting board or similar work surface. Make a well in the center and add the eggs, reduced citrus juice, 1 tablespoon olive oil, chopped citrus zest, and 1 teaspoon salt. Using a fork, combine the eggs, juice, oil, zest, and salt. When thoroughly mixed, begin to work the flour into the center, a small amount at a time. When enough flour has been added that you can handle the dough, begin kneading by hand. Knead the dough by hand until all the flour has been incorporated, about 10 minutes. Cover the dough with film wrap and allow to relax at room temperature for 1 hour.

Preheat the oven to 275 degrees.

While the pasta dough is relaxing, peel and mince 3 shallots. Heat 1 tablespoon butter in a non-stick sauté pan over medium heat. When hot, add the minced shallots, season with salt and pepper, and sauté for 1 minute. Add the wine and bring to a simmer. Lower the heat and simmer until the pan is almost dry, about 15 minutes. Remove from the heat, transfer to a stainless-steel bowl, and cool. When cool, combine with the remaining butter, parsley, and garlic. Cover the garlic butter with film wrap and hold at room temperature until ready to use.

Cut the remaining whole shallots into quarters but do not peel. Place the shallots on a baking sheet and sprinkle with the remaining 2 table-spoons olive oil. Season with salt and pepper. Place the baking sheet in the preheated oven and roast the shallots for 20 minutes. Remove the pan from the oven and allow to cool for a few moments. Trim and peel the shallots and cover with film wrap. Hold at room temperature until ready to use.

Lower the oven temperature to 225 degrees.

Cut the pasta dough into 8 equal portions. Roll and knead each portion of dough through the pasta machine, using the extra ½ cup flour as necessary to prevent the dough from becoming tacky. Cut the sheets of dough into ricciarelle (see page 315). To prevent sticking, toss the cut pasta with the cornmeal, then place the cut pasta portions onto a baking sheet lined with parchment paper. Cover the sheet tightly with film wrap and refrigerate until needed.

Combine the scallops with the vegetable oil. Season with salt and pepper. Divide the scallops into 8 portions and skewer each portion.

Grill the scallop skewers for 4 minutes over a medium charcoal or wood fire. Turn the skewers only once while cooking. Transfer the skewers to a baking sheet along with the roasted shallot quarters. Baste the skewers with ½ cup garlic butter. Hold in the preheated oven while cooking the pasta.

Cook the pasta (see page 315) in 3 quarts boiling salted water until tender but still firm to the bite, 2 to 2½ minutes. Transfer the cooked pasta to a colander, return to the pan, and toss with the remaining garlic butter. Place equal portions of the cooked pasta on each of 8 warm plates. Unskewer each scallop portion into the center of the pasta and garnish with equal portions of the roasted shallots. Serve immediately.

The Chef's Touch

Any single citrus fruit, or a combination of any citrus fruits, may be used for this pasta recipe.

Ricciarelle is a uniquely shaped pasta. Its wavy shape and thicker cut (about $1/16$ inch thick) give it a visual as well as textural identity. If you do not own a ricciarelle cutter you may use a lasagne cutter. Cut each sheet of lasagne lengthwise into two or three strips. Lacking either one of these cutters you can cut the pasta into fettuccine, spaghetti, capellini, or tagliatelle. Remember to adjust the cooking time, as the thinner-cut pastas will cook very rapidly.

Garlic butter may be prepared in advance and stored covered and refrigerated for several days. Soften butter to room temperature before using.

Be careful not to overgrill the scallops; if in doubt, it is better to undercook. The grilling should impart only a slight flavor of the charcoal or wood to the scallops; additional cooking will take place in the oven. If grilling is impractical, the scallops may be fully cooked by broiling in the oven. Place the scallops on a baking sheet under a preheated broiler and broil for four minutes (two minutes on each side).

As a final extra touch to this recipe, you may want to sprinkle chopped fresh parsley and citrus zest over the scallops and pasta.

With all of these flavors at work, an uncomplicated but not austere chardonnay would be perfectly suited. The 1984 Trefethen winery chardonnay is my choice.

Sautéed Salmon Fillet with Fresh Peas and Cream on Sorrel Fettuccine

Serves 8

*¹/₂ pound sorrel leaves (2 cups
 tightly packed), stemmed,
 washed, and dried*
2 tablespoons olive oil
5 cups all-purpose flour
4 eggs
1 teaspoon salt
3 tablespoons lemon juice

*8 5-ounce skinless salmon fillets
 Salt and pepper to season*
1¹/₂ pounds shelling peas, shelled
¹/₂ cup cornmeal
2 cups heavy cream
1 tablespoon vegetable oil
*9 tablespoons unsalted butter,
 softened*

EQUIPMENT: *Cutting board, French knife, measuring cup, measuring spoons, food processor, rubber spatula, fork, film wrap, pasta machine, two baking sheets with sides, parchment paper, two 2¹/₂-quart saucepans, stainless-steel ladle, medium-gauge strainer, stainless-steel bowl, double boiler, three non-stick sauté pans (one large), metal spatula, 5-quart saucepan, tongs, colander*

Cut 8 large sorrel leaves into thin strips. Cover with film wrap and refrigerate until needed.

In the bowl of a food processor fitted with a metal blade, purée the remaining sorrel leaves along with the olive oil for 2 to 3 minutes, scraping down the sides of the processor bowl as necessary with a rubber spatula.

Place 4¹/₂ cups flour on a clean, dry cutting board or similar surface. Make a well in the center and add the eggs, sorrel purée, and 1 teaspoon salt. Using a fork, combine the eggs, sorrel purée, and salt. When thoroughly mixed, begin to work the flour into the center, a small amount at a time. When enough flour has been added so that you can handle the dough, begin kneading by hand. Knead by hand until all the flour has

91

been incorporated, about 10 minutes. Cover with film wrap and allow to relax at room temperature for 1 hour.

While the pasta dough is relaxing, sprinkle the lemon juice over the salmon fillets. Season with salt and pepper and individually film-wrap the fillets. Refrigerate until needed.

Blanch the shelled peas in 2 quarts boiling salted water for 1 minute. Transfer the peas to a strainer; place the strainer in ice water. When the peas are cool, remove from the ice water, drain thoroughly, cover with film wrap, and refrigerate until ready to use.

Cut the pasta dough into 8 equal portions. Roll and knead each portion of dough through the pasta machine, using the extra 1/2 cup flour as necessary to prevent the dough from becoming tacky. Cut the sheets of dough into fettuccine (see page 315). To prevent sticking, toss the cut pasta with the cornmeal, then place the cut pasta portions on a baking sheet lined with parchment paper. Cover the sheet tightly with film wrap and refrigerate until needed.

Heat the heavy cream in a 2 1/2-quart saucepan over medium heat. Lightly season with salt and pepper. Keep a ladle in the saucepan and occasionally stir the cream so that it does not foam over the sides of the pot. Lower the heat if necessary so that the cream is barely simmering. Simmer until reduced by half, about 45 minutes. Strain the reduced cream and hold warm in a double boiler.

Preheat the oven to 225 degrees.

Heat the vegetable oil in a large non-stick sauté pan over high heat. Remove the film wrap from the salmon fillets and season with salt and pepper. When the oil is hot, place the salmon fillets in the pan, skinned side up. Sauté for 1 minute on each side. Transfer the salmon to a baking sheet and hold in the preheated oven while heating the peas and cooking the pasta.

Heat 1 tablespoon butter in a non-stick sauté pan over medium high heat. When the butter is hot, add the peas. Season with salt and pepper and sauté until hot, 2 to 3 minutes.

Cook the pasta (see page 315) in 3 quarts boiling salted water until tender but firm to the bite, 30 seconds to 1 minute. Transfer the cooked pasta to a colander to drain, return to the pan, and toss with the remaining softened butter.

Place equal portions of the cooked pasta on each of 8 warm plates. Spoon 2 tablespoons reduced cream over each serving of pasta. Place a salmon fillet in the center. Portion the peas over all and sprinkle the pasta with the sorrel strips (leave the salmon uncovered). Serve immediately.

The Chef's Touch

For Fannie Farmer, the ingredients in this recipe might have been canned salmon, dried herbs, canned peas, white sauce, and overcooked noodles.

Thankfully, Americans are eschewing their unfortunate culinary past. In its place, fresh products and skillful cookery combine to create recipes that predate the turn-of-the-century decline and recall the early nineteenth century, a time when Mary Randolph was documenting the roots of our true native cuisine in *The Virginia House-wife*.

Shelling peas is time-consuming; however, freshly shelled peas are worth the effort. They are beautiful, delicious, and texturally there is simply no comparison between a fresh sweet pea and the frozen or canned product. If fresh shelling peas are not available, substitute whole snow peas or sugar snap peas.

Reduced cream must be kept warm: hold it in a double boiler. Once reduced cream has cooled, it will not reheat properly. Reheated reduced cream is usually grainy in texture and tends to break down (the fat separating from the non-fat portion).

Although reduced cream adds to the palatability and elegance of this dish, it is not essential. If you are concerned about saturated fats, eliminate the cream and toss the pasta with 1/4 cup olive oil instead of the softened butter.

The direction to place salmon fillets skinned side up into the hot pan is important. To determine which side of the fillet is the skinned side, look for streaks of dark coloration on the flesh. Cooking the fillet skinned side up and turning the fillet once during the sautéing guarantees the flesh side of the fillet will be attractively presented when the cooking is done.

The sour taste of fresh sorrel is just the right foil to the richness of this dish. Spinach leaves may be used as a substitute for color and texture, although the unique taste of the sorrel will be missing.

As a final eye-appealing touch, garnish each plate with whole sorrel and sliced lemons.

A 1983 Charles Shaw gamay beaujolais, a California red wine of subtle character, would be an excellent, though not traditional, match for this contemporary salmon dish.

Grilled Breast of Chicken with Spring Vegetables and Vermouth

Serves 8

8 8-ounce boneless and skinless chicken breasts
1/4 cup fresh lemon juice
1/4 cup dry white wine
   Salt and pepper to season
1/4 pound snow peas, trimmed
1/4 pound tiny green beans, trimmed
1/2 pound asparagus, stems trimmed and peeled

1 large carrot, cut into strips 2 1/2 inches long and 1/8 inch wide
1/2 cup dry vermouth
2 tablespoons safflower oil
1 large red onion, sliced thin
1 medium tomato, peeled, seeded, and chopped (see page 316)
1/4 pound mushrooms, stems trimmed and sliced 1/8 inch thick

EQUIPMENT: *Paring knife, cutting board, French knife, measuring spoons, two stainless-steel bowls, meat cleaver, aluminum foil, film wrap, two baking sheets with sides, two 2 1/2-quart saucepans, medium-gauge strainer, charcoal grill, tongs, large non-stick sauté pan*

Trim any excess fat from the chicken breasts. In a stainless-steel bowl, combine the lemon juice and white wine. Season with salt and pepper and mix thoroughly. Sprinkle over the chicken breasts. Place the chicken breasts, one at a time, between two sheets of lightly oiled aluminum foil or parchment paper. Uniformly flatten each breast (see page 316) with a meat cleaver or the bottom of a sauté pan. Individually film-wrap each chicken breast and refrigerate until needed.

Blanch the snow peas in 2 quarts boiling salted water for 20 to 30 seconds. Transfer to ice water. When the peas are cool, drain thoroughly, cover with film wrap, and refrigerate. Separately blanch the tiny green beans in the same saucepan of boiling water for 2 to 2 1/2 minutes. Transfer to ice water. When cool, drain thoroughly, cover, and refrigerate. Blanch the asparagus for 45 seconds. Cool in ice water, drain thoroughly, cover, and refrigerate.

In a separate saucepan of boiling salted water, blanch the carrots for 1 1/2 minutes. Transfer to ice water. When cool, drain, cover with film wrap, and refrigerate until needed.

Preheat the oven to 350 degrees.

Season the chicken breasts with salt and pepper and grill over a medium hot charcoal or wood fire for 1 1/2 minutes on each side. Transfer to a baking sheet. Pour the vermouth over the chicken and cover tightly with aluminum foil. Place in the preheated oven for 10 minutes.

While the chicken is cooking, heat the safflower oil in a large non-stick sauté pan over medium high heat. When hot, add the onion. Season lightly with salt and pepper and sauté for 1 minute. Add the tiny beans and carrots, season, and sauté for 1 minute. Add the tomato and asparagus, season, and sauté for 2 minutes. Finally, add the snow peas and mushrooms, season, and sauté until all the vegetables are hot, an additional 1 or 2 minutes. Taste and adjust the seasoning if necessary.

Place equal portions of the vegetables on each of 8 warm 10-inch plates. Place a chicken breast on top of each and serve immediately.

The Chef's Touch

On my first trip to Paris, I found American-born Patricia Wells' *The Food Lover's Guide to Paris* indispensable.

After reading Ms. Wells' review of the Parisian restaurant Jacqueline Fenix, I could not wait to try it—not a vegetarian restaurant, but rather one that gave prominent and simple treatment to vegetables and featured them on the same plate as the main course, sometimes as an accompaniment and quite often as a replacement for a sauce.

This contemporary restaurant lived up to my expectations and the review. All of the food was simply prepared from impeccably fresh ingredients, just the type of straightforward approach we offer in this recipe.

The above dish makes an excellent meal for those interested in a low-saturated-fat diet. If you are also counting calories, reduce the size of the chicken breast to 4 ounces.

This very simple recipe can be enhanced by several variations. A bed of fresh pasta covered with a medley of sautéed vegetables, then topped with a grilled chicken breast, would make an appealing combination. A variety of fresh herbs used singly or in combination would add depth to the flavor. Almost any other vegetable could be used as a substitute (such as snap beans for the tiny green beans) or in addition to those called for (such as fresh artichoke hearts, bell peppers, and yellow beans).

Although we suggest using vermouth for this recipe, different nuances can be achieved by the use of other wines. A chardonnay with overtones of oak and vanilla would contribute a distinctive flavor, while the spicy quality of an Alsatian gewürztraminer would be an intriguing touch.

Grilling the chicken is an important element in the success of this recipe. The flavor of the burning charcoal and wood fire should permeate but not overpower the chicken. Do not over-grill or cook over too hot a fire; the end product would be overwhelming in flavor as well as tough and devoid of natural juices.

As each vegetable is seasoned (beginning with the onion), be certain to season lightly. The seasoning should be adjusted after all the vegetables have been added and heated.

Drink a pouilly-fumé from the Loire to complement this unaffected dish.

Grilled Smoked Lamb with Artichokes and Slab Bacon on Fresh Thyme Fettuccine

Serves 8

1 10-pound leg of lamb, boned	¹/₂ cup chopped fresh thyme
2 cups warm water	1 teaspoon salt
1 cup kosher salt	¹/₂ pound hickory-smoked slab
¹/₄ cup granulated sugar	bacon
2 cups cool water	6 medium artichokes, prepared
11 tablespoons olive oil	as on page 317
Salt and pepper to season	¹/₄ cup fresh lemon juice
4 cups all-purpose flour	¹/₂ cup cornmeal
4 eggs	

EQUIPMENT: *Boning knife, cutting board, measuring cup, stainless-steel bowl, whisk, paper towels, two baking sheets with sides, film wrap, "Little Chief" smoker, parchment paper, measuring spoons, charcoal grill, tongs, serrated slicer, fork, pasta machine, paring knife, grapefruit spoon, 2¹/₂-quart saucepan, 5-quart saucepan, large non-stick sauté pan, colander*

Trim all fat, tendons, and membrane from the boned leg of lamb, to yield six 6-ounce pieces of well-trimmed lamb. Combine the warm water, kosher salt, and sugar in a stainless-steel bowl, whisking until the salt and sugar have dissolved. Whisk in the cool water. Place the lamb pieces in the brine for 5 minutes. Remove the lamb from the brine. Drain on paper towels, then refrigerate uncovered for 1 hour.

Line the center shelf of the smoker (see page 320) with parchment paper. Place the lamb pieces on the parchment and smoke for 3 hours, turning the pieces over after 1¹/₂ hours. Transfer the smoked lamb to a baking sheet and refrigerate, loosely covered with film wrap, until completely cool, about 2 hours.

Coat the smoked lamb pieces with 4 tablespoons olive oil, then season liberally with salt and pepper. Grill the lamb over a hot charcoal or wood fire for 1 to 1¹/₂ minutes per side (total cooking time, 2 to 3 minutes).

Place the lamb pieces on a baking sheet and refrigerate for 1 hour. Cut the cooled lamb into 2½-inch-long and ⅜-inch-wide strips and refrigerate, covered, until needed.

Place 3½ cups flour on a clean, dry cutting board or similar work surface. Make a well in the center and add the eggs, 7 tablespoons chopped thyme, 1 tablespoon olive oil, and 1 teaspoon salt. Using a fork, combine the eggs, thyme, oil, and salt. When thoroughly mixed, begin to work the flour into the center, a small amount at a time. When enough flour has been added that you can handle the dough, begin kneading by hand. Knead by hand until all the flour has been incorporated, about 10 minutes. Cover with film wrap and allow to relax at room temperature for 1 hour.

Preheat the oven to 325 degrees.

Prepare the bacon while the dough is relaxing. Trim the rind and excess fat from the bacon and slice into ⅜-inch strips. Cut the strips into ⅜-inch cubes. Cook the bacon cubes on a baking sheet in the preheated oven for 30 minutes. When cooked, place on paper towels to drain. Keep at room temperature until needed.

In a 2½-quart saucepan, bring to a boil 2 quarts lightly salted water with the lemon juice. Add the prepared artichokes and cook until a knife inserted in the center of an artichoke encounters firmness but no resistance, 10 to 12 minutes. Drain the cooked artichokes, then plunge into ice water. When cool, trim, then cut into strips 1½ inches long and ¼ inch wide. Cover with film wrap and refrigerate until needed.

Cut the pasta dough into 8 equal portions. Roll and knead each portion of dough through a pasta machine, using the extra ½ cup flour as necessary to prevent the dough from becoming tacky. Cut the sheets of dough into fettuccine (see page 315). To prevent sticking, toss the cut pasta with the cornmeal, then place the cut pasta portions on a baking sheet lined with parchment paper.

Heat 2 tablespoons olive oil in a large non-stick sauté pan over high heat. Add the bacon and sauté for 30 seconds. Add the lamb strips, artichokes, and remaining tablespoon thyme. Season lightly with salt and pepper and sauté for 3 minutes. Adjust the heat to low. Keep the pan on low heat while cooking the pasta.

Cook the pasta (see page 315) in 3 quarts boiling salted water until tender but still firm to the bite, 30 seconds to 1 minute. Drain the cooked pasta in a colander, return to the pan, and toss with the remaining 4 tablespoons olive oil.

Place equal portions of the pasta on each of 8 warm plates. Divide the lamb mixture over the top of each and serve immediately.

The Chef's Touch

American lamb is a delicious meat that, according to statistics, few Americans eat. Annual consumption of lamb in this country is under 2 pounds per person, versus close to 80 pounds per person for beef. Too many taste buds may have been disappointed by frozen imported lamb, which is often gamy in flavor. The fact is that fresh American lamb has an enjoyable and not overwhelming taste, subtle enough to meld with other ingredients, yet with enough character to establish its own identity.

There is an unfortunate amount of waste from a leg of lamb, especially so with this recipe, because the meat should be free of all fat, sinew, and membrane. Other cuts of lamb such as neck and shoulder meat may also be used, but the lightly marbled leg meat better absorbs the smoke flavor.

The meat is refrigerated after smoking and grilling to control the degree of doneness. The lamb should remain very rare after it has been grilled.

If grilling is not practical, roast the cooled smoked meat for 5 minutes in a preheated 350-degree oven.

If fresh thyme is not available for the pasta, substitute 2 tablespoons dried thyme for flavor and 1 cup finely chopped, lightly packed stemmed spinach leaves for color.

Scarlet-colored ruby chard, cut into thin strips, blanched, and then sautéed with the lamb and artichokes, was added to this dish when we listed it on our spring 1986 menu.

As a final touch, garnish the plate with thyme flowers.

The diversity of flavors in this dish is highlighted by the smoked and charred taste of the lamb as well as the sweet pungent flavor of thyme. A compatible wine is a full-bodied but not overly tannic cabernet sauvignon.

Grilled Calves' Liver with Avocado, Red Onion, and Brown Butter

Serves 8

6 tablespoons cider vinegar
3¹/₂ tablespoons fresh lemon juice
4 teaspoons Dijon-style mustard
¹/₂ teaspoon salt
¹/₄ teaspoon ground black pepper
1³/₄ cups vegetable oil
4 medium red onions, sliced ³/₈ inch thick

8 8-ounce slices calves' liver, ¹/₂ to ³/₄ inch thick
8 8-ounce avocados
Salt and pepper to season
¹/₄ pound unsalted butter, softened
1 tablespoon chopped fresh parsley

EQUIPMENT: *Measuring spoons, measuring cup, stainless-steel bowl, whisk, film wrap, cutting board, paring knife, serrated slicer, French knife, four baking sheets (two with sides), charcoal grill, tongs, metal spatula, non-stick sauté pan*

In a stainless-steel bowl, whisk together the vinegar, 3 tablespoons lemon juice, mustard, ¹/₂ teaspoon salt, and ¹/₄ teaspoon ground black pepper. Add 1¹/₂ cups vegetable oil in a slow and steady stream, whisking continuously until all the oil has been incorporated. Immerse the onion slices in this marinade. Cover the bowl with film wrap and refrigerate for 1 hour.

Coat the liver slices with the remaining ¹/₄ cup vegetable oil. If the liver is not to be used immediately, individually film-wrap each slice and refrigerate until needed.

Preheat the oven to 225 degrees.

Peel and split in half one avocado at a time. Remove the seed. Place the cut sides of the avocado on a cutting board. Thinly slice (about ¹/₈ inch thick) the avocado halves from end to end, keeping the slices together. Using both hands, shape each avocado half into a fan. Place the two avocado fans, opposite each other, along the inside border of a large dinner plate. Repeat the procedure for each dinner plate.

Remove the onion slices from the marinade. Season each slice with salt and pepper and grill over a medium hot charcoal or wood fire for 2½ minutes on each side. Place the grilled onion slices on a baking sheet and hold in the preheated oven while grilling the liver.

Season the liver with salt and pepper and grill over a medium fire for 1 to 2 minutes on each side, depending upon the thickness. Transfer to a baking sheet and hold in the oven with the onions for 5 minutes.

Place a non-stick sauté pan over high heat. When the pan is very hot, add the butter and brown evenly. While the butter is browning, place a grilled liver slice in the center of each plate, between the 2 avocado fans. Place 2 slices grilled red onion on top of the liver. Add the remaining ½ tablespoon lemon juice to the brown butter, shaking the pan vigorously so that the butter does not foam over the sides. Carefully pour equal amounts of brown butter over each portion of onions and liver. Sprinkle the chopped parsley over the onions and liver and serve immediately.

The Chef's Touch

There seems to be no middle ground between those who disdain liver and those who frequently yearn for this unique cut of meat. My wife, Connie, numbers among the latter. When she dines at The Trellis, it is certain that she will order liver if it is on the menu. Connie likes her calves' liver very rare, contrary to the most frequently requested degree of doneness: well done! The fact is, liver should never be overcooked as it develops an unappetizing flavor and aroma when subjected to excessive cooking.

The red onions may be marinated for several hours or from the day before this dish is to be served. The rest of the recipe takes less than thirty minutes to prepare and serve.

Properly trimmed liver should be free of surface membrane, blood vessels, and tough inner membrane. It will oxidize quickly after the surface membrane has been removed. Coating with oil and film wrapping will assure fresh and pleasant-smelling liver (even for up to two or three days, under proper refrigeration). If you purchase a whole liver, trim and slice it the day of purchase. After coating with oil and film-wrapping, freeze whatever portions will not be used immediately.

Liver should be seasoned with salt only a few moments before it is to be grilled. A natural action of salt is to draw moisture. In the case of liver, salting done any length of time before cooking would draw out much of the blood and render the liver quite insipid.

Choose ripe but *firm* avocados or you will end up with guacamole rather than fans. The avocados may be sliced up to a half hour before serving. Held longer than that, they will become unattractively discolored.

Connie suggests that a McDowell Valley Vineyards syrah be enjoyed with this, her favorite of our calves' liver recipes.

Grilled Duck Breast with Raspberries and Macadamia Nuts

Serves 8

4 5-pound ducks
1 cup red wine
2 cups macadamia nuts
2 cups chicken stock (see
     page 305)
1¹/₂ pints red raspberries
1 cup raspberry vinegar

¹/₄ cup minced shallots
¹/₄ teaspoon cracked black
     peppercorns
¹/₄ cup heavy cream
1¹/₂ tablespoons arrowroot
     Salt and pepper to season

EQUIPMENT: *Cutting board, boning knife, measuring cup, two stainless-steel bowls, aluminum foil, meat cleaver, two baking sheets with sides, two 2¹/₂-quart saucepans, measuring spoons, fine strainer, whisk, double boiler, charcoal grill, tongs*

Preheat the oven to 300 degrees.

Remove the breasts from the duck (see page 316). Trim all fat and membrane from the duck breasts. Pour the red wine into a stainless-steel bowl. Dip the duck breasts in the wine, then place the duck breasts, one at a time, in between two sheets of lightly oiled aluminum foil or parchment paper. Uniformly flatten each breast (see page 316) with a meat cleaver or the bottom of a sauté pan. Individually film-wrap each breast and refrigerate until needed.

Toast the macadamia nuts on a baking sheet in the preheated oven until golden brown, 15 to 20 minutes. Hold at room temperature until needed. Lower the oven temperature to 225 degrees.

Heat the chicken stock in a 2¹/₂-quart saucepan over medium high heat. Lower the heat and simmer until reduced to 1 cup, about 20 minutes. Add ¹/₂ pint raspberries to the reduced chicken stock, adjust the heat to low, and allow the raspberries to steep for 15 to 20 minutes.

While the raspberries are steeping, heat the vinegar, shallots, and black peppercorns in a 2¹/₂-quart saucepan over medium high heat. Cook, reducing until the saucepan is almost dry, 15 to 20 minutes.

Combine the chicken stock and raspberries with the vinegar reduction. Bring to a boil over high heat, then strain through a fine strainer. This should yield 1½ cups of liquid. Heat the liquid to a boil in a 2½-quart saucepan over medium high heat.

In a stainless-steel bowl, whisk together the heavy cream and arrowroot. Pour ½ cup of the hot raspberry mixture into the cream and whisk until smooth. Transfer to the saucepan containing the remaining raspberry mixture and whisk until smooth. Strain and hold warm in a double boiler while grilling the duck.

Remove the film wrap from the duck breasts and season with salt and pepper. Grill over a medium charcoal or wood fire for 2 to 2½ minutes on each side. Transfer the grilled duck to a baking sheet and hold in the 225-degree oven while assembling the plates.

Flood the base of each of 8 warm 10-inch plates with ¼ cup raspberry sauce. Arrange a ring of raspberries near the outside edge of each plate. Slice the duck breasts at a slight angle across the grain. Arrange each sliced duck breast in a fan in the center of each plate. Sprinkle the macadamia nuts around the duck breasts and serve immediately.

The Chef's Touch

Some may perceive this recipe to be an affectation of "nouvelle cuisine." Perhaps so, but it is nevertheless a splendid dish: distinct slices of medium rare duck, set off by a stunning sauce enhanced by a purée of fresh berries, all garnished with lush raspberries and buttery macadamia nuts.

After removing the duck breasts from the carcass, cut away the leg and thigh sections. Marinate the duck legs in red wine for three days and grill. They are also delicious cured (see below).

The buttery sweet flavor of macadamia nuts is irreplaceable in this recipe.

Due to strong consumer demand, fresh raspberries are being marketed almost year-round in the United States. California raspberries are usually available in early May, followed by Northwest berries through September. In addition to American raspberries, we have beautiful berries from New Zealand and Chile available from November through April.

The flavor characteristics of this recipe depend upon the use of fresh raspberries.

Many red raspberry vinegars are now available. The best, albeit expensive, is the French Corcellet red raspberry wine vinegar. It has a definite fruit taste and is pleasantly tart. The success of this sauce relies on the use of a high-quality raspberry vinegar.

Arrowroot is an excellent thickening agent derived from the root of a tropical plant. Some cooks mistakenly believe that cornstarch is a valid substitute for arrowroot. It is true that cornstarch thickens in much the same way; however, the texture of a sauce thickened with cornstarch is not as smooth nor as glossy as that of a sauce thickened with arrowroot.

A sublime wine selection for this dish would be a 1982 Château Giscours, a rich, supple example of a red bordeaux still developing into maturity.

CURED DUCK LEGS

Place 8 duck legs in a stainless-steel bowl. Combine the legs with 3 tablespoons kosher salt, 1½ tablespoons sugar, ¾ teaspoon chopped fresh thyme, ½ teaspoon chopped fresh rosemary, and ¼ teaspoon minced garlic. Stir well to mix. Cover with film wrap and refrigerate for 6 hours.

In a non-stick sauté pan over medium heat, heat 3 cups vegetable shortening for 20 minutes, to 300 degrees. Cook the duck legs in the hot shortening, turning regularly, until golden brown and the skin begins to pull back from the bone, 35 minutes.

Transfer the warm duck legs to a heat-resistant crock. Allow the shortening to cool to room temperature. Pour the cooled shortening over the legs. Be certain the legs are completely submerged. Refrigerate. When the shortening solidifies, cover the crock.

The duck legs should remain in the refrigerator for three days before you use them. (They will keep for two to three weeks if the solidified shortening layer is not disturbed.)

Cured duck legs may be grilled, warmed in the oven, braised with dried beans, or the meat may be removed from the bone, cut into thin strips, and served over salads and pastas.

Grilled Asparagus with Tomatoes, Braised Black-eyed Peas, and Basil Rice

Serves 8

1 pound dried black-eyed peas, washed and picked over

2½ pounds asparagus

2 teaspoons salt

6 cups vegetable stock (see page 309)

6 tablespoons olive oil

¼ cup minced shallots
Salt and pepper to season

2 cups converted rice

6 tablespoons chopped fresh basil

1 medium onion, chopped fine

2 medium carrots, chopped fine

2 stalks celery, chopped fine

2 small leeks, white part only, chopped fine

1 small red bell pepper, chopped fine

1 small green bell pepper, chopped fine

1 teaspoon minced garlic

¼ cup balsamic vinegar

3 medium tomatoes, peeled, seeded, and chopped (see page 316)

4 scallions, trimmed and sliced thin

EQUIPMENT: *Two 5-quart saucepans, measuring cup, two 2½-quart saucepans, film wrap, measuring spoons, tongs, stainless-steel bowl, colander, paring knife, French knife, cutting board, wooden spoon, aluminum foil, two non-stick sauté pans (one large), rubber spatula, charcoal grill, baking sheet with sides*

Place the peas in a 5-quart saucepan, cover with 4 cups cold water, and soak for 2 hours at room temperature.

Snap the woody stem from each stalk of asparagus and lightly peel the stalks. Blanch the asparagus in boiling salted water for about 45 seconds, depending upon the thickness; the asparagus should remain very crisp. Immediately transfer to ice water. When cold, drain thoroughly, cover with film wrap, and refrigerate until needed.

Rinse the soaked peas thoroughly. Drain, then return them to the 5-quart saucepan and cover with 6 cups fresh cold water. Add 2 teaspoons salt. Cook the peas over medium high heat until tender but still firm, 18 to 20 minutes. Drain, then cool under cold running water. Cover with film wrap and refrigerate until needed.

Heat 4 cups stock to a boil in a 2½-quart saucepan over high heat. In a separate 2½-quart saucepan, heat 1 tablespoon olive oil over medium high heat. When hot, add 2 tablespoons shallots, season with salt and pepper, and sauté for 1 minute. Add the rice and stir until the rice grains are covered with olive oil. Carefully add the boiling stock. When the stock returns to a boil, add 5 tablespoons chopped basil; season with salt and pepper. Stir well and cover tightly. Reduce the heat to low and cook for 20 minutes. Remove the pot from the heat and keep covered while completing the recipe.

Heat 1 tablespoon olive oil in a large non-stick sauté pan. When the oil is hot, add the chopped onion, carrots, celery, leeks, bell peppers, remaining 2 tablespoons minced shallots, and garlic. Season with salt and pepper and sauté for 4 minutes. Transfer the sautéed vegetables to a 5-quart saucepan and add the black-eyed peas, remaining 2 cups stock, balsamic vinegar, and remaining tablespoon basil. Bring the mixture to a boil over medium high heat, then reduce heat to low. Keep the peas warm over low heat while completing the recipe.

Preheat the oven to 225 degrees.

Coat the asparagus stalks with the remaining 4 tablespoons olive oil. Season with salt and pepper and grill over a medium charcoal or wood fire for 1½ minutes, turning as needed to prevent overcharring. Transfer the grilled asparagus to a baking sheet and hold in the preheated oven.

Heat the tomatoes in a non-stick sauté pan over medium high heat. Season with salt and pepper and sauté until hot, 4 to 5 minutes.

Arrange a 2½-inch-wide semicircle of black-eyed peas and vegetables along the outside edge of each of 8 warm large dinner plates. Parallel to the peas, arrange a 2½-inch-wide semicircle of rice. Place the tomatoes on each plate to fill in the remaining space. Arrange a fan of asparagus over the peas and rice, stem ends touching and clustered at the tomatoes. Sprinkle the scallions over the tomatoes and serve immediately.

The Chef's Touch

Inspired by a week at the Canyon Ranch Fitness Spa in Tucson, Arizona, I wanted to offer our guests an authentic vegetarian selection. Although the ranch does not prepare only vegetarian food, their emphasis on structuring a meal with a minimum of 60% complex carbohydrates clearly put the options in the direction of vegetables, grains, and beans.

Offered at both lunch and dinner at The Trellis, our vegetarian items are called "the garden selection."

The delicious hearty flavor of dried black-eyed peas makes them one of our favorite dried beans. Several other dried beans would work well in this recipe, including black turtle beans and red kidney beans.

The vegetable stock is a flavorful but not essential element in this recipe. If time is short, use well-seasoned water or, if an authentic vegetarian course is not a necessity, use chicken stock.

Other oils low in saturated fats may be substituted for olive oil in this recipe. Safflower oil, sunflower oil, and corn oil are all lower in saturated fats than olive oil and they are also all excellent cooking oils.

Use a less expensive red wine vinegar if balsamic vinegar is not available.

Sautéed Lump Backfin Crabmeat with Irish Smoked Salmon on Toasted Brioche

Serves 8

16 *³/₈-inch-thick slices brioche loaf*
   (see page 228)
¹/₄ *pound unsalted butter, softened*
 2 *pounds lump backfin crabmeat,*
   well picked of shell

¹/₄ *pound smoked salmon, cut into*
   ³/₈-inch cubes
   Salt and pepper to season

EQUIPMENT: *Cutting board, serrated slicer, two baking sheets, measuring spoons, large non-stick sauté pan, slotted spoon*

Preheat the oven to 325 degrees.

Trim the crust from the brioche slices. Cut 8 of the slices in half diagonally to form triangles. Toast on baking sheets in the preheated oven until golden brown, about 15 minutes. Keep the slices at kitchen temperature until ready to use. Lower the oven temperature to 200 degrees.

Heat the butter in a large non-stick sauté pan over medium high heat. When hot, add the crabmeat and smoked salmon and sauté for 4 to 5 minutes. When hot, adjust the seasoning with salt and pepper.

Warm the brioche slices in the 200-degree oven while the crabmeat is being sautéed.

Place a brioche square in the center of each of 8 warm plates, then place a brioche triangle to the left and right of each square. Using a slotted spoon, portion the crab and salmon over the brioche square, leaving the triangles exposed. Serve immediately.

The Chef's Touch

Sautéed crabmeat served over warm brioche is an elegant meal. You may wish to make it a more casual entrée by substituting Chili Corn Bread (see page 241) for the brioche.

Many variations on this theme allow the cook to serve this dish frequently without wearing out the concept. In addition to using another bread, you may want to use country ham or chopped tomatoes and fresh herbs rather than smoked salmon.

Be careful to season this dish very lightly; the smoked salmon will accentuate any added salt.

For breakfast or brunch, serve half of the suggested portion with scrambled eggs.

If you wish, garnish the dish with chopped fresh parsley, half a lemon, and fresh herb leaves.

There is a feeling of celebration about lump crabmeat, smoked salmon, and toasted brioche; in acknowledgment, I would drink a 1978 Laurent-Perrier, Gran Siècle. This champagne is delicate, subtle in flavor, and possesses an abundance of tiny bubbles. You and your guests should derive much pleasure from this food and wine pairing.

Grilled Soft-shell Crabs with Cucumbers, Dill Butter Sauce, Shiitakes, and Country Ham

Serves 8

16 *live jumbo soft-shell crabs*
5 *tablespoons fresh lemon juice*
 Salt and pepper to season
6 *tablespoons fish stock (see page 307)*
2 *tablespoons dry white wine*
11 *tablespoons unsalted butter, softened*
1 *tablespoon all-purpose flour*
1 *tablespoon chopped fresh dill*

2 *tablespoons water*
³/₄ *pound shiitake mushrooms (stems removed), sliced*
¹/₂ *pound country ham, cut into strips 1¹/₄ inches long and ¹/₈ inch thick*
6 *large cucumbers, peeled, split in half lengthwise, seeded, and cut into long, thin strips the length of the cucumber*

EQUIPMENT: *Cutting board, paring knife, measuring spoons, baking sheet with sides, film wrap, French knife, mandolin, stainless-steel bowl, 2¹/₂-quart saucepan, whisk, charcoal grill, tongs, two non-stick sauté pans (one large)*

Dress the crabs (see page 316). Sprinkle 4 tablespoons lemon juice over the crabs and season with salt and pepper. Place on a baking sheet lined with film wrap and cover tightly with film wrap. Refrigerate until needed.

Heat the stock and wine to a boil in a 2¹/₂-quart saucepan over high heat. Combine 1 tablespoon softened butter with the flour and knead until smooth. Whisk the flour and butter mixture into the boiling stock, a quarter of the mixture at a time, whisking continuously until the stock is smooth and slightly thickened. Return to a boil, then remove from the heat. Whisk 6 tablespoons butter, 1 tablespoon at a time, into the hot thickened stock, making certain that each addition is completely incorporated before adding subsequent tablespoons.

When all the butter has been incorporated, add the chopped dill and remaining tablespoon lemon juice. Adjust the seasoning with salt and pepper and combine thoroughly. Transfer the dill butter sauce to a ceramic crock or stainless-steel container, cover with film wrap, and hold at room temperature (for no more than 1 hour).

Preheat the oven to 350 degrees.

Season the crabs with salt and pepper. Grill the crabs over a medium hot charcoal or wood fire for 1 minute on each side, shell side first. Transfer the crabs to a baking sheet and hold in the preheated oven while completing the recipe.

Heat 2 tablespoons butter and 2 tablespoons water in a non-stick sauté pan over medium high heat. When hot, add the mushrooms, season with salt and pepper, and sauté for 2 minutes. Add the ham and sauté for an additional 3 minutes.

While the mushrooms are being sautéed, heat 2 tablespoons butter in a large non-stick sauté pan over high heat. When hot, add the cucumbers, season with salt and pepper, and sauté until just warm, 2 to 3 minutes.

Portion the cucumbers on 8 warm 10-inch plates. Arrange a 1-inch-wide ring of cucumbers along the outside edge of each plate. Portion the shiitake mushrooms and ham inside the cucumbers. Place 2 soft-shell crabs on top of the mushroom and ham mixture, with crabs slightly overlapping each other. Spoon 2 tablespoons dill butter sauce over the cucumbers on each plate and serve immediately.

The Chef's Touch

Use a lightly flavored chicken stock, if fish stock is not available, for the preparation of the dill butter sauce.

Consider using an assortment of fresh herbs, such as basil, dill, and chervil, which would heighten the overall flavors in this recipe. These herbs should be readily available at the same time as soft crabs.

Use, as we do, a salt-cured ham from Virginia for this recipe. If Virginia ham is not available to you, look for a salt-cured ham from your own area to add a regional touch.

Be careful not to overheat the cucumbers. Warm cucumbers are delicious as opposed to hot cucumbers, which are both bland and lacking in texture. To ensure the proper serving temperature, remove the cucumbers from the heat when just warmed.

To modify this recipe for a low-saturated-fat diet, eliminate the ham and the butter sauce. Sauté the mushrooms in 2 tablespoons safflower oil and 2 tablespoons water. Sauté the cucumbers in the same amount of oil and add the chopped dill to the cucumbers when they are warm.

This recipe made its debut at an international soft-shell crab challenge in May 1986 where assistant chef Jonathan Zearfoss and I competed against three other challengers. Our recipe did not win the first prize, but it was nonetheless highly regarded and eagerly eaten by the attendees. Since the challenge, we have served soft crabs prepared in this fashion frequently at The Trellis, partly due to co-owner Tom Power's passionate love of soft crabs prepared in this manner. Tom likes to drink Kistler Vineyards Dutton Ranch chardonnay with this dish. The buttery and lemony finish of the wine makes the two a perfect pairing.

Grouper, Shrimp, and Scallops with Snow Peas, Tomatoes, and Tarragon Butter

Serves 8

1/4 pound unsalted butter, softened
3 tablespoons minced shallots
   Salt and pepper to season
6 tablespoons dry white wine
2 tablespoons chopped fresh
   tarragon
3/4 pound snow peas, trimmed
2 pounds skinless grouper fillet
1 cup fish stock (see page 307)

2 tablespoons water
3/4 pound large shrimp, peeled,
   deveined, and cut in half
   lengthwise
3/4 pound sea scallops (side muscle
   removed), sliced 1/4 inch thick
3 medium tomatoes, peeled,
   seeded, and chopped (see
   page 316)

EQUIPMENT: *Measuring spoons, three non-stick sauté pans (two large), two stainless-steel bowls, film wrap, 5-quart saucepan, cutting board, serrated slicer, paring knife, baking sheet with sides, measuring cup, 2½-quart saucepan, aluminum foil, metal spoon, metal spatula*

Heat 1 tablespoon butter in a non-stick sauté pan over medium heat. When hot, add the minced shallots. Season with salt and pepper and sauté for 1 minute. Add the wine, bring to a simmer, adjust the heat, and simmer until the pan is almost dry, about 15 minutes. Remove the pan from the heat, transfer the reduction to a stainless-steel bowl, and cool. When cool, combine with the remaining butter and chopped tarragon. Cover the tarragon butter with film wrap and keep at room temperature until ready to use.

Blanch the snow peas in boiling salted water until tender but very crisp, 20 to 30 seconds. Drain the peas and transfer immediately to ice water. When the peas are cold, drain thoroughly, cover with film wrap, and refrigerate until needed.

Slice the grouper into ¼-inch-thick slices. Divide the grouper into 8 portions of 3 or 4 slices, with each slice partially overlapping another.

Heat the fish stock to a boil in a 2½-quart saucepan over high heat. While waiting for the stock to come to a boil, place the grouper in a large non-stick sauté pan and season with salt and pepper. Place ½ table-spoon tarragon butter on each grouper portion. Gently pour the boiling hot stock into the pan around the grouper. Cover the pan with aluminum foil, place the pan over medium heat, and allow the fish to cook for 6 to 7 minutes.

While the grouper is cooking, heat the remaining tarragon butter and 2 tablespoons water in a large non-stick sauté pan over high heat. When hot, add the shrimp, scallops, and tomatoes. Season with salt and pepper and sauté for 2½ to 3 minutes. Add the snow peas, adjust the seasoning with salt and pepper, and sauté until the snow peas are hot, about 2 minutes.

Portion the shrimp and scallop mixture onto each of 8 warm 9- or 10-inch soup/pasta plates. Place a grouper portion on top and serve immediately.

The Chef's Touch

The tarragon butter may be prepared several days in advance and kept, covered, under refrigeration. Soften the butter to room temperature before using.

If fresh tarragon is not available, substitute dill, basil, thyme, savory, or chervil, or a combination of these herbs. These and several other herbs are usually easily found during the summer season. As a last resort, use spinach or parsley. Do not use dried herbs; they would most certainly overpower the delicate balance of flavors in this recipe.

Generally speaking, grouper is a fine eating fish. There are, however, several grouper species, and although they are always white fleshed and lean, the eating qualities and the cooked texture of these fish vary substantially. The Florida red grouper seems to yield the best flesh. Ask your fishmonger to thoroughly clean the grouper, which should include removing any fibrous sinew from the fillet.

This is a versatile preparation; experiment with other fish and shell-fish. For an expensive substitution, try lobster, bay scallops, and halibut, and for a more economical preparation, try monkfish, calico scallops, and crab claw meat.

If fish stock is not available, substitute a lightly flavored chicken stock or use water. Adjust the seasoning with salt and pepper as necessary, to both enhance and develop the flavors.

Sauvignon blanc wines are always a good choice with light foods, especially if they are similar in style to the Groth Vineyards 1985 sauvignon blanc. This wine has an ample amount of fruit and an absence of the grassy herbal qualities that sometimes overpower this varietal.

Grilled Tuna and Grilled Potatoes with Tomatoes, Green Beans, and Onion Dressing

Serves 8

4 Idaho baking potatoes, unpeeled
³/₄ cup vegetable oil
5 tablespoons fresh lemon juice
8 6-ounce tuna fillets, about ³/₄ inch thick
Salt and pepper to season
6 tablespoons cider vinegar
4 teaspoons Dijon-style mustard
¹/₂ teaspoon salt
¹/₄ teaspoon ground black pepper
1¹/₂ cups olive oil
1 small onion, sliced thin
2 teaspoons chopped fresh basil

2 teaspoons chopped fresh thyme
¹/₂ tablespoon minced garlic
2 anchovies, minced
1 pound tiny green beans, trimmed
4 medium tomatoes, peeled and each cut into 8 wedges (see page 316)
2 medium heads red leaf lettuce, washed and dried
64 Mediterranean black olives
2 tablespoons chopped fresh chives

EQUIPMENT: *5-quart saucepan, slotted spoon, measuring cup, measuring spoons, film wrap, two baking sheets with sides, paring knife, cutting board, French knife, stainless-steel bowl, whisk, 2¹/₂-quart saucepan, serrated slicer, colander, pastry brush, charcoal grill, tongs*

Cook the potatoes in boiling salted water for 35 minutes. Remove from the cooking water and cool under cold running water for a few minutes. Drain and refrigerate for 1 hour. Slice the cold potatoes ¹/₄ inch thick; each potato should yield 8 slices. Discard the end slices. Lay the slices out on a film-wrapped baking sheet, cover with film wrap, and refrigerate until needed.

Mix together ¹/₄ cup vegetable oil and 2 tablespoons lemon juice and use to marinate the tuna fillets. Season with salt and pepper and individually film-wrap each fillet. Refrigerate the fillets until needed.

In a stainless-steel bowl, whisk together the vinegar, remaining 3 tablespoons lemon juice, Dijon-style mustard, ½ teaspoon salt, and ¼ teaspoon black pepper. Add the olive oil in a slow, steady stream, whisking continuously until all the oil has been incorporated. Add the onion, basil, thyme, garlic, and anchovies and combine thoroughly. Cover with film wrap and refrigerate until needed.

Blanch the tiny green beans in 2 quarts boiling salted water until tender but still crunchy, 2 to 2½ minutes. Drain the beans, then plunge into ice water. Remove from the ice water and drain well.

Set up eight 10-inch plates by arranging 4 tomato wedges, evenly spaced, around the outside edge of each plate. Place a bed of red leaf lettuce leaves in the center of each plate. Sprinkle some tiny green beans over each bed of lettuce. Place 2 olives in between the tomato wedges (8 olives per plate).

Preheat the oven to 225 degrees.

Brush the potato slices on both sides with the remaining ½ cup vegetable oil. Season liberally with salt and pepper. Grill over a hot charcoal fire until golden brown and slightly charred, 2 to 2½ minutes on each side. Transfer to a baking sheet and keep in the preheated oven while grilling the tuna.

Season the tuna with salt and pepper. Grill the tuna fillets over a medium hot charcoal fire for 1½ minutes on each side. The tuna will be medium rare to medium; cook longer if well-done tuna is desired, but do not overcook.

Combine the dressing thoroughly and dress the tiny green beans and red leaf lettuce on each plate with 6 tablespoons dressing. Place a warm potato slice adjacent to each tomato wedge (4 slices per plate; see color photograph). Place a grilled tuna fillet in the center of each plate. Sprinkle the chives over each tuna fillet and serve immediately.

The Chef's Touch

Fresh herbs should be readily available during the summer months. Over the last few years we have been able to purchase a wide variety of fresh herbs on a year-round basis, but never is the variety as bountiful as it is in the summer. For this dressing, you may use a mixture of herbs such as marjoram, oregano, and parsley, in addition to basil and thyme. It is better to use only one fresh herb, however, should only one be available, rather than to add dried herbs.

This onion dressing is quite assertive when first prepared. For that reason, I would suggest making it from 4 to 24 hours before serving. The flavors will mingle and the dressing will mellow. The dressing may be kept, covered and refrigerated, for 3 to 4 days.

We have a fondness for tiny green beans (*haricots verts*) at The Trellis. Their delicate shape and sweet taste make them a favorite of our guests as well. During the summer season you may want to purchase the smallest tender snap beans available; they will make an excellent substitute for the tiny green beans.

After washing the red leaf lettuce, shake dry in a colander, pat dry with paper towels, or, preferably, spin dry in a lettuce spinner.

Once you have eaten a tree-ripened black olive it will be difficult to be truly satisfied with any other kind. Whether they are Greek, Italian, Spanish, or French, the olives of the Mediterranean area have an intensity of flavor that makes them very special.

I would suggest a white burgundy such as the Louis Jadot meursault as the wine to accompany this main course salad. To experience this food and wine pairing is to understand how such combinations can create lasting memories.

Grilled Chicken with Dijon Mustard and Fresh Tarragon

Serves 8

1 cup Dijon-style mustard
$^1/_2$ cup dry white wine
2 tablespoons chopped fresh
   tarragon

Salt and pepper to season
4 2$^1/_2$-pound chickens, halved

EQUIPMENT: *French knife, cutting board, measuring cup, measuring spoons, stainless-steel bowl, whisk, film wrap, charcoal grill, tongs, baking sheet with sides*

Twenty-four hours before serving, whisk together the mustard, wine, and tarragon in a large stainless-steel bowl. Season with salt and pepper and combine thoroughly.

Coat the chicken halves with the mustard marinade. Individually film-wrap them and refrigerate for 24 hours before grilling.

Preheat the oven to 350 degrees.

Season the chicken halves with salt and pepper and grill over a medium charcoal or wood fire for 15 minutes. Turn the chickens as necessary to avoid overcharring. Transfer to a baking sheet and finish cooking in the preheated oven for 10 minutes. Serve hot, or allow to cool and serve at room temperature.

The Chef's Touch

A notable occasion: Bastille Day, July 14, 1986. The purpose, pleasure: a friendly group of Americans breaking away from their temporary home on the barge *Luciole* to enjoy a picnic in the French countryside. The food was plentiful and delicious, prepared by my daughter, Danielle, and myself early that morning on the barge that had been our kitchen during my week of duty as guest chef, cooking and cruising along the Yonne River. What do Americans eat on Bastille Day? Our picnic had a definite Franco-American twist, with grilled Bresse chickens marinated in mustard and herbs, cold roast tenderloin of beef, warm sliced potatoes dressed with crème fraîche, a variety of chilled vegetable salads, several cheeses and very crusty baguettes, wild strawberries and cream, and, of course, well-chilled chablis and beaujolais.

At The Trellis we use Grey Poupon Dijon mustard to marinate chickens for this recipe. Add your own touch by using a favorite mustard or even a combination of mustards.

It is not absolutely necessary to marinate the chickens for twenty-four hours. Even a very short marination (less than an hour) will impart a delicious flavor to the birds. However, the twenty-four-hour marination will ensure maximum tenderness and flavor.

Overly charred food is the bane of every backyard grill cook. Chicken is especially susceptible to a blackened, unattractively charred appearance. To ensure successful grilling of chicken, grill over a medium fire, turn frequently, and do not hesitate to remove the chicken from the fire even before it is fully cooked. The finishing time in the oven can be increased to accommodate the degree of doneness you prefer. Better to have the chicken spend a minute or two longer in the oven than to render it inedible by prolonged grilling.

Grilled Chicken Breast with Peaches, Country Ham, and Black Pepper Butter

Serves 8

8 8-ounce boneless and skinless
  chicken breasts
1 cup dry white wine
¼ cup fresh lemon juice
  Salt and pepper to season
½ pound unsalted butter, softened
6 tablespoons minced shallots

1 tablespoon cracked black
  peppercorns
4 pounds peaches, unpeeled
½ pound country ham, cut into
  strips 1½ inches long and
  ⅛ inch wide

EQUIPMENT: *Paring knife, cutting board, French knife, measuring spoons, three stainless-steel bowls, wooden spoon, film wrap, meat cleaver, aluminum foil, baking sheet with sides, two non-stick sauté pans (one large), charcoal grill, tongs*

Trim any excess fat from the chicken breasts. In a stainless-steel bowl, combine ¼ cup white wine and the lemon juice, season with salt and pepper, and blend thoroughly. Sprinkle over the chicken breasts. Place the chicken breasts (one at a time) between two layers of lightly oiled aluminum foil or parchment paper. Uniformly flatten each breast (see page 316) with a meat cleaver or the bottom of a sauté pan. Individually film-wrap each chicken breast and refrigerate until needed.

Heat 1 tablespoon butter in a non-stick sauté pan over medium heat. When hot, add the minced shallots, season with salt and pepper, and sauté for 1 minute. Add the remaining ¾ cup wine and bring to a simmer. Adjust the heat and simmer until the pan is almost dry, about 15 minutes. Transfer the reduced mixture to a stainless-steel bowl and allow to cool at room temperature. When cool, combine with the remaining butter. Add the cracked peppercorns and combine thoroughly. Cover the black pepper butter with film wrap and keep at room temperature until ready to use.

Wash the unpeeled peaches and cut each peach into 8 sections.

Preheat the oven to 225 degrees.

Season the chicken breasts lightly with salt and pepper and grill over a medium charcoal or wood fire for 2½ to 3 minutes on each side. Transfer the chicken to a baking sheet, baste with half the black pepper butter, then hold in the preheated oven while completing the recipe.

Heat the remaining black pepper butter in a large non-stick sauté pan over medium high heat. When hot, add the ham and sauté for 30 seconds. Add the peaches and sauté until just warm, 3 to 4 minutes.

Portion the warm peaches on each of 8 warm 10-inch plates, arranged toward the outside edge. Place a chicken breast in the center of the peaches and serve immediately.

The Chef's Touch

Long-time Williamsburg restaurateur Jim Seu is, like myself, a transplanted Yankee. Owner of The Colonial, Jim is a practitioner of the "old" Southern cuisine, and his fried chicken is the best I have ever eaten. He has often raised his billowy eyebrows at some of the Trellis interpretations of Southern cooking, but never more so than when I told him about this particular chicken recipe. To me, it utilizes the best foods the contemporary South has to offer and combines them in a new and delicious fashion. To Jim, any departure from skillet-fried chicken labels one a Carpetbagger.

Black pepper butter may be prepared in advance and stored in the refrigerator for several days. Soften butter to room temperature before using.

Purchase ripe but firm peaches for this recipe. Although coloration is not necessarily an indication of ripeness, we have found that deep-red-colored peaches are usually overripe. If peaches are not available, you could use nectarines.

If the peaches are going to be stored for longer than four hours after cutting, they should be dipped in 1 quart water acidulated with 2 tablespoons lemon juice and drained before being placed in a stainless-steel bowl and refrigerated.

Be careful not to overheat the peaches; they will have a better texture and taste if they are served just barely warm. Do not cook the chicken over too hot a fire or too quickly, or it will be tough and dry.

The flavor of the salt-cured ham uniquely complements the peaches. The ham will impart a very specific salt flavor to the chicken; consequently, no additional salt should be added.

The Fetzer Vineyard 1983 cabernet sauvignon, Mendocino, is the style of light-bodied and not overly tannic cabernet sauvignon that I find easy to drink with chicken, peaches, and country ham.

Loin Lamb Chops with Peppers, Onions, Tomatoes, Mushrooms, and Mint

Serves 8

16 8-ounce loin lamb chops
6 tablespoons olive oil
   Salt and pepper to season
4 medium onions, sliced thin
1 medium tomato, peeled, seeded,
   and chopped into 1/4-inch pieces
   (see page 316)
1/4 pound mushrooms, stems
   trimmed and sliced 1/4 inch
   thick

2 tablespoons chopped fresh mint
2 medium red bell peppers, cut
   into long, thin strips
2 medium green bell peppers, cut
   into long, thin strips

EQUIPMENT: *Measuring spoons, baking sheet with sides, paring knife, cutting board, French knife, charcoal grill, tongs, two non-stick sauté pans (one large), metal spoon*

Preheat the oven to 225 degrees.

Coat the chops with 4 tablespoons olive oil. Season with salt and pepper and grill over a medium charcoal or wood fire for 2 to 3 minutes on each side. Transfer to a baking sheet and hold in the preheated oven while sautéing the vegetables.

Heat 1 tablespoon olive oil in a large non-stick sauté pan over high heat. When the oil is hot, add the sliced onions, season with salt and pepper, and sauté for 4 minutes. Add the tomato, mushrooms, and mint, season lightly with salt and pepper, and sauté for 2 to 3 minutes.

While sautéing, heat the remaining tablespoon olive oil in a separate non-stick sauté pan. When the oil is hot, add the peppers, season lightly with salt and pepper, and sauté for 2 minutes. Combine the sautéed peppers with the onion and mushroom mixture.

Divide the sautéed vegetables onto each of 8 warm 10-inch plates. Place 2 grilled lamb chops on top and serve immediately.

The Chef's Touch

This recipe was inspired by a dish served at the Blythe Benmiller Inn, located in Ontario, Canada. At the inn, crisply charred, thick lamb chops were served in a buttery sauce of mushrooms, garlic, and mint. In our adaptation, textures are highlighted. Cooked for only a few moments without assertive flavors, the vegetables retain their own identity and become an integral part of the eating experience without taking a commanding role.

Have your butcher cut the lamb chops between 1¼ and 1½ inches thick. (If the chops are too thin, they will become dry and overdone very quickly when cooked over a charcoal fire.) The chops should also be trimmed of excess fat. Allow no more than a ¼-inch-wide border of fat. The reason for well-trimmed chops is twofold: too much fat will cause excessive flare-ups over the hot coals, and lamb fat has an assertive flavor and aroma that many people do not find enjoyable. This flavor is much less pronounced in the layer of fat closest to the flesh.

The success of such a simple preparation of the lamb in this recipe presupposes the purchase of high-quality meat. That is, fresh young American lamb with a clean and interesting lamb flavor rather than the strong and gamy flavor characteristic of older or frozen imported lamb.

If the availability of lamb is limited to the latter, then it is advisable to marinate the chops in an oil, herb, and garlic marinade for two to three hours before cooking.

Loin lamb chops are at their best when served medium rare: for 6-ounce chops, two minutes on each side; for 8-ounce chops, three minutes' grilling per side. This amount of grill time will result in fairly rare meat; the completion of the cooking will take place in the oven. Thick-cut lamb chops are at their best when quickly seared on the outside over a charcoal fire, then slowly finished to the preferred degree of doneness in a preheated 225-degree oven, as suggested in this recipe.

If the availability of peppers is limited to green, adjust the amount of peppers to a total of 3 and use 2 tomatoes.

Other fresh herbs such as tarragon or thyme may be used in place of the mint. Dried herbs are not recommended for this recipe.

Spearmint seems to be the most common variety of mint available during the summer season. If you have your own herb garden, you are probably growing 2 or 3 varieties. Do not hesitate to use them, although you should taste them to determine the strength and flavor characteristics and use more or less depending upon your preference.

For a final touch, garnish the plate with 2 or 3 whole fresh mint sprigs.

After your first bite of lamb and peppers, roll a supple 1981 Jordan cabernet over your palate. The effect is extraordinary.

Grilled Pork Tenderloin with Corn and Smoked Chili Salsa on "Hot" Pepper Fettuccine

Serves 8

1 large poblano chili, split in half lengthwise and seeded

1 cup lightly packed stemmed spinach, washed and dried

2 jalapeño peppers, roasted and seeded (see page 314)

5 tablespoons olive oil

4½ cups all-purpose flour

4 eggs

1 teaspoon salt

2 ears fresh corn, husk and silk removed

6 medium tomatoes, peeled, seeded, and chopped (see page 316)

1 small red onion, minced

2 tablespoons red raspberry vinegar

½ teaspoon cracked black peppercorns

Salt and pepper to season

½ cup cornmeal

3 pounds pork tenderloin

¼ cup vegetable oil

EQUIPMENT: *Cutting board, French knife, parchment paper, "Little Chief" smoker, measuring cup, measuring spoons, food processor or blender, rubber spatula, fork, 5-quart saucepan, tongs, paring knife, stainless-steel bowl, two baking sheets (one with sides), film wrap, meat cleaver, charcoal grill, serrated slicer, colander*

Line the middle rack of a smoker (see page 320) with parchment paper. Place the poblano chili halves on the rack and smoke for two hours, turning after the first hour. Remove the chili halves from the smoker and cool. Cut into 1-inch-long thin strips. Refrigerate, covered, until needed.

While the poblano is smoking, combine the spinach, jalapeños, and 1 tablespoon olive oil in a food processor fitted with a metal blade or in a blender. Process the mixture to a fine paste, scraping down the sides of the bowl as needed to incorporate.

Place 4 cups flour on a clean, dry cutting board or similar work surface. Make a well in the center and add the eggs, spinach mixture, and salt. Using a fork, combine the eggs, spinach, and salt. When thoroughly mixed, begin to work the flour into the center, a small amount at a time. When enough flour has been added that you can handle the dough, begin kneading by hand. Knead by hand until all the flour has been incorporated, about 10 minutes. Cover with film wrap and allow to relax at room temperature for 1 hour.

While the dough is relaxing, blanch the ears of corn in 3 quarts boiling salted water for 1 minute. Drain the corn, then cool under cold running water. When the corn is cool enough to handle, cut the kernels from the cob. In a stainless-steel bowl, combine the corn kernels, smoked poblano chili strips, tomatoes, red onion, raspberry vinegar, and cracked black pepper. Adjust the seasoning with salt and pepper and combine thoroughly. Cover and refrigerate until needed.

Cut the pasta dough into 8 equal portions. Roll and knead each portion of dough through the pasta machine, using the extra $1/2$ cup flour as necessary to prevent the dough from becoming tacky. Cut the sheets of dough into fettuccine (see page 315). To prevent sticking, toss the cut pasta with the cornmeal, then place the cut pasta portions on a baking sheet lined with parchment paper. Cover the sheet tightly with film wrap and refrigerate until needed.

Thoroughly trim the fat and membrane from the pork tenderloin. Cut the tenderloin into eight 4-ounce portions and coat with the vegetable oil. Place the tenderloin, one portion at a time, between 2 sheets of lightly oiled aluminum foil. Uniformly flatten each tenderloin (see page 316) to about a $3/4$-inch thickness with a meat cleaver or the bottom of a sauté pan.

Preheat the oven to 225 degrees.

Season the pork with salt and pepper and grill over a low to medium charcoal or wood fire for 3 to $3 1/2$ minutes on each side. Remove from the grill and slice into $1/2$-inch-thick slices, maintaining the original shape of each portion. Place the sliced pork portions on a baking sheet and hold in the preheated oven while cooking the pasta.

Cook the pasta (see page 315) in 3 quarts boiling salted water until tender but still firm to the bite, 30 seconds to 1 minute. Drain the cooked pasta in a colander and toss with the remaining 4 tablespoons olive oil.

Portion the pasta into each of 8 warm 9- or 10-inch soup/pasta plates. Divide the chilled salsa over the pasta. Place the grilled pork on top of the salsa and serve immediately.

The Chef's Touch

The oft-quoted expression "where there is smoke there is fire" surely applies when one considers the ingredients and techniques in this recipe. It is the dish most frequently ordered by Trellis co-owner Mary Ellen Power. Mary Ellen has attuned her palate to fiery foods; to her, a gourmet vacation would best be enjoyed on Avery Island, Louisiana. It is the product of that island, Tabasco sauce, which she boldly adds to this pork dish. "Some like it hot."

Poblano chilies are fairly large and usually mild in comparison to most chilies. If they are not available, substitute a large Anaheim chili, which is also a fairly mild chili, or smoke a small green bell pepper.

Add one or even two additional jalapeño peppers to the pasta recipe, depending upon your affinity for "heat."

If red raspberry–flavored vinegar is not available, use a high-quality red wine vinegar in the salsa. Prepare the salsa two or three days in advance for optimum blending of flavors.

It is unfortunate that fresh pork has become difficult to purchase, both at the retail and commercial level. Pork is a highly perishable meat; even when vacuum sealed, its fresh shelf life is quite a bit shorter than beef's. Consequently, although most meat purveyors purchase a fresh product, many of them freeze the pork upon receipt or soon after it has been butchered. Freezing diminishes the flavor of pork as well as damaging its texture. For the best product, insist on fresh pork.

The texture of pork does not favor extreme heat. Be certain to grill pork over a mellow fire, somewhere between low and medium in intensity. Otherwise, exposure to high heat will toughen a potentially delicious piece of pork.

The preferred beverage with pork on "hot" pepper fettuccine is ice-cold Michelob.

Sautéed Rabbit with Cabbage, Apples, Pearl Onions, and Plums

Serves 8

4 2-pound dressed rabbits
40 pearl onions, peeled
1 tablespoon fresh lemon juice
2 Granny Smith apples, unpeeled
1 Red Delicious apple, unpeeled
2 cups chicken stock (see page 305)
2¹/₂ pounds green cabbage (discolored and tough outer leaves removed), cored, quartered, and sliced ¹/₄ inch thick

Salt and pepper to season
2 tablespoons unsalted butter, softened
12 small ripe Santa Rosa plums, halved, pitted, and each half cut into 4 sections

EQUIPMENT: *Boning knife, cutting board, film wrap, paring knife, 2¹/₂-quart saucepan, colander, French knife, stainless-steel bowl, measuring spoons, 5-quart saucepan, measuring cup, two slotted spoons, large non-stick sauté pan*

Bone the rabbits. Remove all the meat with the exception of the front legs, which have negligible meat. Trim away all tendons and silver skin membrane from the loins, tenderloins, and hind leg and thigh sections. Cut the trimmed meat into ³/₄-inch pieces (the yield of well-trimmed meat from the 4 rabbits should be about 2 pounds). Cover the meat with film wrap and refrigerate until needed.

Blanch the pearl onions in boiling salted water for 1¹/₂ minutes. Transfer to ice water. When cool, drain thoroughly and refrigerate until needed.

Acidulate 1 quart water with 1 tablespoon lemon juice. Core and quarter the unpeeled apples. Slice widthwise about ¹/₄ inch thick and immediately place into the acidulated water. Refrigerate until needed.

Heat the chicken stock in a 5-quart saucepan over high heat. When the stock begins to boil, add the cabbage. Season with salt and pepper and cook for 5 to 6 minutes, stirring occasionally. Drain the apples in a colander and rinse under cold running water. Shake dry. Add the apples and the pearl onions to the cabbage, season with salt and pepper, stir to mix, and adjust the heat to low.

Heat the butter in a non-stick sauté pan over medium high heat. When hot, add the rabbit, season with salt and pepper, and sauté for 6 minutes. Add the plums and gently combine so as not to mash them. Sauté until the plums are warm, about 1½ minutes.

Portion the cabbage mixture into each of 8 warm 9- or 10-inch soup/pasta plates. Portion the rabbit and plum mixture into the center and serve immediately.

The Chef's Touch

When culinary tour specialist Polly Stewart Fritch approached me about spending a week as a guest chef on a barge cruising the waterways of the Yonne River in Burgundy, I immediately said, "Yes!" The total experience was exceptional, with only the daily shopping excursions proving to be far from ideal. The limited storage facilities on the barge necessitated several shopping trips each day. Although this routine proved difficult at times, it also was one of the more satisfying aspects of the trip. I had outlined several potential menus before leaving Williamsburg. Once on the barge, however, it was obvious that it would be much more practical to plan the menus based on each shopping excursion. It was on one of these trips, to the large regional market in Clamecy, that I purchased the most diminutive rabbits I had ever seen in a butcher's case. Later, as I roamed the produce stalls, this recipe for sautéed rabbit with cabbage, apples, pearl onions, and plums was developed.

When The Trellis opened in 1980, I could not find a source for fresh rabbit. Today, we have several dealers selling us fresh rabbit on a year-round basis. We find the best rabbits weigh less than 2½ pounds (dressed weight). Although the meat yield is better on larger-sized rabbits, the meat is not as tender. Frozen rabbit can be used for this recipe, but to really appreciate this delicate yet flavorful meat it is best to use fresh rabbit.

We have used purple pearl onions in this recipe for additional eye appeal. The meaty-tasting Barlette onions from Italy would also add a delicious touch.

Be careful not to overcook the cabbage. It should still be green and crunchy when served.

The apples are added when the heat is adjusted to low so that they will maintain their texture; they should be just warm when served.

Several plum varieties are available during the summer months. The red-skinned and yellow-fleshed Santa Rosa plum seems to be the most commonly available, and it is the variety we have used for this recipe.

If rabbit is not available or desirable, use chicken breast meat for a delicious alternative.

Barge captain Graham Bessant's selection from the *Luciole*'s amply stocked wine cellar was an immensely enjoyable 1983 Domaine Defaix chablis. This still-youthful wine had the acidity necessary to counteract the compelling flavors of the rabbit ensemble.

Sautéed Lump Backfin Crabmeat with Zucchini, Spinach, Broccoli, and Cream

Serves 8

2 cups heavy cream
    Salt and pepper to season
4 pounds zucchini, washed and
    lightly peeled
2½ pounds broccoli, stems trimmed

4 cups loosely packed stemmed
    spinach, washed and dried
¼ pound unsalted butter, softened
1½ pounds lump backfin crabmeat,
    well picked of shell

EQUIPMENT: *Two 2½-quart saucepans, measuring cup, stainless-steel ladle, vegetable peeler, mandolin, cutting board, paring knife, French knife, two large non-stick sauté pans, colander, tongs*

Heat the heavy cream in a 2½-quart saucepan over medium heat. Lightly season with salt and pepper. Place a ladle in the saucepan and occasionally stir the cream so that it does not foam over the sides. Lower the heat if necessary so that the cream barely simmers. Simmer until it has reduced by half, about 45 minutes.

While the cream is simmering, finish preparing the vegetables. Using a mandolin, cut the zucchini into long, thin, spaghetti-like strands the length of the zucchini and about ⅛ inch wide. Trim the broccoli heads into florets. Cut the spinach leaves into thin strips.

About 15 to 20 minutes before the cream is ready, in a 2½-quart saucepan over high heat bring 2 quarts lightly salted water to a boil.

Melt 4 tablespoons butter in each of two large non-stick sauté pans over medium high heat. When hot, place the zucchini and spinach in one pan and the crabmeat in the other pan. Season with salt and pepper and sauté until hot, about 5 minutes.

Cook the broccoli florets in the pot of boiling salted water until tender but still crunchy, about 2½ to 3 minutes. Transfer to a colander and drain thoroughly.

Make a 1½-inch-wide ring of zucchini and spinach along the outer edge of each of 8 warm 9- or 10-inch soup/pasta plates. Spoon 2 tablespoons reduced cream over the zucchini. Arrange the broccoli florets in a ring, stem ends toward the center, on the inside of the zucchini ring. Portion the crabmeat inside each ring of broccoli and serve immediately.

The Chef's Touch

Lump backfin crabmeat is, by itself, an elegant food. Perhaps that is the reason it is, more often than not, enjoyed simply sautéed with a bit of butter and some chopped shallots or served chilled with a squeeze of lemon and some fresh tarragon mayonnaise. This sublime seafood also has the versatility to join with other more pronounced flavors and textures.

A mandolin (see page 320) is the most desirable tool available for cutting vegetables into long, spaghetti-like strands. Guide the zucchini lengthwise over the cutter blades of the mandolin, rotating the zucchini a quarter turn after each pass. Continue to cut the now square-shaped zucchini until the seeds in the center of the zucchini are visible. Discard the heavily seeded center section. A sharp French knife or serrated slicer may also be used; cut 1/8-inch-thick strips the length and width of the zucchini. Rotate the zucchini a quarter turn after each slice. Continue to cut the square-shaped zucchini until the seeds are visible. Discard the seeded center section of the zucchini. Cut the strips into long, thin strands.

Broccoli stems are delicious. Cook them separately from the florets in boiling salted water for about 10 minutes. Cool the cooked stems in ice water to stop the cooking action. Peel the tough fibrous outer layer from the stems, then cut into the desired shape. Use in salads, egg dishes, as a garnish in soups, or in combination with other sautéed vegetables.

You may cut and trim the vegetables several hours in advance. If you do so, cover and refrigerate the prepared vegetables until needed.

For dietary considerations, you may eliminate the cream. Instead of cream, sauté one cup chopped, peeled, and seeded tomatoes with the zucchini and spinach. For a totally vegetarian meal, eliminate the cream, butter, and crabmeat. Sauté the vegetables in olive or safflower oil. Replace the crabmeat with 3 cups chopped, peeled, and seeded tomatoes, 1/2 pound sliced shiitake mushrooms, and 1 tablespoon chopped fresh tarragon. Sauté this mixture in olive oil separately from the zucchini and put the hot mixture in the center of the broccoli ring in place of the crabmeat.

In this recipe, crabmeat is the centerpiece to an ensemble of flavors and textures that not only pleases the palate but immediately awakens the senses in a stunning presentation. A clean, light, and fruity Kenwood Vineyards dry chenin blanc would further ensure an amicable dining experience.

Pan Roast of Oysters with Wild Mushrooms, Spinach, Leeks, and Cream

Serves 8

2 cups heavy cream
   Salt and pepper to season
2 large leeks, white part only,
   split in half and cut into thin
   strips 2 inches long
2 tablespoons unsalted butter,
   softened
2 tablespoons dry white wine

1/2 pound wild mushrooms (stems
   trimmed or removed, as
   necessary), sliced
 3 pints shucked oysters
16 spinach leaves, stemmed,
   washed, dried, and cut into
   thin strips

EQUIPMENT: *Measuring cup, two 2¹/₂-quart saucepans, stainless-steel ladle, medium-gauge strainer, stainless-steel bowl, cutting board, French knife, double boiler, measuring spoon, large non-stick sauté pan, metal spoon*

Heat the heavy cream in a 2¹/₂-quart saucepan over medium heat. Lightly season the cream with salt and pepper. Place a ladle in the saucepan and occasionally stir the cream so that it does not foam over the sides. Lower the heat if necessary so that the cream barely simmers. Simmer until it has reduced by half, about 45 minutes. Strain the reduced cream and hold warm in a double boiler (see page 322).

While the cream is simmering, blanch the leeks in boiling salted water until tender but slightly crunchy, 30 to 40 seconds. Drain the leeks into a strainer and immerse the strainer in ice water. When the leeks are cool, remove from the ice water, drain well, and refrigerate until needed.

Heat the butter and white wine in a large non-stick sauté pan over medium high heat. When the mixture comes to a full boil, add the sliced wild mushrooms, season with salt and pepper, and sauté for 1¹/₂ to 2 minutes.

Add the leeks and oysters, season with salt and pepper, and heat at a simmer (adjust the heat if necessary) until the edges of the oysters begin to curl, 4 to 5 minutes. Add the reduced cream and simmer for an additional 2 minutes. Adjust the seasoning with salt and pepper.

Portion the oyster mixture into each of 8 individual warm soup plates. Sprinkle the spinach strips over the top and serve immediately.

The Chef's Touch

Very few foods on the Eastern seaboard have the culinary roots of oysters. Esteemed by American Indians long before our ancestors waged the "oyster wars" of the seventeenth century, oysters are one of the most "native" of our native foods.

This historical association carries through to our present-day watermen, none of whom seems to be a newcomer to his vocation. The oysters served at The Trellis are purchased from the Terry Brothers in Willis Wharf, Virginia, a third-generation family business started in 1903. The Terrys market their oysters under the brand name Sewansecott, which was the Indian name under which their grandfather had registered to sell his product years ago. The unique aspect of the Terry Brothers' operation is that they are fully integrated producers; they plant oyster shells to cultivate seed, stock the growing beds with those seeds, harvest the mature oysters, then package and ship them.

The seeds are cultivated in deeded nursery grounds on the Machipongo River. They are then transplanted and grow to maturity on leased tidal flats in the bay. During the seeding and growing, the oysters are in waters with high saline content, which gives these mollusks the salty-twangy flavor we prefer.

To facilitate the organization of this recipe, reduce the cream up to two hours before serving. Hold the reduced cream in a double boiler. Reduced cream must be kept warm: once it has cooled it will not reheat properly. Reheated reduced cream is usually grainy in texture and is susceptible to breaking down (the fat separating from the non-fat portion).

Two of the best fresh wild mushrooms for this stewlike preparation are the now widely available shiitake mushrooms and oyster tree mushrooms. Their taste and texture especially complement the oysters. Use only one variety of fresh wild mushrooms if the availability of fresh product is limited. Although we presently use only fresh wild mushrooms at The Trellis, when we first opened our only option was dried mushrooms. If fresh wild mushrooms are not available, use dried rather than canned.

Be certain that you are patient and wait for the wine to come to a boil before you add the mushrooms. If the wine is not sufficiently heated, it will retain the alcohol and impart a sharp taste to the mushrooms, which absorb flavors like a sponge.

For dieters concerned with saturated fats, eliminate the butter and replace the reduced cream with 1 cup half-and-half.

An appropriate wine selection for our oyster stew–like preparation would be a Virginia wine. I would recommend a wine with crisp acidity, obvious fruit, and a reasonably dry finish, such as the 1986 seyval blanc from Oakencroft Vineyards.

Three Steamed Seafish with Nappa Cabbage and Black Pepper Butter

Serves 8

½ pound unsalted butter, softened
6 tablespoons minced shallots
Salt and pepper to season
¾ cup dry white wine
1 tablespoon cracked black peppercorns
2 medium carrots, peeled and cut into strips 2½ inches long and ⅛ inch wide
8 sun-dried tomatoes, packed in olive oil
1 cup fish stock (see page 307)

8 2-ounce skinless salmon fillets
8 2-ounce skinless flounder fillets
8 2-ounce skinless red snapper fillets
3 tablespoons fresh lemon juice
¼ cup water
3 pounds Nappa cabbage (discolored outer leaves removed), cored and sliced ¼ inch thick
1 tablespoon chopped fresh parsley

EQUIPMENT: *Measuring spoons, three non-stick sauté pans (two large), two stainless-steel bowls, wooden spoon, film wrap, cutting board, vegetable peeler, French knife, two baking sheets with sides, 2½-quart saucepan, paper towels, measuring cup, aluminum foil, metal spatula, slotted spoon*

Heat 1 tablespoon butter in a non-stick sauté pan over medium heat. When hot, add the minced shallots, season with salt and pepper, and sauté for 1 minute. Add the wine and bring to a simmer; adjust the heat and simmer until the pan is almost dry, about 15 minutes. Remove from the heat, transfer the reduction to a stainless-steel bowl, and cool. When the mixture is cool, combine with the remaining butter and cracked black peppercorns. Cover the black pepper butter with film wrap and keep at room temperature until needed.

Blanch the carrot strips in boiling salted water for 1½ minutes. Drain and transfer immediately to ice water. When cold, drain thoroughly.

Drain the sun-dried tomatoes on paper towels, then cut into thin strips.

137

Preheat the oven to 350 degrees.

Heat the fish stock to a boil in a 2½-quart saucepan over high heat. While waiting for the stock to boil, place the fish fillets on a baking sheet. Sprinkle with the lemon juice and season with salt and pepper. Place 1 teaspoon black pepper butter on each fish fillet. Gently pour the fish stock into the baking sheet. Tightly cover the sheet with aluminum foil. Place the sheet in the preheated oven and bake the fish for 8 to 9 minutes.

While the fish is baking, heat 4 tablespoons black pepper butter and 2 tablespoons water in each of two large non-stick sauté pans over high heat. When hot, divide the carrots between both pans. Season with salt and pepper and sauté for 1 minute. Divide the cabbage between the two pans, season, and then sauté for 1½ minutes. Divide the sun-dried tomatoes between the two pans, combine thoroughly, and remove the pans from the heat.

Portion the vegetables into each of 8 warm 9- or 10-inch soup/pasta plates. Place one fillet of each fish, with the salmon fillet in the center, on the bed of vegetables on each plate. Garnish with the chopped parsley and serve immediately.

The Chef's Touch

Versatile is not an adjective that one normally associates with cabbage. Certainly, it is a vegetable thought of as a staple rather than a star. However, a culinary tour of Paris in 1986 proved that cabbage has risen from the humble *choux farcis* to center stage in two- and three-star restaurants. At Joel Robuchon's Jamin, lightly steamed cabbage was the garnish for an appetizer of langoustine and ravioli; Alain Senderens served a foie gras wrapped in cabbage and simply garnished with coarse salt and crushed black pepper at the historic Lucas Carton; at the two-star "Jewel Box," Duquesnoy, cabbage leaves were wrapped around thin fillets of salmon, poached, sliced, and presented with a fennel butter sauce. At the lively bistro Polidor, cabbage was more traditionally presented with thick-cut bacon and served with a "falling off the bones," delicious braised guinea hen.

Black pepper butter may be prepared in advance and stored, covered, in the refrigerator for several days. Soften the butter to room temperature before using (about two hours).

If fish stock is not available, use a lightly flavored chicken stock or well-seasoned water.

The fish fillets should be of equal thickness. Cut fillets a minimum of

¼ inch thick to a maximum of ½ inch thick. Although other varieties of fish can be used in this recipe, it is best to use a subtly flavored and delicately textured fish. Turbot, sole, and baby halibut are all acceptable substitutions.

For those concerned about saturated fats, omit the black pepper butter and substitute equal amounts of fish stock. In this case, sprinkle ½ tablespoon cracked black peppercorns over the cabbage and carrots in each pan while they are cooking.

Nappa cabbage, also referred to as Chinese or celery cabbage, is a delicately flavored vegetable that is sometimes confused with the more assertive-tasting bok choy. Nappa cabbage is sweet and delicious; take care in cooking not to subject it to high and prolonged heating. The secret to serving this dish at its best is to heat the cabbage until it is just barely hot. Do not hesitate to remove the pans of cabbage from the heat if the mixture is getting too hot. Better to serve the cabbage lukewarm and preserve its delicate taste and texture.

In this recipe, delicate Nappa cabbage is accented by a snappy black pepper butter which sets the tone for the subtly cooked fish. The forward fruit of Robert Mondavi's chenin blanc makes for a very harmonious pairing.

Pan-fried Local Catfish with Walnuts and Hickory-Smoked Bacon

Serves 8

8 10-ounce whole catfish, skinned, cleaned, and heads removed
Salt and pepper to season
4½ tablespoons fresh lemon juice
1½ pounds hickory-smoked slab bacon
1½ cups walnut halves
2 eggs
1 cup whole milk

¾ cup all-purpose flour
¾ cup yellow cornmeal
1 cup clarified butter (see page 312)
1 cup vegetable oil
¼ pound unsalted butter, softened
4 whole lemons, halved
1 large bunch watercress, stems trimmed, washed, and dried

EQUIPMENT: *Film wrap, measuring spoons, paper towels, three baking sheets (two with sides), metal spatula, two stainless-steel bowls, measuring cup, whisk, three non-stick sauté pans (two large), tongs*

Rinse the catfish under cold running water. Pat dry with paper towels. Sprinkle inside and out with salt, pepper, and 4 tablespoons lemon juice. Individually wrap the catfish in film wrap; refrigerate until needed.

Preheat the oven to 325 degrees.

Trim the rind and excess fat from the bacon. Slice the bacon into strips, then cut into ⅜-inch cubes. Cook on a baking sheet for 30 minutes in the preheated oven. Transfer to paper towels to drain. Keep the drained bacon at room temperature until needed. Lower the oven temperature to 300 degrees.

Toast the walnut halves on a baking sheet in the 300-degree oven for 30 minutes. Remove from the oven and keep at room temperature until needed. Raise the oven temperature to 350 degrees.

Whisk the eggs and milk together in a stainless-steel bowl. Season with salt and pepper and combine thoroughly.

Mix the flour and cornmeal together. Season with salt and pepper and combine thoroughly.

Heat ½ cup clarified butter and ½ cup vegetable oil in each of two large non-stick sauté pans over medium high heat. While the butter-oil mixture is heating, dip the catfish into the egg-milk mixture and then into the flour-cornmeal mixture; coat evenly, lightly, and thoroughly. When the butter and oil mixture is sizzling hot, place 4 fish in each pan. Pan-fry until golden brown, 2½ to 3 minutes on each side. Transfer to a baking sheet and place in the 350-degree oven. Bake until the inside of the fish cavities shows no pink coloration, 10 to 12 minutes.

Place one cooked catfish on each of 8 warm plates. Sprinkle the bacon pieces and walnuts over each fish. Heat the unsalted butter in a large non-stick sauté pan over high heat. Allow to brown evenly. Add the remaining ½ tablespoon lemon juice to the brown butter, shaking the pan vigorously so that the butter does not foam over the sides of the pan. Carefully pour equal amounts of brown butter over each portion of catfish. Garnish each plate with half a lemon and a spray of watercress. Serve immediately.

The Chef's Touch

Our local catfish supplier, Pete Hazelwood, has been in the business of catching catfish for over forty years. The current popularity of catfish is keeping Pete and his son Garland quite busy these days. Fishing with both baited nets and traps, the Hazelwoods are hauling in catfish from the clean waters of the Chickahominy, Pamunkey, and Rappahannock rivers. The subject of clean water is dear to Pete's heart, because the channel catfish that he catches can thrive only in unpolluted, clear running water, as opposed to other catfish such as bullheads that thrive in murky ponds.

Fresh catfish may be found in most good supermarkets or fish markets. For this recipe, purchase them whole and ready to cook; that is, dressed, head and skin removed. Skinning catfish is definitely a task for your fishmonger to perform. The skin of a catfish is thick, slippery, and strong, much like that of an eel. To perform this task yourself you would need a sturdy board, hammer, ten-penny nail, pliers, French knife, and patience. Better to leave it to the experts; even The Trellis buys catfish skinned! If fresh catfish are not available, purchase comparably sized fresh perch.

You may use catfish fillets for this recipe; purchase sixteen individual 4-ounce fillets or fillet eight whole 10-ounce fish. Prepare the fillets as directed for the whole fish. Sauté eight fillets in each large pan. Cook for 2½ to 3 minutes on each side. The fillets will be ready to serve and, unlike the whole fish, will not need any additional oven time.

Hickory-smoked slab bacon may be purchased in supermarkets or in specialty food stores. It is usually available in 2- or 4-pound pieces. If you do not use all the purchased bacon, it may be kept refrigerated, tightly wrapped, for three to four weeks.

If you are lucky enough to have a very large cast-iron skillet, it would make sense to use it for pan-frying the catfish, as you will be able to do all of the fish in the same pan at the same time. (Of course, some cooks would not consider pan-frying in anything but a well-seasoned cast-iron skillet.) More important than the skillet, however, is the temperature of the butter-oil mixture in which the fish is fried. If you fry at too low a temperature, the fish will absorb too much fat, making the crust soggy and listless. On the other hand, if you fry the fish at too high a temperature, the crust will brown too rapidly, possibly imparting a disagreeable taste to the fish and also leaving the inside temperature of the fish quite cold, thereby rendering our prescribed cooking time irrelevant. For best results, bring the temperature of the butter-oil mixture to 360 degrees before frying the fish. A frying thermometer will be needed to get an accurate reading.

At The Trellis we have served this catfish with Corn and Tomato Fritters (see page 210). Not entirely unlike the more traditional hush puppies, these fritters are an appropriate accompaniment to this regional food.

A Robert Pecota sauvignon blanc from the Napa Valley has the perfect acidity to pair with the sweet-tasting, delicate flesh of our pan-fried catfish.

Grilled Monkfish with Cabbage, Tomatoes, and Slab Bacon

Serves 8

1 pound hickory-smoked slab
 bacon
3 pounds monkfish fillet, cut into
 1- to 1½-inch pieces
¼ cup vegetable oil
2 tablespoons fresh lemon juice
 Salt and pepper to season
2 tablespoons clarified butter
 (see page 312)
2 pounds green cabbage
 (discolored and tough outer
 leaves removed), cored, quartered, and sliced ¼ inch thick

¼ cup water
3 medium tomatoes, peeled,
 seeded, and chopped
 (see page 316)
4 whole lemons, halved
1 bunch watercress, stems
 trimmed, washed, and dried

EQUIPMENT: *Cutting board, serrated slicer, French knife, baking sheet with sides, spatula, paper towels, stainless-steel bowl, measuring spoons, eight 9-inch metal or bamboo skewers, film wrap, charcoal grill, tongs, two large non-stick sauté pans*

Preheat the oven to 325 degrees.

Trim the rind and excess fat from the bacon. Slice the bacon into strips, then cut into ³⁄₈-inch cubes. Cook on a baking sheet in the preheated oven for 30 minutes. Transfer the cooked bacon to paper towels to drain. Keep the drained bacon at room temperature until needed. Lower the oven temperature to 225 degrees.

Combine the monkfish with the vegetable oil and lemon juice and season with salt and pepper. Divide the fish pieces into 8 equal portions and skewer. Season the skewered portions with salt and pepper, then grill for 4 minutes over a medium charcoal or wood fire. Turn the skewers occasionally while cooking. Transfer the skewers to a baking sheet and hold in the 225-degree oven while preparing the cabbage.

In each large non-stick sauté pan, heat 1 tablespoon clarified butter over medium high heat. When hot, add the diced bacon and sauté for 30 seconds. Add equal amounts of the cabbage to each pan, season with salt and pepper, and heat for 2 minutes. Add 2 tablespoons water to each pan and braise the cabbage and bacon for 3 to 5 minutes. Divide the chopped tomatoes between the two pans, season with salt and pepper, and continue to heat until the mixture is hot, about 2 to 3 minutes.

Portion the cabbage mixture onto each of 8 warm 9- or 10-inch soup/pasta plates; remove the grilled monkfish from the skewers and place a portion on each plate. Garnish with the lemon and watercress and serve immediately.

The Chef's Touch

It took a tremendous public relations effort to put monkfish on American menus. Whole monkfish defies description—it looks like a throwback to the prehistoric era. Several years ago, Julia Child was pictured in *Time* magazine displaying a whole monkfish. From that time on, monkfish was transformed from an unwanted "trash" fish into a much sought-after delicacy, with a taste and texture that many describe in the same terms as they do lobster meat. Try it as we have prepared it in this recipe, and you may agree.

Only slab bacon can be cut into the size cube necessary for this recipe. If slab bacon is unavailable, use the thickest-sliced bacon you can purchase. If it is good-quality bacon, the taste will be very similar; however, the texture will be significantly different.

It is best to purchase monkfish already cleaned and filleted from your fishmonger. Well-cleaned monkfish fillets, trimmed of tough membranes, have very attractive white, firm flesh and a very distinctive texture when cooked. Be certain to ask your fishmonger to clean your monkfish properly. That is, have all of the previously mentioned membrane removed; otherwise, the fish will be quite rubbery when cooked.

Technically, braising is a moist-heat method of cooking. Whenever the term applies to vegetables, it is usually further defined as cooking slowly in a small amount of liquid. In this recipe, however, the cooking is done relatively quickly. At The Trellis, we usually cook cabbage very briefly. It seems that the longer cabbage cooks the more it develops a rather strong and assertive flavor and aroma that unappetizingly remind me of old-world cookery. However, the cooking time for the cabbage may be increased depending on your own preference. The cooking of the cabbage for this recipe can be varied by the substitution of white wine and/or fish stock for the recommended water.

A refreshing and dry Virginia wine like a Meredyth seyval blanc would complement the diverse but uncomplicated flavors in this recipe.

Grilled Breast of Chicken with Wild Mushrooms, Applejack, and Pears

Serves 8

8 8-ounce boneless and skinless
   chicken breasts
5 tablespoons fresh lemon juice
1/4 cup dry white wine
   Salt and pepper to season
4 large pears, unpeeled

1³/₄ cups apple cider
1/4 cup apple brandy
1¹/₂ pounds wild mushrooms (stems
   trimmed or removed, as
   necessary), sliced

EQUIPMENT: *Paring knife, cutting board, French knife, measuring spoons, two stainless-steel bowls, aluminum foil, meat cleaver, film wrap, baking sheet with sides, measuring cup, charcoal grill, tongs, colander, two large non-stick sauté pans, slotted spoon*

Trim any excess fat from the chicken breasts. In a stainless-steel bowl, combine 4 tablespoons lemon juice with the white wine, season with salt and pepper, and combine thoroughly. Sprinkle over the chicken breasts. Place the chicken breasts, one at a time, between two sheets of lightly oiled aluminum foil or parchment paper. Flatten each breast (see page 316) with a meat cleaver or the bottom of a sauté pan. Individually film-wrap each chicken breast and refrigerate until needed.

Acidulate 1 quart water with the remaining 1 tablespoon lemon juice. Core and quarter the unpeeled pears. Cut the quartered pears into 1/2-inch dice and immediately place the diced pears into the acidulated water.

Combine the cider and brandy in a stainless-steel bowl, then cover with film wrap and keep at room temperature until needed.

Preheat the oven to 350 degrees.

Season the chicken breasts with salt and pepper and grill over a medium hot charcoal or wood fire for 1¹/₂ minutes on each side. After grilling, transfer the chicken breasts to a baking sheet. Pour 1 cup of the cider and brandy mixture over the chicken. Cover the baking sheet tightly with aluminum foil and place in the preheated oven for 10 minutes.

While the chicken is cooking, drain the pears and then rinse under cold running water. Heat $1/2$ cup of the cider-brandy mixture in each of two large sauté pans over medium high heat. When the mixture has boiled for 30 seconds, add the sliced wild mushrooms to one pan and the pears to the other pan. Season the ingredients in both pans with salt and pepper. Adjust the heat and simmer for 3 to 4 minutes.

Portion the sautéed wild mushrooms onto individual warm 10-inch plates. Form a ring with the mushrooms toward the outside edge of each plate. In the center of each ring, portion the diced pear mixture. Place a chicken breast on top and serve immediately.

The Chef's Touch

Most of the pears grown in the United States are Bartlett pears. At The Trellis, we like to use a combination of both the red Bartlett and the more commonly available greenish-yellow–colored Bartletts. During the height of the pear season, August through November, additional varieties become available, including Anjou, Bosc, Comice, and Seckel. We do not peel the pears in this recipe for both textural and aesthetic reasons.

Apple brandy is distilled from apple cider. The most famous, and considered by some to be the finest, apple brandy in the world is Calvados, produced in the Normandy region of France. In the United States, apple brandy is usually referred to as applejack, although in post-Revolutionary colonial America the term ''applejack'' referred to apple cider. In this recipe we have covered all of the bases by combining apple cider and apple brandy (we use Captain Apple Jack apple brandy), and we have used the term ''applejack'' in the title.

This is a very simple recipe which relies on the affinity of wild mushrooms and fresh pears to lift it above the norm. Therefore, fresh wild mushrooms are an important component in this dish. Cultivated white mushrooms would have neither the taste nor the texture necessary to make this spartan preparation interesting.

A mixture of apricot-colored chanterelles, for their aromatic woodsy flavor, and white trumpets, for their delicate texture and appearance, is my choice in this recipe. Both mushrooms are available fresh during the autumn season.

Be certain that the charcoal or wood fire is not too hot or the chicken meat will toughen. Better to err with too little fire and take a few moments longer for grilling than to have too much fire, resulting in overly charred and tough meat.

Although the flavors in this preparation are straightforward, the infusion of the cider and brandy into the chicken breast gives the dish an edge best countered with a fairly complex chardonnay which has an obvious oak flavor and finishes clean on the palate. Recommended: a 1984 Château Bouchaine chardonnay.

AUTUMN

Braised Lamb with Onions, Potatoes, Cabbage, and Herbs

Serves 8 to 12

3¹/₂ pounds well-trimmed lamb
    meat, cut into 1-inch pieces
10 cups chicken stock (see
    page 305)
2 teaspoons minced garlic
    Salt and pepper to season
2 tablespoons unsalted butter,
    softened
2 tablespoons water
2 large onions
2 stalks celery, chopped
2 small parsnips, chopped
2¹/₂ pounds green cabbage
    (discolored and tough outer
    leaves removed), cored,
    quartered, and sliced ¹/₄ inch
    thick

2 pounds potatoes, peeled, cut
    into 1-inch cubes, and covered
    with cold water
1 tablespoon chopped fresh
    parsley
¹/₂ tablespoon chopped fresh
    rosemary
¹/₂ tablespoon chopped fresh thyme

EQUIPMENT: *Two 5-quart saucepans, measuring cup, paring knife, vegetable peeler, cutting board, French knife, wooden spoon, food processor, rubber spatula, large non-stick sauté pan*

Blanch the lamb in 3¹/₂ quarts lightly salted water for 2 minutes. Drain in a colander and rinse with cold water.

Heat 4 cups stock in a 5-quart saucepan over medium heat. When the stock begins to simmer, add the lamb and garlic. Season with salt and pepper and return to a simmer. Adjust the heat and simmer until tender, 45 minutes to 1 hour.

While the lamb is simmering, heat 1 tablespoon butter with 1 tablespoon water in a 5-quart saucepan over medium high heat and chop one of the onions. When the butter is hot, add the chopped onion,

148

celery, parsnips, and half the cabbage. Season with salt and pepper and sauté until hot, about 5 minutes. Add the remaining 6 cups chicken stock. Drain the potatoes, rinse with cold water, and add to the pan. Bring the mixture to a boil, then reduce the heat and simmer slowly for 30 minutes.

Purée the hot potato and cabbage mixture in a food processor fitted with a metal blade (depending upon the size of the processor, this may have to be done in 2 or 3 batches). Return the puréed mixture to the 5-quart saucepan and bring to a simmer. Drain the cooked lamb in a colander, add the lamb to the puréed potatoes and cabbage, and allow to barely simmer while completing the recipe.

Heat the remaining tablespoon butter with 1 tablespoon water in a large non-stick sauté pan over medium high heat and slice the remaining onion. When the butter is hot, add the sliced onion, season with salt and pepper, and sauté for 3 minutes. Add the remaining raw cabbage, season with salt and pepper, and sauté for 5 to 6 minutes. When the cabbage and onion are hot, combine with the lamb and puréed potatoes and cabbage. Add the chopped herbs; adjust the seasoning with salt and pepper. Allow to simmer for an additional 10 minutes.

Portion the braised lamb and vegetables onto 8 warm 9- or 10-inch soup/pasta plates. Serve immediately.

The Chef's Touch

Whether you believe in the mystical power of the Blarney Stone or not, living in New York City will make you Irish for at least one day of the year. This Irish stew–like preparation was the result of a collaboration between the German sous chef at the Hotel Pierre and me on Saint Patrick's Day in 1968. I was then *entremetier* (assistant to both the sauce chef and the soup chef) at that venerable hotel on Madison Avenue, and found that the assignment sheet for the day called for me to prepare Irish lamb stew, a dish I had never cooked. I did a little research and asked sous chef Walter Gurnee for help with a recipe that turned out to be delicious, though more French than Irish.

The blanching and rinsing of the lamb are done both to remove some of the blood, which would darken the vegetable purée, and to lessen the assertive lamb flavor.

The economical shoulder meat may be used for this recipe. The slow simmering (about 60 minutes for shoulder meat) of the lamb will help to break down the connective tissue, rendering the meat quite tender. Leg meat may also be used, but the cooking time should be adjusted (about 45 minutes for leg meat) so as not to allow the meat to overcook and dry out.

The sweet flavor of the parsnip is an interesting taste component in this stew, although it is not essential. You may want to experiment with other root vegetables such as rutabagas and turnips, or eliminate this component altogether (the omission of the small amount suggested will not dramatically affect the consistency of the finished stew).

Be certain not to overcook the potato and cabbage mixture. The suggested 30 minutes of slow simmering should cook the vegetables just to the point that they can be puréed. Overcooking and boiling rather than simmering will affect both the taste and the texture of the puréed vegetables.

This recipe may be prepared a day in advance of serving. Prepare as directed in the recipe, but omit adding the herbs. Cool properly (see page 315) and refrigerate, covered. To serve, bring to a simmer, then add the herbs and allow to simmer for four to five minutes before serving.

My suggestion is that you drink a glass or two of stout along with this hearty preparation.

Grilled Medallions of Pork with Sweet Potatoes, Cranberries, and Pine Nuts

Serves 8

3 pounds well-trimmed boneless
    pork loin, cut into 32 $^1/_2$-inch-
    thick medallions
$^1/_4$ cup olive oil
6 medium sweet potatoes, peeled
$^1/_2$ cup light brown sugar

$^1/_2$ pound unsalted butter, softened
    Salt and pepper to season
2 cups fresh cranberries
2 tablespoons granulated sugar
$^1/_2$ cup pine nuts

EQUIPMENT: *Cutting board, boning knife, serrated slicer, measuring cup, film wrap, two baking sheets with sides, vegetable peeler, Japanese turning slicer, measuring spoons, 2$^1/_2$-quart saucepan, food processor, rubber spatula, charcoal grill, tongs, 5-quart saucepan, colander*

Coat the pork medallions with the olive oil and divide into 8 portions of 4 medallions. Individually film-wrap each portion and refrigerate until needed.

Trim the ends of the raw, peeled sweet potatoes so that the ends are flat. Reserve the ends. Cut the sweet potatoes into long, thin strands on a Japanese turning slicer. Reserve the uncut center sections. Place the sweet potato strands in a stainless-steel bowl with ice water to cover; refrigerate until needed.

Cook the sweet potato ends and uncut center sections in 1 quart boiling salted water with $^1/_4$ cup brown sugar for 4 minutes. Transfer to ice water. When cool, drain thoroughly, then place in a food processor fitted with a metal blade. Pulse the potatoes for 1 minute. Add the softened butter and salt and pepper to season. Pulse until thoroughly mixed. Transfer the sweet potato butter to a stainless-steel bowl, cover with film wrap, and keep at room temperature until needed.

Preheat the oven to 300 degrees.

Cut the cranberries in half. In a stainless-steel bowl, combine the granulated sugar and cranberries. Set aside until needed.

Toast the pine nuts on a baking sheet in the preheated oven until golden brown, 10 to 12 minutes. Remove from the oven and hold at room temperature until needed. Lower the oven temperature to 225 degrees.

Season the pork medallions with salt and pepper and grill over a medium charcoal or wood fire for 1 to 1½ minutes on each side. Transfer the medallions to a baking sheet, baste with half the sweet potato butter, and hold in the 225-degree oven while completing the recipe.

Cook the sweet potato strands in 3 quarts boiling salted water with the remaining ¼ cup light brown sugar for 1 minute. Drain the cooked sweet potatoes in a colander and toss with the remaining sweet potato butter.

Portion the sweet potato strands onto each of 8 warm 9- or 10-inch soup/pasta plates. Place 4 medallions of pork on each portion of sweet potatoes and sprinkle with cranberries and pine nuts. Serve immediately.

The Chef's Touch

My first invitation to teach in California came from Karen and Rich Keehn, the proprietors of McDowell Valley Vineyards. I met the Keehns in early 1983, when Trellis partner John Curtis and I toured their vineyard. Karen was very hospitable to us the day we visited and we spent several hours talking about food and wine. I was impressed with Karen's philosophy: "Fine food and fine wine are the products of time, attention to detail, and commitment; both are the results of the creative process." I was also impressed with the quality of their wine. So, when an invitation arrived a few months later for me to conduct a weekend of cooking classes at their beautiful vineyard in Mendocino, I wasted no time in developing a menu that would showcase the Trellis style of cooking. This recipe for grilled pork medallions was demonstrated and served along with several other courses to an enthusiastic audience.

A well-trimmed boneless pork loin will weigh from 3 to 3½ pounds.

Sweet potatoes cut on a Japanese turning slicer (see page 321) will have a unique appearance, not unlike long, thin strands of spaghetti. If the turning slicer is not available, use a French knife to cut the raw sweet potatoes into long, thin strips. Blanch and sauté the strips as recommended for the strands. However, cooking time may be slightly longer.

Although sweet potatoes and yams are similar, it is primarily the sweet potato that is marketed in the United States. (The sweet potato is actually a root vegetable, whereas the yam is a tuber.) Raw unpeeled sweet potatoes should not be refrigerated, as storage at cold temperatures will impair the taste and texture. Store in a cool, dry place.

The availability of fresh cranberries is limited. Early October to late December is the primary period. For the ensuing months, frozen cranberries can be purchased. These tart little berries freeze fairly well. Although the texture of frozen berries is not as firm, there is little deterioration in taste.

It is important that each berry be cut in half; otherwise, the sugar will not penetrate the interior of the berry. Whole berries are capable of shocking the unsuspecting palate.

Be careful that the charcoal or wood fire is not too hot or it will toughen the meat.

If grilling is impractical, sear the medallions in a dry non-stick sauté pan over medium heat. Lightly brown the meat on each side, then finish in the oven as suggested in the recipe.

The deep-rose–colored McDowell grenache served with the pork made for a superb pairing.

Sautéed Pheasant with Shiitake Mushrooms, Seasonal Squash, and Cashew Butter

Serves 8

4 1½-pound whole pheasants
1 cup roasted, unsalted cashew
    pieces
½ pound unsalted butter, softened
    Salt and pepper to season
1 pound tiny green beans,
    trimmed
1 tablespoon peanut oil
½ pound shiitake mushrooms
    (stems removed), sliced ¼ inch
    thick

2 tablespoons water
1½ pounds butternut squash,
    peeled, seeded, and cut into
    strips 2 inches long and ⅛ inch
    wide (see page 317)
¾ pound acorn squash, peeled,
    seeded, and cut into strips 2
    inches long and ⅛ inch wide

EQUIPMENT: *Boning knife, cutting board, serrated slicer, film wrap, measuring cup, baking sheet, measuring spoons, two stainless-steel bowls, vegetable peeler, French knife, paring knife, 5-quart saucepan, colander, three non-stick sauté pans (one large), tongs*

Preheat the oven to 300 degrees.

Remove the leg, thigh, and breast meat from the pheasant (see page 316). Trim any excess fat and skin from the meat and slice into ½-inch-thick strips. Film-wrap the meat and refrigerate until needed.

Toast the cashew pieces on a baking sheet in the preheated oven until golden brown, 15 to 18 minutes. Cool, then chop fine. Combine with the softened butter, season with salt and pepper, and blend thoroughly. Keep the cashew butter at room temperature until needed.

Blanch the tiny green beans in boiling salted water until tender but still crisp, 2 to 2½ minutes. Transfer to ice water. When cool, drain thoroughly, then refrigerate until needed.

Heat the peanut oil in a large non-stick sauté pan over high heat. When hot, add the pheasant, season with salt and pepper, and sauté until lightly browned, about 2 minutes. Add the shiitake mushrooms and a third of the cashew butter and sauté until hot, 3 to 4 minutes.

While the pheasant is cooking, divide the remaining cashew butter between two non-stick sauté pans. Add 2 tablespoons water to one of the pans. Heat both pans over medium high heat. When the butter is hot, add the tiny beans to the pan with butter and water, season with salt and pepper, and sauté until the beans are thoroughly hot, 5 minutes. Place the squash in the other pan, season with salt and pepper, and sauté until hot, 4 to 5 minutes.

Portion the pheasant and shiitake mushrooms in the center of each of 8 warm 10-inch dinner plates. Arrange the squash in a tight ring around each portion of pheasant. Finish by arranging the tiny green beans in a ring around the squash. Serve immediately.

The Chef's Touch

At The Trellis, we have developed a philosophy about cooking game birds very delicately to preserve their flavors and natural moisture without marinades or larding. Our quick-sauté method is simple. The result is a tender and juicy product every time. We purchase, based on availability, the small (about 1½ pounds each) wild Michigan pheasant as well as the larger (about 2 pounds) farm-raised California birds. Each 1½-pound pheasant should yield about 8 ounces of boneless and skinless meat.

This recipe is an excellent quick-sauté for pheasant. However, for the sake of variety and economy, chicken or rabbit would make an excellent alternative.

Purchase cashew pieces, if available, for this recipe. The cost of cashew pieces is about half the price of whole cashews.

Several other nuts, including pistachios, pecans, and hazelnuts, could be used in place of the cashews.

Substitute thin snap beans if the tiny green beans (*haricots verts*) are not available.

Peanut oil is used to sauté the pheasant, not only for flavor but also because butter would burn before it got hot enough to brown the pheasant. Clarified butter or other high-quality vegetable oils could also be used.

The wild Michigan pheasants are our favorites because of their gamy, but not overpowering, flavor. The soft, smooth finish of the 1983 Gundlach-Bundschu merlot makes it very compatible with this pheasant presentation.

Whole Stuffed Quail with Crispy Potato Cakes and Wild Mushroom Sauce

Serves 8

1 pound fresh bulk sausage
1¼ cups clarified butter (see page 312)
¼ cup minced onion
4 teaspoons minced shallots
½ teaspoon minced garlic
   Salt and pepper to season
2 tablespoons dry white wine
6 teaspoons brandy
½ pound cultivated white mushrooms, chopped fine
½ teaspoon chopped fresh tarragon

¼ teaspoon chopped fresh rosemary
1 tablespoon all-purpose flour
¼ pound pistachios, shelled, skinned, and crushed
8 whole quail, partially boned
1 pound wild mushrooms (stems trimmed or removed, as necessary), sliced
4 cups heavy cream
8 4-ounce Crispy Potato Cakes (see page 233)

EQUIPMENT: *Paring knife, cutting board, French knife, two large non-stick sauté pans, wooden spoon, colander, measuring spoons, stainless-steel bowl, teaspoon or pastry bag, two baking sheets with sides, film wrap, 5-quart saucepan, measuring cup, stainless-steel ladle, double boiler, metal spatula, tongs*

Crumble the sausage into a large non-stick sauté pan. Cook over medium heat until thoroughly cooked but not browned, 5 to 6 minutes. Drain the sausage in a colander.

Heat 1 tablespoon clarified butter in a large non-stick sauté pan over medium high heat. When it is hot, add the onion, 1 teaspoon shallots, and the garlic. Season with salt and pepper and sauté for 1 minute. Add the white wine and 2 teaspoons brandy; heat for 1 minute. Add the chopped cultivated white mushrooms and herbs and season with salt and pepper. Reduce the heat to medium and simmer until almost all the liquid has evaporated, 7 to 8 minutes. Add the flour, stirring to combine.

Add the cooked sausage; sauté for an additional 3 to 4 minutes. Transfer the stuffing mixture to a stainless-steel bowl and allow to cool at room temperature for a few minutes before covering and refrigerating to cool completely.

Add the pistachios to the cooled sausage mixture. Season the inside of each quail with salt and pepper. Using a teaspoon or a pastry bag, fill the cavity of each bird with the sausage stuffing. Cover the quail with film wrap and refrigerate until needed.

Heat 1 tablespoon clarified butter in a 5-quart saucepan over medium heat. When hot, add the remaining shallots and brandy and sauté for 30 seconds. Add three-quarters of the sliced wild mushrooms, season with salt and pepper, and sauté for 3 minutes. Add the cream, bring to a simmer, then adjust the heat so the cream will simmer slowly. Place a ladle in the saucepan and occasionally stir the cream so that it does not foam over the sides. Simmer slowly for 1 hour. Add the remaining mushrooms, adjust the seasoning with salt and pepper, and simmer for 5 additional minutes. Transfer the wild mushroom sauce to a double boiler and hold warm while completing the recipe.

Heat ½ cup clarified butter in a large non-stick sauté pan over medium high heat. When hot, fry 4 potato cakes until evenly golden brown, 3½ to 4 minutes on each side. Transfer the fried cakes to a baking sheet and hold at room temperature. Discard any remaining butter from the pan, wipe the pan dry, and repeat the procedure with the remaining 4 cakes. Keep the fried cakes at room temperature while sautéing the quail.

Preheat the oven to 350 degrees.

Heat the remaining 2 tablespoons clarified butter in a large non-stick sauté pan over high heat. Season the quail with salt and pepper. When the butter is hot, place the quail in the pan, breast side down. Sauté the quail until golden brown, 2½ minutes on each side (total time about 5 minutes). Transfer to a baking sheet. Place separate baking sheets of potato cakes and quail in the preheated oven. Heat the quail for 5 to 7 minutes, then remove from the oven and hold at room temperature while the potato cakes cook for another 5 minutes.

Portion the sauce onto each of 8 warm 10-inch plates. Push the mushrooms toward the outside edge of the plate to form a circular border. Place a hot and crispy potato cake in the center of each plate, then place a quail on top of the potato cake and serve immediately.

The Chef's Touch

At The Trellis, we use fresh pork sausage from Wallace Edwards in Surry, Virginia (see page 324). If this sausage is not available, use a lightly seasoned breakfast sausage. Although bulk sausage is more convenient for this recipe, link sausage may also be used with the casings removed.

Dried herbs are acceptable for the stuffing. Use ¼ teaspoon dried tarragon and a pinch or two of dried rosemary. In any case, the herbs are intended to play a subtle part in the seasoning of the recipe.

If no fresh wild mushrooms are available, use ¼ pound sliced dried wild mushrooms rehydrated in 8 cups warm water for 1 hour. Remove the mushrooms from the liquid and drain thoroughly by squeezing gently (this liquid may be heated and reduced to about 3 to 4 tablespoons and added to the cream as it reduces). Slice the mushrooms and use as directed in the recipe.

Farm-raised quail are now available in many large supermarkets. Unfortunately, they will be found in the frozen food case. We are able to purchase fresh quail from a number of purveyors (see page 324). The partially boned quail that are available through these purveyors are ideal for this recipe. All of the bones in the interior of the breast cavity have been removed, allowing for delicious and easy eating. Some specialty food stores may also carry this style of fresh quail.

To accompany this delicate dish, I suggest that you select an appropriate red bordeaux, one that is light and velvety, such as a 1981 Château Gloria.

Sautéed Gulf Shrimp with Fennel and Smoked Tomatoes on Wild Mushroom Fettuccine

Serves 8

- ½ cup olive oil
- ½ pound wild mushrooms (including stems), chopped
  Salt and pepper to season
- 2 tablespoons brandy
- 2 cups water
- 6 medium tomatoes
- 1 teaspoon salt
- 2 eggs
- 5 cups all-purpose flour
- 1 large fennel bulb, cored, cut into strips 1¼ inches long and ⅛ inch wide
- ½ cup cornmeal
- 2½ pounds large shrimp, peeled, deveined, and halved lengthwise

EQUIPMENT: *Cutting board, French knife, 2½-quart saucepan, measuring spoons, measuring cup, 5-quart saucepan, paring knife, "Little Chief" smoker, film wrap, medium-gauge strainer, food processor, rubber spatula, fork, pasta machine, baking sheet with sides, parchment paper, two non-stick sauté pans (one large), tongs, colander*

Heat 1 tablespoon olive oil in a 2½-quart saucepan over high heat. When the oil is hot, add the chopped wild mushrooms, season with salt and pepper, and sauté for 5 minutes, stirring constantly. Add the brandy and simmer for 1 additional minute. Add the water, bring to a boil, then adjust the heat and simmer until the pan is almost dry, about 1 hour. Cool the mushroom reduction, uncovered, in the refrigerator for a half hour.

While the mushrooms are simmering, smoke the tomatoes. Line the wire shelves of a "Little Chief" smoker (see page 320) with parchment paper. Peel and seed the tomatoes (see page 316). Arrange the tomato halves in a single layer on the parchment, cut side down. Smoke the tomatoes for 2 hours, turning them after the first hour. Remove the tomatoes from the smoker and cut into ¼-inch cubes. Cover with film wrap and refrigerate until needed.

Strain the liquid from the cooled mushroom reduction and discard the liquid (press down on the mushrooms while straining to remove as much liquid as possible). Transfer the mushrooms to a food processor fitted with a metal blade. Add 1 tablespoon olive oil and 1 teaspoon salt. Purée for 1 minute. Add the 2 eggs and pulse for 15 seconds, scraping down the sides of the bowl as needed.

Place 4½ cups flour on a clean, dry cutting board or similar work surface. Make a well in the center and add the processed mushroom mixture. Using a fork, work the flour into the center, a small amount at a time. When enough flour has been added that you can handle the dough, begin kneading by hand. Knead the dough by hand until all the flour has been incorporated, about 10 minutes. Cover with film wrap and allow to relax at room temperature for 1 hour.

While the pasta dough is relaxing, blanch the fennel in boiling salted water until tender but still slightly crisp, 2½ to 3 minutes. Transfer to ice water. When cool, drain thoroughly and refrigerate until needed.

Cut the pasta dough into 8 equal portions. Roll and knead each portion of dough through a pasta machine, using the extra ½ cup flour as necessary to prevent the dough from becoming tacky. Cut the sheets of dough into fettuccine (see page 315). To prevent sticking, toss the cut pasta with cornmeal, then place the cut pasta portions on a baking sheet lined with parchment paper. Cover the sheet tightly with film wrap and refrigerate until needed.

Heat 1 tablespoon olive oil in a large non-stick sauté pan over medium high heat. When hot, add the shrimp, season lightly with salt and pepper, and sauté for 5 to 6 minutes.

While the shrimp are cooking, heat 1 tablespoon olive oil in a separate non-stick sauté pan over high heat. When hot, add the fennel, season lightly with salt and pepper, and sauté for 1 minute. Add the smoked tomatoes, season with salt and pepper, and sauté for 4 to 5 minutes.

Cook the pasta (see page 315) in 3 quarts boiling salted water until tender but still firm to the bite, 30 seconds to 1 minute. Drain the cooked pasta in a colander and toss with the remaining ¼ cup olive oil.

Portion the pasta into 8 warm 9- or 10-inch soup/pasta plates. Portion the tomatoes and fennel over the pasta. Place equal amounts of shrimp on, and in the center of, the tomatoes and fennel. Garnish with fennel leaves (if available) and serve immediately.

The Chef's Touch

Although desirable, it is not necessary to use fresh wild mushrooms for this recipe. A couple of options may be considered: use only stems, which have been accumulated and frozen over a period of time, or use dried mushrooms. Rehydrate 2 ounces dried wild mushrooms in 4 cups warm water for one hour; drain thoroughly before cooking.

Whether using fresh, frozen, or dried wild mushrooms, the flavor and color of the pasta will be enhanced by the addition of 1 teaspoon ground imported mushrooms (usually found in the spice section at the supermarket).

Carefully seed the tomato halves so as not to destroy their shape. This will result in more consistent smoking. The tomatoes may be smoked two to three days in advance of serving. Keep the smoked tomatoes refrigerated in a tightly sealed plastic container.

If the smoke flavor of the tomatoes is more intense than desired, adjust by adding enough unsmoked chopped, peeled, and seeded tomatoes to satisfy your own taste preferences. Lightly salt this dish; the smoke flavor accentuates saltiness.

If wild mushrooms are bountiful, sauté ½ pound sliced wild mushrooms along with the tomatoes and fennel.

This recipe calls for a fennel bulb; you may, however, replace or supplement the suggested amount with fennel stalks (if available). Slice fennel stalks widthwise as you would a stalk of celery.

All the energy and dedication needed to be a successful vineyard is present at Fetzer Vineyards in Mendocino. The Fetzer clan has been producing quality wines at reasonable prices for several years. A fresh and lemony 1985 chardonnay from Fetzer is the right wine for a recipe such as this one, with so many flavors at play.

Sewansecott Oyster and Gulf Shrimp Gumbo

Serves 8

9 tablespoons vegetable oil

14 tablespoons (1 cup less 2 tablespoons) all-purpose flour

1/2 teaspoon cayenne pepper

1/2 teaspoon celery salt

1 tablespoon water

2 medium onions, sliced thin

4 stalks celery, sliced
Salt and pepper to season

2 small red bell peppers, cut into thin strips

2 small green bell peppers, cut into thin strips

2 medium leeks, white part only, halved and cut into thin strips

6 cups fish stock (see page 307)

3 tablespoons gumbo filé powder

2 medium tomatoes, peeled, seeded, and chopped (see page 316)

1 1/4 pounds large shrimp, peeled and deveined

1 1/2 pints shucked Sewansecott oysters

EQUIPMENT: *Paring knife, cutting board, French knife, 2 1/2-quart double-gauge aluminum saucepan or a cast-iron skillet, measuring spoons, two whisks, 5-quart saucepan, slotted spoon, two stainless-steel bowls, measuring cup, large non-stick sauté pan*

Make a roux by heating 1/2 cup vegetable oil in a 2 1/2-quart saucepan over medium high heat. Heat until the oil is smoking and very hot; this will take about 20 minutes. Whisk the flour into the hot oil. Continue to whisk vigorously while cooking the roux until it is a uniformly deep brown color. This will take from 5 to 10 minutes depending on the temperature of the oil when the flour was added. Add the cayenne pepper and celery salt; whisk until thoroughly combined. Remove the roux from the heat and keep at kitchen temperature until needed.

Heat the remaining 1 tablespoon oil and 1 tablespoon water in a 5-quart saucepan over medium high heat. When the oil and water are hot, add the onions and celery, season with salt and pepper, and sauté for 6 minutes. Add the peppers and leeks, season with salt and pepper, and sauté all the vegetables for 6 additional minutes. Transfer the sautéed vegetables to a stainless-steel bowl and keep at kitchen temperature until needed. Add 5½ cups stock to the 5-quart saucepan and bring to a boil.

Blend 2 cups boiling stock into the roux, whisking vigorously until smooth. Then whisk into the remaining boiling stock; continue to whisk until smooth. Bring the thickened stock to a boil, then reduce the heat and simmer for 10 minutes.

Whisk together, in a stainless-steel bowl, the remaining ½ cup stock with the gumbo filé. Then whisk into the thickened stock, combining thoroughly.

Add the sautéed vegetables to the thickened stock. Stir to combine thoroughly. Bring to a boil, then reduce the heat and simmer for 5 minutes. At this point, the mixture may be cooled (see page 315) and refrigerated, if desired.

Heat the tomatoes in a large non-stick sauté pan over medium high heat. Season with salt and pepper and sauté for 2 minutes. Add the shrimp, season with salt and pepper, and sauté for 2 minutes. Add the oysters, season, and heat for 2 more minutes. Transfer the shrimp and oysters to the pot with the hot vegetable and thickened stock mixture. Combine all ingredients thoroughly. Adjust the seasoning with salt and pepper. Serve immediately in warm soup plates.

The Chef's Touch

When preparing a dark roux for a gumbo, several precautions must be taken. Be certain your kitchen exhaust system is in good working order. Use a heavy-duty double-gauge aluminum pot or a cast-iron skillet. Use a good-quality vegetable oil (peanut oil works very well). Use a deep-frying thermometer to determine the temperature of the oil. The optimum temperature for making roux for gumbo is between 500 and 550 degrees. The oil must be this hot in order to successfully brown the roux in a very short period of time.

Be very careful when adding the hot stock to the roux, as the mixture will spatter; especially so, if the roux has not been allowed to cool before adding the boiling hot stock. The burning effect of this mixture on the skin is vicious—*be careful!*

Gumbo filé powder, made from ground sassafras leaves, gives the stewlike preparation called gumbo its distinctive flavor. The quality of filé varies from one brand to the next and from one batch to the next. If you have any doubt as to the intensity of the filé, add half the suggested amount, then taste after the gumbo has cooked for a few minutes before adding the remaining amount.

Any high-quality, but preferably East Coast, oyster would be an adequate replacement for the favored Sewansecott oysters.

We have served our version of gumbo with both Black Pepper Brioche (see page 228) and Chili Corn Bread (see page 241).

In 1983, on my first trip to New Orleans I immediately headed for K-Paul's Louisiana Kitchen. The reputation of its famous owner-chef, Paul Prudhomme, lured me to stand in the obligatory line to await the fiery gastronomy being created within. When I was seated, it was coincidentally with another chef, Mark Miller, who like me was in town to attend the second Symposium on American Cuisine. I had not previously met Mark, who was at the time the owner-chef of The Fourth Street Grill in Berkeley, California. We wasted no time in becoming friends, and Mark wasted no time in telling me that my choice of white wine to accompany rabbit jambalaya was akin to using a garden hose to put out a three-alarm fire! I soon switched to Dixie beer and went on to have an extraordinary afternoon of Cajun food and great conversation. I likewise recommend Dixie beer to accompany this dish. If it is not available in your area, then lots of cold Michelob should accompany this gumbo.

Sautéed Oysters with Spinach, Artichokes, and Herbed Butter Sauce

Serves 8

2 cups heavy cream
  Salt and pepper to season
7 tablespoons fresh lemon juice
6 medium artichokes, prepared
  as on page 317
24 cups loosely packed stemmed
  and washed spinach
  (approximately 3 10-ounce
  packages)
  Pinch grated nutmeg

6 tablespoons fish stock (see
  page 307)
2 tablespoons dry white wine
¼ pound unsalted butter, softened
2 teaspoons all-purpose flour
1 tablespoon chopped fresh
  tarragon (or 1 teaspoon dried)
1½ tablespoons minced shallots
2½ pints shucked oysters
¼ cup water

EQUIPMENT: *Measuring cup, two 2½-quart saucepans (one stainless-steel), stainless-steel ladle, double boiler, two stainless-steel bowls, measuring spoons, paring knife, grapefruit spoon, slotted spoon, cutting board, French knife, film wrap, colander, food processor, rubber spatula, ceramic crock, whisk, three large non-stick sauté pans, tongs*

Heat the heavy cream in a 2½-quart saucepan over medium heat. Lightly season with salt and pepper. Place a ladle in the saucepan with the cream and occasionally stir the cream so that it does not foam over the sides. Lower the heat if necessary so that the cream barely simmers. Simmer until reduced by half, about 45 minutes. Strain the reduced cream and hold warm in a double boiler (see page 322).

While the cream is reducing, bring 8 cups lightly salted water with ¼ cup lemon juice to a boil in a 2½-quart stainless-steel saucepan. Cook the artichokes in the boiling water until a knife inserted in the center of an artichoke encounters firmness but no resistance, 10 to 12 minutes. Drain the cooked artichokes, then plunge into ice water. When cool, remove from the water, cut into thin strips, cover with film wrap, and refrigerate until needed.

Chop 16 cups spinach into small pieces in a food processor fitted with a metal blade (this may have to be done in batches, depending upon the size of the processor), or with a French knife (to yield about 4 cups). Heat the chopped spinach in a large non-stick sauté pan over medium heat; season with salt and pepper. When the spinach is warm and slightly wilted, about 3 minutes, add the reduced cream. Allow the spinach and cream to simmer for 5 minutes; adjust the heat if necessary. Add the pinch of nutmeg, adjust the seasoning with salt and pepper, and hold warm in a double boiler.

Heat the stock and wine to a boil in a 2½-quart saucepan over high heat. Combine 2 teaspoons softened butter with the flour and knead the mixture until smooth. Whisk the flour and butter mixture into the boiling stock, a quarter at a time, whisking continuously until the stock is smooth and slightly thickened. Return to a boil, then remove from the heat. Whip 6 tablespoons butter, 1 tablespoon at a time, into the hot thickened stock, making certain each tablespoon is completely incorporated before adding more butter. When 6 tablespoons butter have been incorporated into the stock, add the chopped tarragon and 1 tablespoon lemon juice. Adjust the seasoning with salt and pepper and combine thoroughly. Transfer the herbed butter sauce to a ceramic crock or a stainless-steel container, cover with film wrap, and hold at room temperature for up to an hour before serving.

Heat the remaining 4 teaspoons butter in a large non-stick sauté pan over medium high heat. When hot, add the shallots and sauté for 1 minute. Add the oysters and artichokes, season with salt and pepper, and sauté until warm, about 5 minutes.

While the oysters are heating, heat ¼ cup water in a separate large non-stick sauté pan. When the water is hot, add the remaining 8 cups spinach leaves. Season with salt and pepper and steam just enough to wilt the spinach, about 3 minutes.

Arrange 4 to 5 tablespoons creamed spinach in a ring toward the outside edge of each warm 10-inch plate, leaving a 3- to 4-inch-wide circle in the center of the plate. Place some spinach leaves in the center of each plate, arranging the leaves into a small, neat bed. Using a slotted spoon, portion the oyster and artichoke mixture on top of the steamed spinach leaves. Spoon 2 tablespoons herbed butter sauce over the oysters and artichokes and serve immediately.

The Chef's Touch

It is best to use whole nutmeg and grate as needed. The flavor intensity and aroma of freshly grated nutmeg are wonderful. If necessary, use ground nutmeg as a substitute.

If fish stock is not available, use a very lightly flavored chicken stock or water in place of the fish stock.

You can purchase already shucked oysters from your local fish market or supermarket's fresh fish department. Shucked oysters should be kept in a sealed container immersed in ice. If stored in this fashion, they should keep fresh for several days.

The textures of the spinach leaves and the julienne of artichoke combined with fat oysters and the creamy spinach set up a sensual stimulation of the palate. Heighten this experience with champagne, Moët & Chandon brut to be specific.

Pan Roast of Black Sea Bass Fillet with Lemon and Marjoram

Serves 8

1 cup dry white wine
1 cup fish stock (see page 307)
8 6-ounce black sea bass fillets
2 lemons, zested and juiced (see page 314)

Salt and pepper to season
1 tablespoon chopped fresh marjoram

EQUIPMENT: *Zester or vegetable peeler, cutting board, French knife, medium-gauge strainer, measuring spoons, measuring cup, two large non-stick sauté pans, aluminum foil, slotted spatula*

Heat ½ cup white wine and ½ cup fish stock in each of two non-stick sauté pans over medium high heat, until the liquid comes to a boil. Reduce the heat to medium. Carefully place 4 fillets in each pan. Sprinkle half the lemon juice over the fish in each pan. Season with salt and pepper. Sprinkle the lemon zest and chopped marjoram over each fillet. When the liquid in each pan returns to a simmer, cover the pans with aluminum foil. Reduce the heat to low and cook for 4 to 5 minutes.

Remove each fillet from the cooking liquid with a slotted spatula. Place each fillet on a warm plate. If desired, garnish the plates with whole stems of fresh marjoram and roses fashioned out of lemons. Serve immediately.

The Chef's Touch

The black sea bass we have used in this recipe is a true sea bass, not to be confused with striped bass (also called rockfish). Substitute tilefish or red snapper if the delicately flavored black sea bass is not available.

If fish stock is not available, use water and adjust the seasoning with salt and pepper.

Adjust the cooking time according to the thickness of the fish; you may have to cook a little more or a little less, depending upon the thickness of the portion. The sea bass fillets used at The Trellis are about ¹/₂ inch thick.

The success of this recipe is based upon its simplicity and the usage of fresh ingredients. If sweet-scented fresh marjoram is not available, use its close cousin, fresh oregano. Do not use dried marjoram or dried oregano as the flavor will overpower. Instead, use fresh parsley or fresh dill, both of which always seem to be available in supermarkets. For that matter, almost any fresh herb could be used in this style of preparation.

Choose a well-balanced chardonnay to accompany the sea bass. A wine that is not overly complicated and one with an abundance of fruit would be my choice. With that in mind a Davis Bynum chardonnay would be selected.

Baked Flounder Fillet with Herb and Mushroom Sauce

Serves 8

8 6-ounce skinless flounder fillets
2 tablespoons fresh lemon juice
  Salt and pepper to season
4 cups heavy cream
3 tablespoons unsalted butter, softened
1/4 cup minced shallots
2 cups fish stock (see page 307)
6 tablespoons chopped fresh spinach

2 tablespoons chopped fresh dill
2 tablespoons chopped fresh parsley
2 tablespoons chopped fresh thyme
1 pound mushrooms, stems trimmed, sliced 1/4 inch thick

EQUIPMENT: *Measuring spoons, two baking sheets with sides, film wrap, measuring cup, 5-quart saucepan, stainless-steel ladle, two non-stick sauté pans (one large), rubber spatula, stainless-steel bowl, cutting board, French knife, medium-gauge strainer, double boiler, 2½-quart saucepan, aluminum foil*

Sprinkle the lemon juice over the flounder fillets and season with salt and pepper. Individually film-wrap each fillet and refrigerate until needed.

Heat the cream in a 5-quart saucepan over medium heat. Season the cream with salt and pepper. Place a ladle in the saucepan with the cream and occasionally stir the cream so that it does not foam over the sides. Adjust the heat if necessary so that the cream barely simmers. Simmer the cream until it has reduced to half, about 1 hour.

While the cream is reducing, heat 1 tablespoon butter in a non-stick sauté pan over medium heat. When hot, add the shallots, season with salt and pepper, and sauté for 1 minute. Add 1 cup fish stock, 5 tablespoons chopped spinach, 1 tablespoon chopped dill, 1 tablespoon chopped parsley, and 1 tablespoon chopped thyme. Adjust the heat and simmer slowly until the pan is almost dry, 20 to 25 minutes. Remove the pan from the heat and hold at room temperature until the cream has finished reducing.

Strain the reduced cream. Add the herb reduction and the remaining chopped herbs to the cream. Adjust the seasoning with salt and pepper and hold in a double boiler, tightly covered with film wrap, over low heat while completing the recipe.

Preheat the oven to 350 degrees.

Heat the remaining cup of fish stock to a boil. Place the flounder fillets on a baking sheet. Carefully pour the boiling hot fish stock over the flounder. Cover the baking sheet with aluminum foil. Bake in the preheated oven for 12 to 14 minutes. Remove the pan from the oven and leave it covered with foil.

Heat the remaining 2 tablespoons butter in a large non-stick sauté pan over medium high heat. When hot, add the mushrooms, season with salt and pepper, and sauté for 2 minutes. Add the cream and herb mixture and bring the sauce to a simmer.

Portion the sauce onto each of 8 warm 10-inch dinner plates. Push the mushrooms toward the outside edge of the plate to form a circular border. Place a flounder fillet in the center of each plate. Sprinkle with the remaining chopped spinach and serve immediately.

The Chef's Touch

It is no exaggeration to say that herb and mushroom sauce is an elixir for the range cooks at The Trellis. Whenever this sauce makes an appearance on the Trellis menu, our cooks scramble for any sauce that remains after an evening's service!

The subtle quality of the fish stock adds a nuance of flavor to the sauce which allows it to be eaten with a diversity of foods. Although we serve it only with fish at The Trellis, our cooks have been known to savor the sauce with whatever the evening's employee fare might be, whether a grilled skirt steak or a sautéed chicken breast.

There are as many types of flounder as there are recipes to prepare them. This mild, delicate, and delicious fish is marketed under a variety of names as well as sizes. This recipe is adaptable to turbot, halibut, plaice, grey sole (not a true sole but a flounder), brill, or any tasty fish, whether flatfish of the flounder family or not.

The texture of flounder will vary depending upon the variety and also the season. It is wise to check the fish after it has cooked for 10 minutes. If overcooked, the fish texture may be tacky instead of flaky.

A lightly flavored chicken stock may be used rather than the fish stock.

The sauce may be held in a double boiler for up to an hour before serving the fish. Hold on low heat to prevent further reduction (if the sauce becomes too thick add a little extra stock or cream) or evaporation. Cover the double boiler tightly with film wrap to prevent the top of the sauce from congealing.

The 1985 Château du Mayne Graves is an economical and very easy-to-drink white bordeaux. The crisp dryness and well-balanced acid-to-fruit finish make the wine quite enjoyable with richly sauced foods such as this dish.

Salmon Fillet with Steamed Carrots, Turnips, Leeks, Fresh Herbs, and Lemon

Serves 8

¹/₄ cup fresh lemon juice
    Salt and pepper to season
8 4-ounce skinless salmon fillets
4 medium carrots, peeled and cut
    into 3-inch sections
4 medium turnips, peeled and
    ends trimmed
2 cups fish stock (see page 307)

6 teaspoons lemon zest (see
    page 314)
2 teaspoons chopped fresh dill
2 teaspoons chopped fresh thyme
4 medium leeks, white part only,
    cut into thin strips 2¹/₂ inches
    long

EQUIPMENT: *Zester, vegetable peeler, medium-gauge strainer, film wrap, baking sheet with sides, paring knife, cutting board, French knife, Japanese turning slicer, two stainless-steel bowls, measuring spoons, measuring cup, 5-quart saucepan with lid, large non-stick sauté pan, aluminum foil, tongs, ladle, metal spatula*

Sprinkle the lemon juice and salt and pepper over the salmon fillets. Individually film-wrap each fillet and refrigerate until needed.

Cut the carrots and turnips into long, thin strands on a Japanese turning slicer. Place the vegetable strands in separate bowls of ice water and refrigerate until needed.

In a 5-quart saucepan over high heat, heat 1¹/₂ cups fish stock to a simmer. While waiting for the stock to simmer, thoroughly drain the carrots and turnips, keeping them separate. When the stock begins to simmer, place the carrots into, and to one side of, the saucepan, then place the turnips in the other half of the saucepan. Sprinkle 4 teaspoons lemon zest, 1 teaspoon dill, and 1 teaspoon thyme over the vegetables. Season with salt and pepper. Cover the saucepan tightly. Steam the vegetables on high heat for 3 minutes, then turn off the heat. Do not remove the cover while steaming or after shutting off the heat. The vegetables must remain covered until you are ready to portion them onto the plates.

While the vegetables are steaming, heat the remaining ½ cup fish stock in a large non-stick sauté pan over medium high heat. When the stock is hot, carefully place the salmon fillets in the pan. Season with salt and pepper. Sprinkle the leeks and remaining lemon zest and herbs over the fillets. Cover the pan with aluminum foil, reduce the heat to medium, and cook for 3 to 4 minutes.

Using tongs, portion the carrot strands into, and to one side of, each of 8 individual warm 9- or 10-inch soup/pasta plates. Portion the turnips into the other half of each plate. Spoon 3 to 4 tablespoons vegetable cooking liquid over the vegetables. Center a salmon fillet over the vegetables on each plate. Serve immediately.

The Chef's Touch

Dining in the garden at Les Trois Marches in Versailles on a balmy June night a few years ago was an epicurean indulgence of no small proportion. Trellis co-owner John Curtis and his wife, Julia, were hosting several Parisian friends, including Jean Labee. As a self-proclaimed *gout* (taster), Jean Labee had collaborated with his friend chef Gerard Vie to plan an exceptional gustatory event. Magnums of 1978 Calon-Ségur accompanied our first course, a terrine of lamb that was served in individual sterling-silver saucepans (used only for service). Every course was eagerly anticipated, although as evening ran into morning the lighter courses, such as a barely cooked salmon paillard with lightly steamed vegetables and a light citrus butter sauce, were the most appreciated. This is my re-creation of the dish.

Many fish fillets other than salmon can be steamed and served with these vegetables. Halibut, flounder, red snapper, black sea bass, and tilefish would all be complementary.

The variety of root vegetables available during the winter months is extensive. Salsify, small rutabagas, parsnips, and celery root are the most common and, happily, inexpensive.

The Japanese turning slicer (see page 321) is the necessary piece of equipment for cutting the recommended vegetables into long, thin, and seemingly endless strands. Lacking this piece of equipment, you may cut the vegetables into long, thin strips with a sharp French knife. Increase, by five to six minutes, the amount of time needed to cook the vegetables when using knife-cut root vegetable strips.

If fish stock is not available, use a light-flavored chicken stock, or water well seasoned with salt and pepper.

The use of salt is critical to the piquancy of this recipe. The flavors of the components are very subtle. The steaming, however, will infuse the lemon and herb flavor into the vegetables and fish. By adding salt during the cooking process, these flavors will be intensified.

We drank a 1978 Côte de Beaune with our salmon at Les Trois Marches. A much more affordable 1985 Mâcon Villages would be my choice from the Trellis wine list.

Grilled Skewers of Catfish with Sautéed Winter Greens, Wine-soaked Raisins, and Toasted Pine Nuts

Serves 8

1 cup raisins
³/₄ cup dry white wine
¹/₂ cup pine nuts
3 pounds catfish fillet, cut into
    1- to 1¹/₂-inch pieces
¹/₄ cup vegetable oil
2 tablespoons fresh lemon juice

Salt and pepper to season
¹/₄ cup water
1 tablespoon unsalted butter
2 pounds collard greens,
    stemmed, washed, dried, and
    torn into 2- to 3-inch pieces.

EQUIPMENT: *Small non-stick sauté pan, measuring cup, two baking sheets with sides, cutting board, French knife, stainless-steel bowl, measuring spoons, eight 9-inch bamboo or metal skewers, film wrap, colander, charcoal grill, tongs, 5-quart saucepan, wooden spoon*

Preheat the oven to 300 degrees.

Heat the raisins and white wine in a small non-stick sauté pan over medium heat for 10 minutes. Remove the raisins from the heat and hold in the pan at room temperature until needed.

Toast the pine nuts on a baking sheet in the preheated oven for 10 to 12 minutes. Remove from the oven and keep at room temperature until ready to use. Lower the oven temperature to 225 degrees.

Combine the catfish pieces with the vegetable oil and lemon juice, season with salt and pepper, and combine thoroughly. Divide the fish pieces into 8 portions. Skewer each portion.

Season the skewered portions with salt and pepper, then grill for 4 minutes over a medium charcoal or wood fire. Turn the skewers occasionally while cooking. Transfer the skewers to a baking sheet and hold in the 225-degree oven while preparing the greens.

Heat the water and butter in a 5-quart saucepan over medium heat. When hot, add the greens and season with salt and pepper. Steam until the volume of greens is reduced by two-thirds, 8 to 10 minutes.

While the greens are cooking, heat the raisins over low heat until warm.

Portion the greens onto each of 8 warm 10-inch plates. Remove the grilled catfish from the skewers and place a portion on each plate. Sprinkle the warm raisins and toasted pine nuts over each portion and serve immediately.

The Chef's Touch

It has been over thirty years since I caught my last catfish, so it seems somewhat hard to believe that "catfishing" was such a passion and significant part of my growing-up. Of the many experiences relating to those times, I best remember my first catfish cooking lesson from *mon oncle* Gerry. My cousin Paul and I had just returned from a successful fishing adventure. This trip was so successful that Uncle Gerry decided to teach two ten-year-olds how to prepare catfish for cooking. The lesson included: skinning, which to us seemed cruel and unusual punishment; removal of the roe, which was soon pan-fried and devoured; and the salting of the fish, which, according to Uncle Gerry, was essential in removing the muddy flavor these bottom-dwelling bullheads were likely to have (an unnecessary procedure when using channel catfish or the abundantly available farm-raised catfish). I certainly had no idea at that time that cooking as a livelihood was in my future. But I loved the experience of what may have been my very first cooking lesson.

I suggest using the dark Thompson seedless raisins, but not the golden seedless variety (also sun-dried from Thompson seedless grapes), which are, unfortunately, treated with sulphur dioxide. Dried currants would also work well in this recipe.

If catfish fillets are not available, use fresh perch or a delicately flavored sea fish such as tilefish. If you purchase whole catfish, it will take 6 to 8 cleaned fish, weighing 10 to 12 ounces each with head removed, to yield the necessary amount of filleted fish.

You may wish to use your favorite greens for this recipe. Many greens are available almost year-round. Some of the best greens are also easy to find, especially in the South; they are kale, mustard greens, the recommended collard greens, and, just recently, we have been able to find rapini (broccoli rabe). The primary cautionary note in cooking the greens is not to overcook. Prolonged cooking will cause an accentuation of the inherent bitterness in greens. Cook over low to medium heat, just until they are tender. When cooking the greens for this recipe, it may be necessary to wilt some of them slightly before they will all fit into the cooking pot.

The combinations of flavors in this recipe, particularly the sweet and slightly bitter greens, necessitate a chardonnay with a great deal of varietal flavor, such as Virginia's Burnley Vineyards Special Reserve chardonnay.

Loin of Lamb with Fennel and Curry

Serves 8

2 large fennel bulbs, cored and
    cut into strips 1¹/₄ inches long
    and ¹/₄ inch wide
1 cup sliced almonds
4 cups chicken stock (see
    page 305)
1¹/₂ cups wild rice

Salt and pepper to season
4 teaspoons curry powder
4 cups heavy cream
3 tablespoons clarified butter
    (see page 312)
4 boneless and well-trimmed
    lamb loins (about 2¹/₂ pounds)

EQUIPMENT: *Two 2¹/₂-quart saucepans, film wrap, two baking sheets (one with sides), measuring cup, double boiler, two non-stick sauté pans (one large), measuring spoons, rubber spatula, 5-quart saucepan, stainless-steel ladle, colander, stainless-steel bowl, tongs, instant-read test thermometer, cutting board, serrated slicer*

Preheat the oven to 300 degrees.

Blanch the fennel strips in boiling salted water until tender but slightly crisp, 2¹/₂ to 3 minutes. Transfer to ice water. When cool, drain thoroughly and refrigerate until needed.

Toast the almonds on a baking sheet in the preheated oven until golden brown, about 15 minutes. Hold at room temperature until needed. Raise the oven temperature to 375 degrees.

Heat the chicken stock to a boil in a 2¹/₂-quart saucepan over high heat. Heat a double boiler with 2 inches of water in the bottom portion over medium heat. Place the wild rice and 3¹/₂ cups boiling chicken stock in the top half, season lightly with salt and pepper, and cover tightly. Cook the rice over medium heat for 1 hour. Turn off the heat and leave the double boiler covered.

While the rice is cooking, prepare the sauce. Heat the remaining ¹/₂ cup chicken stock in a non-stick sauté pan over medium heat. When the stock begins to simmer, whisk in the curry powder. Reduce the heat if necessary to allow the mixture to simmer until the pan is almost dry, about 15 minutes. While the curried stock is reducing, heat the heavy cream in a 5-quart saucepan over medium heat. Lightly season with salt and pepper. When the cream begins to boil, whisk in the curry reduction. Continue to whisk until the cream is smooth. Place a ladle in the saucepan and occasionally stir the cream so that it does not foam over the sides. Adjust the heat if necessary so that the cream barely simmers. Simmer the cream until it has reduced to half, about 1 hour. Adjust the heat to keep the curried cream warm.

Heat 2 tablespoons clarified butter in a large non-stick sauté pan over high heat. Season the lamb loins with salt and pepper. When the butter is very hot, place the lamb loins in the pan and sear until evenly browned, 1½ to 2 minutes on each side. Transfer the meat to a baking sheet and place in the 375-degree oven until the meat reaches an internal temperature of 120 degrees, 6 to 8 minutes. Remove the lamb from the oven and hold at room temperature.

Heat the remaining 1 tablespoon clarified butter in a non-stick sauté pan over medium high heat. When hot, add the fennel, season lightly with salt and pepper, and sauté for 3 minutes.

Slice the lamb loins into 12 pieces (not including the end pieces; save those for a great sandwich). Arrange a 1-inch-wide ring of wild rice around the outside edge of each of 8 warm 10-inch dinner plates. Sprinkle toasted almonds over each ring of rice. Flood the center of each plate with ¼ cup curried cream. Arrange a 2-inch-wide strip of fennel in the center of each plate within the ring of rice. Place 6 lamb slices, each slightly overlapping the other, in the center of the plate over the fennel and the curried cream (the sliced lamb and fennel strips will form an **X**). Serve immediately.

The Chef's Touch

My first experience with fennel was at the Culinary Institute of America. Chef instructor Dominick De Maio, who was in charge of the cold foods class, called fennel by its Italian name, *finocchio*. At that time (1963), fennel was not a well-known vegetable in the United States. However, in cities with large Italian populations such as New Haven (then the home of the Culinary Institute), it was available, sought after, and frequently eaten. Chef De Maio's enthusiasm for this licorice-tasting vegetable rubbed off on at least one of his students, for I have enjoyed preparing and eating fennel ever since.

Fennel is being sold almost year-round in most areas of the United States, although late fall and winter are the best seasons. At that time, fennel is usually sold in its entirety: that is, the bulb, stalk, and leaves attached. In this recipe we use the bulb, which is the bottom portion of the fennel closest to the root. The bulb is a bit on the fibrous side and it is sometimes recommended to lightly peel it as you might celery. Fennel stalks are more intensely colored and more fibrous than the bulbs. They are also more assertively licorice-tasting. Slice the stalks and serve them raw in salads; they are a pleasant surprise on the palate. The leaves from the stalks resemble dill in appearance and have a mild sweet taste that is very appealing. Use the leaves combined with other herbs in recipes that call for an assortment of fresh herbs. They also make a very attractive garnish for grilled fish.

The success of this recipe depends on drawing diverse ingredients to marry well with each other. With this in mind, it is important that the fennel be cooked until tender and only slightly crisp; otherwise, the raw flavor would compete with the spiciness of the curry.

Once cooked, the wild rice will stay warm and in good textural condition if removed from the heat but left covered in the double boiler for up to 20 or 30 minutes. For the sake of time and organization, the rice can be cooked several hours in advance (or even the day before), cooled (see page 315), and refrigerated. For service, heat the chilled rice in a non-stick sauté pan with ¼ cup chicken stock or water.

The amount of curry powder suggested for this recipe will create a pleasant but definite impression on the palate. Curry powder is a mixture of dried spices. The intensity of flavor varies from one brand to the other. Taste the curry before using to determine its strength by diluting 1 teaspoon in a cup of hot chicken stock or water. Increase or decrease the amount used in the reduction based upon your own taste preferences.

The lamb will continue to cook for several minutes after it has been removed from the oven. For that reason, it is important that it not be overcooked. An internal temperature of 120 degrees taken with an instant-read test thermometer (see page 322) will produce a degree of doneness somewhere between medium rare and medium. For rare to medium rare, cook to an internal temperature of 110 degrees.

Choose a full-bodied chardonnay such as the Château St. Jean 1985 Sonoma chardonnay. It has the overall character and durable acidity necessary to present a counterpoint to the assertive flavors present in this recipe.

Grilled Medallions of Veal with Apples, Mushrooms, and Cream on Buckwheat Fettuccine

Serves 8

3¹/₂ cups all-purpose flour
1 cup buckwheat flour
5 eggs
1 tablespoon olive oil
1 teaspoon salt
¹/₂ cup cornmeal
2 cups heavy cream
   Salt and pepper to season
1 tablespoon fresh lemon juice
2 Red Delicious apples, unpeeled

2 Granny Smith apples, unpeeled
2 pounds well-trimmed boneless
   veal loin, cut into 32
   medallions ¹/₄ inch thick
¹/₄ cup vegetable oil
10 tablespoons unsalted butter,
   softened
1 pound mushrooms, stems
   trimmed, sliced

EQUIPMENT: *Cutting board, measuring cup, measuring spoons, fork, film wrap, pasta machine, two baking sheets with sides, parchment paper, 2¹/₂-quart saucepan, stainless-steel ladle, paring knife, stainless-steel bowl, charcoal grill, tongs, colander, large non-stick sauté pan, medium-gauge strainer, 5-quart saucepan, large metal spoon*

Combine 3 cups all-purpose flour with the buckwheat flour. Place the combined flours on a clean, dry cutting board or similar work surface. Make a well in the center and add the eggs, olive oil, and 1 teaspoon salt. Using a fork, combine the eggs, oil, and salt. When thoroughly mixed, begin to work the flour into the center, a small amount at a time. When enough flour has been added that you can handle the dough, begin kneading by hand. Knead by hand until all the flour has been incorporated, about 10 minutes. Cover with film wrap and allow to relax at room temperature for 1 hour.

Cut the pasta dough into 8 equal portions. Roll and knead each portion of dough through the pasta machine, using the extra ¹/₂ cup flour as necessary to prevent the dough from becoming tacky. Cut the sheets of dough into fettuccine (see page 315). To prevent sticking, toss the cut pasta with the cornmeal, then place the cut pasta portions on a baking sheet lined with parchment paper. Cover the sheet tightly with film wrap and refrigerate until needed.

Heat the heavy cream in a 2½-quart saucepan over medium heat. Lightly season the cream with salt and pepper. Place a ladle in the saucepan with the cream and occasionally stir the cream so that it does not foam over the sides. Adjust the heat if necessary so that the cream barely simmers. Simmer the cream until it has reduced to half, about 45 minutes.

While the cream is simmering, acidulate 4 cups water with 1 tablespoon lemon juice. Core and quarter the unpeeled apples. Slice the apples widthwise into the acidulated water. Refrigerate until needed.

Lightly coat the medallions with the vegetable oil. Season with salt and pepper. Quickly sear the medallions over a hot charcoal or wood fire. Transfer the medallions to a baking sheet and hold at room temperature.

Preheat the oven to 350 degrees.

Drain the sliced apples in a colander and rinse under cold running water. Shake dry. Heat 2 tablespoons butter in a large non-stick sauté pan over high heat. When hot, add the apples and mushrooms, season with salt and pepper, and sauté for 3 minutes. Strain the reduced cream into the pan with the apples and mushrooms. Reduce the heat to medium and allow to heat while preparing the pasta.

Place the veal in the preheated oven. Cook the pasta (see page 315) in 3 quarts boiling salted water until tender but still firm to the bite, 30 seconds to a minute. Drain the cooked pasta in a colander and return to the pan. Cut the remaining butter into pieces, add to the pasta, and toss to coat.

Portion the pasta into 8 warm 9- or 10-inch soup/pasta plates. Spoon an equal amount of the apples, mushrooms, and cream over each portion of pasta. Place 4 warm veal medallions on each portion and serve immediately.

The Chef's Touch

In order to feature veal frequently on the menu at The Trellis, it is necessary for us to develop economical yet sophisticated recipes. This is done through portion control and creativity. This recipe exemplifies that philosophy: a 4-ounce portion of veal accented by a somewhat classical apple, mushroom, and cream combination featured on strands of earthy buckwheat pasta. It is very appetizing, eye-appealing, and popular.

Buckwheat flour is usually found in the health-food section at major supermarkets, or it can be purchased at health-food stores.

If the reduction of the cream is completed before you are ready to add it to the apples and mushrooms, place the cream in a double boiler, cover tightly with film wrap, and hold over low heat until ready to use.

Peel the apples if you object to the texture of apple peel.

For this recipe, purchase medallions cut from milk-fed veal. The texture and flavor are far superior to that of grass-fed calves.

Veal medallions cut from the loin result in elegant but expensive eating. For budgetary reasons, consider using slices of meat cut from the veal leg.

It should take no more than thirty seconds to properly sear each side of the veal medallions. Be very cautious in the timing; overcooked veal is rather tasteless. If you are a bit nervous about the timing, I suggest that only a few pieces of veal be seared at once. Since the veal will be finished in the oven, it is not necessary that it be seared simultaneously. Better to take a little extra time during the grilling than to ruin an expensive culinary investment.

Either a light cabernet sauvignon or a rich chardonnay would be a companionable beverage with a serving of this delicious veal and pasta.

Roast Loin of Pork with Acorn Squash, Butternut Squash, and Roasted Walnut Butter

Serves 8

1 whole fresh boneless pork loin
2 tablespoons olive oil
2 cups walnut halves
1 pound unsalted butter, softened
  Salt and pepper to season
1 tablespoon cracked black peppercorns
2 medium butternut squash, peeled, seeded, and cut into strips 2½ inches long and ⅛ inch wide (see page 317)

2 medium (2 pounds) acorn squash, peeled, seeded, and cut into strips 2 inches long and ⅛ inch wide
1 large bunch watercress, stems trimmed, washed and dried

EQUIPMENT: *Cutting board, boning knife, French knife, film wrap, measuring cup, two baking sheets (one with sides), two stainless-steel bowls, wooden spoon, vegetable peeler, paring knife, measuring spoons, tongs, instant-read test thermometer, two large non-stick sauté pans, serrated slicer*

Preheat the oven to 300 degrees.

Remove any remaining fat and membrane from the pork loin. Cut into two equal-size pieces (so they will fit in a sauté pan), and coat with the olive oil. Film-wrap and refrigerate until needed.

Toast the walnut halves on a baking sheet in the preheated oven for 15 to 20 minutes. Remove from the oven and allow to cool. When the walnuts are cool, finely chop all but 24 halves. Combine the chopped walnuts with the softened butter. Season with salt and pepper and combine thoroughly. Cover the walnut butter with film wrap and hold at room temperature until needed. Raise the oven temperature to 350 degrees.

Season the pork loin halves with cracked black pepper and salt. Heat a large sauté pan over high heat until very hot, 2 to 3 minutes. Reduce the heat to medium high. Place the pork loin halves in the sauté pan and cook until evenly browned, 3 minutes on each side (total cooking time, 6 minutes). Transfer the loin halves to a baking sheet, baste with half the walnut butter, and place in the 350-degree oven until the meat reaches an internal temperature of 130 degrees, 14 to 16 minutes. Remove the pork from the oven and hold at room temperature.

Divide the remaining butter between two large non-stick sauté pans. Heat the butter over medium high heat. When hot, divide the squash between the pans, season with salt and pepper, and sauté until thoroughly warm, 6 to 7 minutes.

Slice each pork loin half into 12 slices. Portion the squash onto 8 warm 10-inch plates. Place 3 pork slices on top and in the center of the squash. Garnish each plate with a spray of watercress and 3 toasted walnut halves. Serve immediately.

The Chef's Touch

The subject of colonial Virginia cookery was well documented by the late Dr. Jane Carson, noted author and historian. I met Dr. Carson in 1971 when she served as an adviser on *The Williamsburg Cookbook*. I was assisting on the food styling for the photographs taken for the book by Taylor Lewis. Dr. Carson, a stickler for detail, was very insistent that all elements of the book reflect the Southern tradition.

Over the years, I had the pleasure of engaging in several impromptu food discussions with Dr. Carson. Although her expertise was colonial cookery, she nonetheless had many opinions about the contemporary cooking scene. It was Dr. Carson who suggested that we serve roast pork at The Trellis with an accompaniment of squash and walnuts. All the ingredients in this recipe are traditional (if not colonial; fresh pork was seldom served in the eighteenth century), although the techniques and the presentation are contemporary.

An average pork loin will weigh 10 to 13 pounds. Have your butcher bone out the loin or do it yourself. A boneless pork loin should weigh about 6 pounds before being trimmed of excess fat and membrane. Usable meat yield of the pork loin after being well trimmed is about 3 to 3½ pounds.

Do not hesitate to use varieties of squash other than the two suggested for this recipe. Consider pumpkin or hubbard as excellent alternatives or as additions.

The recommended cooking time and temperatures for the pork will result in moist and tender meat. It is important to use an instant-read test thermometer (see page 322) to determine the degree of doneness. At 130 degrees, the pork will be moist, pink, and medium rare to medium. The meat will continue to cook once it has been removed from the oven, so although 130 degrees will usually indicate that meat is medium rare, the actual serving doneness will be closer to medium after it has been held at room temperature for the few minutes it will take to sauté the vegetables. If medium well done pork is desired, bring the internal temperature to 150 degrees before removing from the oven.

The squash should be gently sautéed and not overcooked; otherwise, it will break apart and be much less attractive.

Although pork is excellent with the squash and walnut butter, for variety serve a grilled boneless and skinless chicken breast in the same fashion.

The 1982 Clos Du Val merlot is a pleasant and easy wine with a particular affinity to nuts, making it perfect to drink with this pork dish.

Braised Tenderloin of Beef with Mushrooms, Raisins, Figs, and Red Wine

Serves 8 to 12

2 tablespoons water
4 medium carrots, peeled and cut into slices ¼ inch thick
2 medium onions, chopped
Salt and pepper to season
6 cups red wine
2 pounds beef tenderloin, cut into ¾-inch cubes
½ pound smoked sausage, cut into slices ½ inch thick

1 small jalapeño pepper, roasted, seeded, and cut into thin strips (see page 314)
1 cup raisins
10 dried figs, split in half lengthwise
½ pound mushrooms, stems trimmed, cut into quarters

EQUIPMENT: *Paring knife, vegetable peeler, cutting board, French knife, tongs, 7-quart saucepan, measuring spoons, wooden spoon, measuring cup*

Heat 2 tablespoons water in a 7-quart saucepan over medium heat. When hot, add the carrots and onions, season with salt and pepper, and braise for 10 minutes.

Add the red wine, adjust the heat to high, and bring to a boil. Add the beef, sausage, jalapeño pepper, raisins, and figs, season with salt and pepper, and adjust the heat so that the mixture will simmer slowly for 30 minutes (occasionally stir gently while simmering). Add the quartered mushrooms and simmer for an additional 10 minutes.

Remove the mixture from the heat and cool properly (see page 315). Refrigerate for 24 hours before serving.

Reheat the desired amount of braised beef over medium heat. When thoroughly heated, serve in warm 9- or 10-inch soup plates.

The Chef's Touch

Aromas play a significant role in food memories: onions sautéing in butter, a freshly chopped bunch of basil, a loaf of walnut bread as it bakes in the oven. These and countless other smells serve as reminders of the pleasures of good food and cooking. One aroma I will never forget is that of this braised beef recipe or "drink in the pot" as it was called by Mrs. Mary Humelsine, wife of the chairman of the Colonial Williamsburg Foundation. Mrs. Humelsine had requested that I prepare this dish for the annual Colonial Williamsburg board of directors' meeting in 1973. This is one of Mrs. Humelsine's favorite recipes. I am certain that once you savor the aroma of this delicious preparation, it will also become one of yours.

Since 1980 the only beef appearing on the Trellis seasonal menus has been beef tenderloin steak, a continual best-seller. We use only center-cut fully trimmed tenderloins for this steak; consequently, we generate quite a bit of end pieces and good trimmings. This is the reason we use beef tenderloin in this recipe.

For the home cook, for both convenience and economy, other beef cuts may be utilized. Top round, trimmed of all fat and connective tissue, can be successfully used with a slight change in the cooking procedure. If using a less tender cut of meat such as top round, follow the recipe directions as stated. However, the carrots should not be braised with the onions; rather, they should be added after the mixture (red wine, beef, etc.), minus the carrots, has simmered for 20 minutes. After the carrots have been added, allow the mixture to simmer slowly for an additional 40 minutes before adding the mushrooms and completing the recipe as directed.

A variety of smoked pork and beef-pork sausage is available in most good supermarkets. Look for a dry-pack product that has a minimum amount of fat streaks.

Although the braised beef can be eaten immediately following preparation, the flavors of the mixture will mellow and be much more enjoyable if allowed to meld for about 24 hours in the refrigerator.

In this unorthodox cooking preparation, the quality of the wine is most important. Choose a light-bodied red wine such as a California gamay or a French Beaujolais. The drinking characteristics to look for would be: dry, but not tannic, and fruity, without being sweet. A wine with these characteristics would be my choice for drinking as well.

Sautéed Calves' Liver with Fresh Pears and Surry Sausage

Serves 8

8 links (about 1 pound) Surry
    sausage
4 tablespoons unsalted butter,
    softened
1 tablespoon chopped fresh sage
    Salt and pepper to season
1 tablespoon fresh lemon juice

4 large pears, unpeeled
2 pounds well-trimmed calves'
    liver
2 tablespoons water
1 medium onion, sliced thin
    Fresh sage leaves, for garnish

EQUIPMENT: *Paring knife, fork, baking sheet with sides, measuring spoons, cutting board, French knife, serrated slicer, two stainless-steel bowls, film wrap, colander, two large non-stick sauté pans, slotted spoon*

Preheat the oven to 300 degrees.

Puncture each sausage several times with a fork. Place sausages on a baking sheet with ¼ cup water. Place in the preheated oven and cook for 20 minutes. Remove from the oven and allow the sausages to cool at room temperature. When cool, refrigerate for 30 minutes before cutting each sausage into 4 or 5 pieces.

Combine the butter and chopped sage in a stainless-steel bowl. Season with salt and pepper and blend thoroughly. Cover the sage butter with film wrap and keep at room temperature until ready to use.

Acidulate 4 cups water with 1 tablespoon lemon juice. Core and quarter the unpeeled pears. Slice each quarter lengthwise into 8 slices, and place in the acidulated water. Cover with film wrap and refrigerate until needed.

Cut the trimmed liver into 1-inch cubes. Cover with film wrap and refrigerate until needed.

Heat 2 tablespoons sage butter with 2 tablespoons water in a large non-stick sauté pan over high heat. When the butter mixture is hot, add the onion, season with salt and pepper, and sauté until tender and somewhat translucent, 3½ to 4 minutes.

Drain the pears in a colander and then rinse under cold running water. Shake dry. Add the pears to the onion and sauté until hot, about 2½ to 3 minutes.

While the onion is sautéing, heat the remaining 2 tablespoons sage butter in a separate large non-stick sauté pan over medium high heat. Season the liver with salt and pepper. When the butter is hot, add the liver and sausage and sauté for 4 minutes. Constantly shake the pan so that the liver and sausage will evenly color while cooking.

Portion the onion and pear mixture onto 8 warm 10-inch plates. Portion the liver and sausage on top of the onion and pear mixture on each plate. Garnish with sage leaves and serve immediately.

The Chef's Touch

"A liver for all seasons," almost, for calves' liver has appeared on sixteen of the Trellis seasonal menus as well as having been featured countless times as a daily special. Or perhaps we should say, "Fifty ways to love your liver."

Each appearance on a seasonal menu has featured calves' liver prepared in a different manner: with mustard butter, skewered with bacon and mushrooms, with artichokes and brown butter, skewered with sweetbreads, and with buttered whole scallions. These preparations, along with the recipes featured in this book, are but a few of the delicious ways we have offered this often neglected meat.

Sausage-making is experiencing a welcome surge of popularity. Professional chefs as well as home chefs all over America are producing unique and flavorful products. This current interest has also been encouraging for small, quality-oriented commercial sausage makers, who are finding that the increased attention has led to increased sales of a quality product.

For this recipe we use a fresh sausage from Surry, Virginia. Identify the best product available in your area and use it, thereby regionalizing this recipe.

The reason the sausage is refrigerated after blanching is to facilitate the cutting. Fresh sausages are usually delicate and have a tendency to crumble if cut when still warm. Refrigerate the sausage after cutting if it will not be served within an hour. Otherwise, keep the sausage at room temperature until ready to use.

I suggest using red Bartlett pears if they are available; they will add a great deal of eye appeal to the finished product. If these pears are not available, use the commonly available greenish-yellow-colored Bart-letts.

To trim a whole liver, use a very sharp knife to cut under the thin membrane, then use your fingers to get in between the membrane and the meat. Work your fingers and eventually your hand under the membrane. If this is done slowly, it is often possible to remove most of the membrane. Use the knife to cut away membrane that does not come free. Also, use a boning knife to remove blood vessels and tough interior membrane. Sometimes it is necessary to cut into the meat to be able to remove most of the interior membrane; do this carefully so as not to cut too deeply.

It will take approximately 2½ pounds of untrimmed liver to yield the necessary 2 pounds for this recipe. A whole calves' liver will weigh about 6 pounds. If you buy a whole liver, trim properly; cut the necessary 2 pounds of cubes, then cut the remaining amount of liver into slices and coat each slice with oil. Film wrap each slice and keep refrigerated for up to 3 days, or freeze each wrapped portion immediately.

While on the subject of neglect, a wine comes to mind—zinfandel. Regrettably, the American wine consumer had a very short love affair (or should I say flirtation) a few years ago with this robust and sometimes aggressively tannic wine. It is unfortunate to note that zinfandel sales have been on the decline. The styles of zinfandels do vary dramatically from one wine maker to the next. Perhaps a more consistent product would gain more adherents. A zinfandel that I have found to be exceptional in quality and reliably good to drink is Paul Draper's, from Ridge Vineyards. These always rich and intense wines are undeniably the best that can be produced from this grape.

ACCOMPANIMENTS

Sautéed Asparagus with Black Pepper, Lemon, and Toasted Almonds

Serves 8

2 pounds asparagus
1 cup sliced almonds
2 tablespoons unsalted butter,
   softened
1 tablespoon water

Salt and pepper to season
Zest of 1 lemon (see page 314)
1 teaspoon cracked black
   peppercorns

EQUIPMENT: *French knife, cutting board, vegetable peeler, zester, 5-quart saucepan, tongs, stainless-steel bowl, baking sheet, measuring cup, measuring spoons, large non-stick sauté pan*

Preheat the oven to 300 degrees.

Snap the woody stem from each stalk of asparagus. Lightly peel the asparagus and blanch in boiling salted water for about 45 seconds, depending upon the thickness; the asparagus should remain very crisp. Immediately transfer to ice water. When cold, drain thoroughly and refrigerate until needed.

Toast the almonds on a baking sheet in the preheated oven until golden brown, 12 to 15 minutes. Remove from the oven and keep at room temperature until needed.

Heat the butter and 1 tablespoon water in a large non-stick sauté pan over medium high heat. When hot, add the asparagus and season lightly with salt and pepper. Sprinkle with the lemon zest and cracked pepper and sauté until hot, about 3 to 4 minutes. Adjust the seasoning with salt and pepper. Portion the asparagus onto individual plates and sprinkle the almonds over the top. Serve immediately.

The Chef's Touch

To modify this dish for a low-saturated-fat diet, use olive or safflower oil instead of butter. In that case, there will be no need to use the water when sautéing.

The lemon from which the zest has been removed may be saved; although it has no skin, the juice will still be fine.

Sautéed Mirliton Squash with Black Beans, Tomatoes, and Garlic

Serves 8

½ cup dried black turtle beans, washed and picked over
½ teaspoon salt
2 pounds mirliton squash
2 tablespoons olive oil

1 teaspoon minced garlic
Salt and pepper to season
1 medium tomato, peeled, seeded, and chopped (see page 316)

EQUIPMENT: *Measuring cup, stainless-steel bowl, medium-gauge strainer, 2½-quart saucepan, 5-quart saucepan, paring knife, cutting board, French knife, measuring spoons, large non-stick sauté pan, slotted spoon*

Soak the beans overnight in 2 cups water, covered, in the refrigerator. Drain and rinse, then place in a 2½-quart saucepan with 4 cups fresh, cool water and ½ teaspoon salt. Cook over medium heat until tender, 50 to 60 minutes, then cool in the cooking liquid for 45 minutes at room temperature. Drain and set aside until needed.

Blanch the whole mirliton squash in boiling salted water until a paring knife inserted into the center encounters firmness but no resistance, about 30 minutes. Transfer the squash to ice water. When cool, remove from the water. Using a paring knife, peel the whole squash and split it in half along the natural dividing line. Use a paring knife to remove the seed, being sure to remove all of the fibrous seed matter. Cut the squash into strips ½ inch by ¼ inch and the length of the squash.

Heat the olive oil in a non-stick sauté pan over medium high heat. When hot, add the garlic and sauté for 5 seconds. Add the squash strips, season lightly with salt and pepper, and sauté for 2 minutes. Add the beans and tomato, season lightly with salt and pepper, and sauté until hot, about 3 minutes. Adjust the seasoning with salt and pepper if necessary. Portion onto individual serving dishes and serve immediately.

The Chef's Touch

Any inventory of the produce walk-in refrigerator at The Trellis will show some type of squash on hand. It is also a rare day when one of the many varieties of squash does not find its way onto our menu. Mirliton is one of my favorites, especially when prepared as in this tantalizing recipe.

Mirliton or chayote squash grows in warmer climates all over the world. Most of the mirliton served at The Trellis is from Costa Rica, although we also receive squash from Mexico and from Florida.

The skin of this pear-shaped fruit may be a creamy light green or an extremely dark green, but you should always choose squash that is free from exterior discoloration: a mottled appearance indicates brown spots in the flesh.

The yield from 1/2 cup dried black beans will be approximately 1 cup cooked beans.

Marinated Chopped Tomatoes

Yields 2 cups

1 small jalapeño pepper
3 tomatoes, cored
1 small red onion, diced fine
2 teaspoons red raspberry vinegar

¾ teaspoon freshly cracked black
   peppercorns
½ teaspoon salt

EQUIPMENT: *Tongs, 5-quart saucepan, cutting board, paring knife, French knife, measuring spoons, stainless-steel bowl, wooden spoon, film wrap*

Char the jalapeño pepper over a gas flame, charcoal fire, or an electric range element until black. When the pepper is thoroughly black, rinse under cold running water to remove its skin. Cut the rinsed pepper in half and remove the seeds (see page 314). Finely mince and set aside.

Place the cored tomatoes in boiling water until the skin begins to come loose, about 45 seconds. Remove the tomatoes from the boiling water and plunge into ice water. When the tomatoes are cool, remove from the water. Peel, cut in half horizontally, seed, and cut into ¼-inch pieces.

In a stainless-steel bowl whisk together the raspberry vinegar, black pepper, and salt. Add the tomatoes and minced jalapeño and blend well. Cover with film wrap and refrigerate for 3 hours, or until ready to use.

The Chef's Touch

This is the Trellis version of tomato salsa. It is subtle enough to be served as a side dish with an entrée such as Grilled Calves' Liver with Avocado, Red Onion, and Brown Butter (see page 100).

This salsa is also interesting enough to liven up simply prepared dishes while adding very few calories and no saturated fats. I often make liberal use of this spicy condiment as an accompaniment to a grilled chicken paillard.

We use this salsa, which can be held in the refrigerator for up to a week, as a condiment or ingredient in a wide variety of preparations: Corn and Tomato Fritters (see page 210), on our vegetarian Chef's Garden Selections, with sautéed crabmeat, in mayonnaise, and even on hamburgers. Keep some on hand at all times!

To seed the tomatoes, gently squeeze each horizontally-cut half under cool running water. Allow the water to flush the seeds out from the tomato sections.

Irish Soda Bread with Herbs

Yields 1 round loaf

4 cups plus 1 tablespoon bread
    flour
1 tablespoon chopped fresh dill
1 tablespoon chopped fresh
    tarragon
1 tablespoon chopped fresh thyme
1 teaspoon baking powder

1 teaspoon salt
½ teaspoon baking soda
1½ cups buttermilk
¼ cup vegetable oil
1 egg yolk
1 tablespoon water

EQUIPMENT: *Cutting board, French knife, measuring cup, electric mixer with paddle, measuring spoons, two stainless-steel bowls, baking sheet, parchment paper, whisk, pastry brush*

Preheat the oven to 325 degrees.

In the bowl of an electric mixer fitted with a paddle, combine 4 cups flour, the chopped herbs, baking powder (see page 319), salt, and baking soda (breaking up any lumps). Mix on low speed for 2 minutes.

Place the buttermilk and vegetable oil in a stainless-steel bowl and whisk gently to combine. Gradually add the buttermilk mixture to the combined dry ingredients while mixing on low speed and continue to mix until the dough forms a ball, 30 to 40 seconds. Scrape the dough away from the paddle and turn the dough ball over. Mix on low speed for an additional 30 seconds.

Flour a clean, dry surface with the remaining tablespoon flour. Transfer the dough ball to the floured surface and knead with the heels of your hands until smooth. Form the dough into a round loaf. Pinch a small handful of dough and gently twist, being careful not to tear the dough from the loaf. Place the loaf, pinched side down, on a baking sheet lined with parchment paper.

Whisk the egg yolk with 1 tablespoon water, then lightly brush the mixture over the top of the loaf. Score the loaf by cutting a ¼-inch-deep **X** into the top.

Bake the loaf in the preheated oven for 50 to 55 minutes. The bread is done if a hollow sound is heard when the bottom is tapped with your finger. Allow the bread to cool to room temperature before slicing.

The Chef's Touch

The Trellis pastry chef, Andrew O'Connell, claims that his Irish heritage entitles him to add fresh herbs to the traditional Irish soda bread without raising the ire of his ancestors.

Fresh herbs give a wonderful flavor, aroma, and appearance to this bread. Use the recommended variety or use only one herb.

Rather than using dried herbs, if fresh are not available, use an equivalent amount of chopped spinach.

To prepare *Scallion Soda Bread,* replace the fresh herbs with ¼ cup thinly sliced scallions. Two scallions should yield this amount.

To prepare *Raisin Soda Bread,* replace the herbs with ⅓ cup raisins. *Caraway Seed Soda Bread* may also be prepared, using 2 tablespoons caraway seeds instead of the fresh herbs.

The dough must be kneaded vigorously by hand; this should take about 2 minutes.

Pinching and twisting the loaf to form a base will give the finished bread a tighter and taller shape. This procedure is not necessary; however, the finished loaf will be much flatter if the base is not pinched and twisted as suggested.

If a table-model electric mixer is not available, this recipe may also be prepared by hand, using a wire whisk (mixing time may double).

Roasted Garlic Breadsticks

Yields about 120 sticks

2 large cloves garlic, unpeeled
  Salt and pepper to season
1³/₄ teaspoons olive oil
1 cup warm water
1 teaspoon granulated sugar

2 teaspoons active dry yeast
3 cups all-purpose flour
1 teaspoon salt
¹/₂ cup cornmeal

EQUIPMENT: *Pie tin, measuring spoons, cutting board, French knife, measuring cup, electric mixer with dough hook, stainless-steel bowl, 100% cotton kitchen towel, film wrap, pasta machine, aluminum foil, two baking sheets*

Preheat the oven to 325 degrees.

Place the garlic cloves on a pie tin. Season with salt and pepper and coat with ¹/₄ teaspoon olive oil. Roast in the preheated oven for 20 to 25 minutes. Remove from the oven and cool for a few moments. Peel, then press to a paste with the edge of a French knife.

In the bowl of an electric mixer fitted with a dough hook, dissolve 1 teaspoon sugar in ¹/₂ cup warm water (see page 318). Add the yeast and stir gently to dissolve. Allow the mixture to stand until it begins to foam, 2 to 3 minutes. Add 2 cups plus 6 tablespoons flour, 1 teaspoon salt, and the roasted garlic paste. Mix on low speed for 30 seconds, then scrape down the sides of the bowl. Mix on low for 30 seconds and again scrape down the sides of the bowl. Add the remaining ¹/₂ cup warm water and mix on low until the dough forms a ball, 4 to 5 minutes.

Flour a clean, dry work surface with 2 tablespoons flour. Transfer the dough to the floured surface and knead by hand until smooth and slightly tacky, 4 to 5 minutes. Coat the inside of a stainless-steel bowl with the remaining 1¹/₂ teaspoons olive oil. Place the dough in the bowl and wipe the bowl with the dough. Turn the dough so that the oiled portion is facing up. Cover with a cotton towel. Allow the dough to rise in a warm location until the dough has doubled in volume, about 40 to 50 minutes.

Punch down the dough, cover with the cotton towel, place in a warm location, and again allow to rise until doubled in volume, about 20 minutes.

Punch down the dough and divide into 4 equal pieces. Knead each piece into an evenly rounded portion. Place on a baking sheet, cover with film wrap, and refrigerate for a half hour.

Preheat the oven to 350 degrees.

Roll and knead each portion of dough to a thickness of ¹/₈ inch through the pasta machine, using the remaining ¹/₂ cup flour as necessary to prevent the dough from becoming tacky. Cut the sheets of dough on the fettuccine cutter (see page 315) and toss the strands of dough with the cornmeal as soon as cut. Use a sharp knife to cut the strands into 6-inch lengths. Distribute the strands of dough on separate sheets of aluminum foil cut to fit a baking sheet, being careful to position the strands of dough ¹/₄ inch apart. Allow the dough strands to rise at room temperature until slightly rounded, 15 to 20 minutes.

Place a sheet of aluminum foil on each available baking sheet and bake the breadsticks, using as many sheets as oven space allows, in the preheated oven until the strands begin to turn golden brown, 13 to 16 minutes.

Remove the breadsticks from the oven and allow to cool thoroughly at room temperature before storing in an airtight container.

The Chef's Touch

For several years, Irish soda bread and fruit breads were the two components of the Trellis breadbasket. Following a long search for a third distinctive bread, a trip to Italy inspired the inclusion of this version of the classic breadstick.

BREADSTICK VARIATIONS:

Shallot: Replace the minced garlic with 2 tablespoons minced shallot.
Black Pepper: Replace the minced garlic with 1 tablespoon cracked black peppercorns.
Cheese: Replace the minced garlic with ¹/₄ cup freshly grated Parmesan cheese.

In this recipe, the dough is allowed to rise in a warm location until it has doubled in volume. Then the dough strands are allowed to rise until rounded. This procedure is called proofing, and it should be done at a room temperature of 75 to 80 degrees.

If the dough is tacky, do not hesitate to use additional flour while rolling and kneading it.

If a table-model electric mixer is not available, this recipe may also be prepared by hand (mixing time may double).

Spaghetti Squash with Tomatoes, Basil, and Parmesan Cheese

Serves 8

2 2½-pound spaghetti squash
2 cups water
2 tablespoons olive oil
2 medium tomatoes, peeled, seeded, and chopped (see page 316)

Salt and pepper to season
16 basil leaves, cut into long, thin strips
1 cup freshly grated Parmesan cheese

EQUIPMENT: *Paring knife, baking sheet with sides, measuring cup, cutting board, French knife, large metal spoon, cheese grater, large non-stick sauté pan, measuring spoons, tongs*

Preheat the oven to 350 degrees.

Puncture the skin of each squash 8 to 10 times with a paring knife, which will allow the steam to escape and prevent the squash from rupturing while baking. Place the squash on a baking sheet with 1 cup water and bake in the preheated oven for 1 hour. Add the remaining cup water to the baking sheet after the first half hour. To test the squash for doneness, penetrate the skin with a paring knife; the squash is done if the knife meets little or no resistance after penetrating the skin, but the skin should still be fairly firm. Cool the squash under cold running water for 10 minutes, and then refrigerate for 1 hour.

Cut off the ends of the spaghetti squash. Split the squash in half lengthwise. Remove the seeds with a large metal spoon. Use the spoon to scrape the squash flesh away from the skin. Break up the flesh by hand into thin, spaghetti-like strands.

Heat the olive oil in a large non-stick sauté pan over medium high heat. When hot, add the tomatoes, season with salt and pepper, and sauté for 1 minute. Add the squash and basil strips, adjust the seasoning with salt and pepper, and sauté until hot, 5 to 6 minutes.

Portion the squash and tomatoes onto 8 warm serving dishes, sprinkle with the Parmesan cheese, and serve immediately.

The Chef's Touch

Smaller spaghetti squash may be boiled, although I prefer the oven method. Boil squash in a large pot for about thirty minutes. Test for doneness as with the baked squash. In either cooking method, if the squash skin ruptures, revealing the flesh, it is a good indication that the squash is overcooked.

After removing the squash flesh and separating it into strands, the strands may be refrigerated for up to three days in a tightly sealed plastic container.

For a dish that is very low in saturated fat, omit the Parmesan cheese.

This vegetable makes an excellent base for a main course. Serve a grilled boneless and skinless chicken breast or grilled flounder over the squash and tomatoes, which have been portioned onto four warm 10-inch dinner plates. Top the fish or chicken with a flavored butter and finish with grated Parmesan.

Marinated Summer Vegetables

Serves 8

1 pound zucchini, lightly peeled and cut into ½-inch dice

¾ pound yellow squash, lightly peeled and cut into ½-inch dice

½ pound green bell peppers, seeded and cut into ¼-inch dice

½ pound red bell peppers, seeded and cut into ¼-inch dice

½ pound red onion, cut into ¼-inch dice

1 medium tomato, peeled, seeded, and chopped (see page 316)

1 cup Trellis Vinaigrette (see page 311)

1 tablespoon chopped fresh basil

1 teaspoon minced garlic

Salt and pepper to season

EQUIPMENT: *Vegetable peeler, paring knife, cutting board, French knife, two stainless-steel bowls (one large), measuring cup, measuring spoons, whisk, rubber spatula, film wrap*

Combine the zucchini, yellow squash, bell peppers, red onion, and tomato in a large stainless-steel bowl.

In another stainless-steel bowl, whisk together the vinaigrette, basil, and garlic. Pour the vinaigrette over the vegetables and mix well. Cover tightly with film wrap and refrigerate for at least 4 hours.

Adjust the seasoning with salt and pepper and serve well chilled.

The Chef's Touch

This style of recipe is meant to be tampered with, so do not hesitate to substitute vegetables; add and delete at will. We often add eggplant to this mixture, which results in a chilled, uncooked ratatouille.

This dish could be prepared and served in less than an hour and would make an excellent accompaniment to many grilled foods. I suggest, however, that the vegetables be allowed to marinate for at least four hours and preferably overnight. The acidity of the Trellis vinaigrette "cooks" the vegetables. After two days, however, it should be noted that the texture of the vegetables will begin to degenerate.

This dish also makes an excellent salad when served on a bed of crisp red leaf lettuce with a sprinkling of Parmesan.

Corn and Tomato Fritters

Yields 32 fritters

³/₄ cup Marinated Chopped
  Tomatoes (see page 199)
3 medium ears fresh corn, husks
  and silk removed
3 cups bread flour
4 teaspoons baking powder
2 teaspoons granulated sugar
2 teaspoons cornstarch
2 teaspoons salt
¹/₂ teaspoon cracked black
  peppercorns

³/₄ cup grated Monterey Jack
  cheese
¹/₄ cup grated Oregon Tillamook
  Cheddar cheese
2 scallions, root ends trimmed,
  sliced thin
³/₄ cup whole milk
³/₄ cup Budweiser beer
4 to 6 cups vegetable shortening

EQUIPMENT: *Measuring cup, French knife, cutting board, medium-gauge strainer, three stainless-steel bowls, 5-quart saucepan, tongs, paring knife, measuring spoons, electric mixer with paddle, rubber spatula, film wrap, deep fryer or heavy-gauge 4-quart saucepan, candy/deep-frying thermometer, #50 (1¹/₂ tablespoons) ice cream scoop, paper towels, baking sheet with sides*

Chop the marinated tomatoes as fine as possible by hand, to yield ¹/₂ cup. Place the chopped tomatoes in a strainer and allow to drain in the refrigerator for 1 hour.

Blanch the corn in 3 quarts boiling salted water for 1 minute. Transfer to ice water. When cool, remove from the water and drain thoroughly. Scrape the kernels from the cob using a paring knife.

Combine the flour, baking powder, sugar, cornstarch, salt, and black pepper in the bowl of an electric mixer fitted with a paddle. Add the grated cheese, scallions, chopped marinated tomatoes, and corn and mix on low for 1 minute. Add the milk and beer and mix on low for 1 minute. Scrape down the sides of the bowl, then mix for another 30 seconds. Cover the fritter batter with film wrap and let stand at room temperature for 20 to 30 minutes before using.

place in a warm location. Allow the dough to rise until it reaches the top of the loaf pan, about 1 hour.

Preheat the oven to 325 degrees.

Bake in the preheated oven for 45 to 55 minutes. Cool in the loaf pan for 15 minutes before removing. When removed, allow to cool to room temperature before slicing.

The Chef's Touch

Developed for a luncheon sandwich, this bread is best when toasted. We serve it with sliced turkey, Surry bacon, and Gruyère cheese.

Depending upon the nature of the dough and the activity of the yeast, proofing can be done in a variety of warm environments. This particular bread should be proofed in a warm (about 70 to 80 degrees), dry place, away from any cool drafts.

To test the bread for doneness, gently remove the loaf from the baking pan. Lightly tap the bottom of the loaf; a hollow sound will indicate that the bread is done.

If a table-model electric mixer is not available, this recipe may also be prepared by hand (mixing time may double).

Sautéed Butternut Squash and Salsify

Serves 8

1 teaspoon fresh lemon juice
1 pound salsify
4 tablespoons unsalted butter, softened
2 tablespoons water

1¹/₂ pounds butternut squash, peeled, seeded, and cut into strips 2¹/₂ inches long and ¹/₄ inch thick (see page 317)
Salt and pepper to season

EQUIPMENT: *Measuring cup, measuring spoons, stainless-steel bowl, French knife, cutting board, vegetable peeler, 5-quart saucepan, colander, large non-stick sauté pan, slotted spoon*

Acidulate 4 cups cold water with 1 teaspoon lemon juice. Peel the salsify with a vegetable peeler and cut into strips 2¹/₂ inches long and ¹/₄ inch wide. Place the strips in acidulated water as they are cut.

Thoroughly drain the salsify, then rinse under cold running water. Blanch the salsify in boiling salted water until tender but still firm, 3¹/₂ to 4 minutes. Transfer to ice water. When cool, drain well and shake dry.

Heat the butter and 2 tablespoons water in a large non-stick sauté pan over high heat. When hot, add the butternut squash strips, season with salt and pepper, and sauté for 2 minutes. Add the salsify, season with salt and pepper, and sauté until the vegetables are hot, 4 to 5 minutes. Portion onto individual serving dishes and serve immediately.

The Chef's Touch

Fresh salsify has an excellent taste. It is easy to prepare and has a delicate flavor that is adaptable in combination with many other foods. Why, then, is so little salsify available in the marketplace? The answer probably relates to the fact that for many years the only salsify that was prepared in restaurants and hotels came out of a can. It is said that the flavor of salsify resembles that of an oyster. Perhaps that perception came from eating the canned product, which does indeed have a metallic flavor. Fresh salsify has a distinct taste that more resembles fresh artichoke than it does a mollusk.

The salsify root that is grown in America has a pale brown skin. It is available in autumn and winter. We also purchase fresh *scorzonera,* which is called black salsify because its skin is black. This root comes to us fresh from Europe and is available during most of the year. Both vegetables are interchangeable, with very little perceptible taste difference. These root vegetables should be bathed in acidulated water before cooking to prevent discoloration.

Crispy Potatoes

Serves 8

4 *large Idaho baking potatoes*
2 *tablespoons vegetable oil*

3 *tablespoons olive oil or clarified*
   butter (see page 312)
   Salt and pepper to season

EQUIPMENT: *5-quart saucepan, paring knife, measuring spoons, two baking sheets with sides, pastry brush, mandolin or a very sharp slicer*

Boil the whole unpeeled potatoes in enough water to cover for 25 minutes.

Remove the potatoes from the water and allow to cool for 1 hour under refrigeration.

Peel the potatoes, then slice on a mandolin (see page 320) or with a slicer to about a $\frac{1}{16}$-inch thickness.

Brush the baking sheets with vegetable oil.

On each baking sheet make 4 double rows of potatoes, using 12 to 14 slices, allowing about half a potato for each portion. Each slice should slightly overlap the previous one, so as to resemble shingles. (At this point, the potatoes may be covered with film wrap and refrigerated for several hours.)

Preheat the oven to 375 degrees.

Brush the potatoes with olive oil or clarified butter. Season with salt and pepper and bake in the preheated oven until golden brown, 20 to 25 minutes. Serve immediately, hot and crispy.

The Chef's Touch

If the sliced potatoes darken during refrigeration, the potatoes were not sufficiently cooked. A slight darkening will not impair the taste or the cooked appearance of the potatoes. However, if the potatoes were significantly undercooked, they will get black and not be suitable for serving.

Crispy potatoes may be held, warm and crispy, in a 200-degree oven for thirty to forty minutes after baking.

To adjust this recipe for low-saturated-fat diets, omit the olive oil or clarified butter. Use safflower oil as the oil to brush on both the baking sheet and the potatoes.

Wild Rice

Serves 8

2¹/₂ cups chicken stock (see
  page 305)
1¹/₂ cups wild rice
  Salt and pepper to season
2 tablespoons unsalted butter,
  softened

1 medium onion, minced fine
2 stalks celery, minced fine
²/₃ cup dry white wine

EQUIPMENT: *Paring knife, cutting board, French knife, two 2¹/₂-quart saucepans, double boiler, measuring cup, measuring spoons, wooden spoon, large non-stick sauté pan*

Heat the stock to a boil in a 2¹/₂-quart saucepan.

Heat 2 inches of water in the bottom half of a double boiler (see page 322) over medium heat. Combine the boiling stock and wild rice in the top half of the double boiler. Season lightly with salt and pepper and cover tightly. Cook the rice over medium heat for 1 hour.

As soon as the rice begins to cook, heat 2 tablespoons butter in a 2¹/₂-quart saucepan over medium high heat. When hot, add the onion and celery, season with salt and pepper, and sauté for 3 minutes. Add the white wine, reduce the heat to low, and allow to simmer until almost all the liquid has evaporated, 45 to 50 minutes.

Combine the rice and vegetables, adjust the seasoning with salt and pepper, and serve immediately; or cool (see page 315) and keep refrigerated, covered, for up to 3 days.

The Chef's Touch

Every dinner guest at The Trellis is given the choice of a fresh vegetable or wild rice to accompany his or her main course selection. Consequently, we use a considerable amount of wild rice. Recently the price for pure wild rice has dropped appreciably. Nevertheless, it is still an expensive item. With the cost in mind, be certain that the rice is cooked to the point that it begins to "bloom"; that is, when the rice grains begin to split open and appear variegated rather than the solid dark brown color of uncooked wild rice. If the rice is undercooked, it will have considerably less volume than the sufficiently cooked rice.

Several variations can be made on our basic wild rice recipe. Nuts (such as almonds, pecans, and hazelnuts) are very complementary to the somewhat nutty taste of the wild rice. Add these at the last minute to the already heated rice. Depending upon the dish that the rice will accompany, consider adding raisins or currants to the rice as it is being reheated. Serve with duck or game dishes. You can also use wild rice cold as a salad. Add 2 tablespoons of an herbed mayonnaise or 1 tablespoon of Trellis Vinaigrette (see page 311) to each cup of chilled, cooked wild rice.

To reheat wild rice, heat ¼ cup chicken stock or water in a large non-stick sauté pan over medium high heat. When the water begins to simmer, add the rice and heat until hot, 4 to 5 minutes. Adjust the seasoning with salt and pepper if necessary and serve immediately.

AUTUMN

Pumpkin Bread

1½ cups water
2 tablespoons tightly packed light brown sugar
1 pound peeled pumpkin meat, cut into ½-inch pieces
1 teaspoon salt
¾ cup pecan halves
1 teaspoon vegetable shortening
3 cups plus 1 tablespoon all-purpose flour

1½ teaspoons cinnamon
1 teaspoon baking powder
1 teaspoon baking soda
½ teaspoon nutmeg
1¼ cups granulated sugar
3 eggs
½ cup vegetable oil
¾ cup raisins

EQUIPMENT: *French knife, cutting board, paring knife, 2½-quart sauce-pan, measuring cup, measuring spoons, wooden spoon, baking sheet, two stainless-steel bowls (one large), food processor, rubber spatula, film wrap, 9 × 5 × 3-inch loaf pan, sifter, wax paper, electric mixer with paddle*

Preheat the oven to 325 degrees.

Heat ½ cup water with the brown sugar in a 2½-quart saucepan over medium high heat. When hot, add the pumpkin and salt. Heat for 5 minutes, then reduce the heat to medium and allow to cook for 25 minutes, stirring occasionally. Transfer the mixture to a stainless-steel bowl and cool in an ice-water bath (see page 315) for about 15 minutes.

While the pumpkin mixture is cooling, toast the pecans on a baking sheet in the preheated oven for 10 to 12 minutes. Hold at room temperature until needed. Do not turn off the oven.

In a food processor fitted with a metal blade, purée the cooled pumpkin mixture until smooth, about 1 minute, to yield 1¼ cups. Transfer to a stainless-steel bowl and cover with film wrap.

Lightly coat a loaf pan with vegetable shortening. Dust the pan with 1 tablespoon flour and shake out the excess.

Sift together the remaining 3 cups flour, and the cinnamon, baking powder, baking soda, and nutmeg over a piece of wax paper.

In the bowl of an electric mixer fitted with a paddle, combine the granulated sugar and eggs. Beat on medium for 2 minutes, then scrape down the sides of the bowl. Add the vegetable oil and mix on low to combine, about 10 seconds. Add the pumpkin mixture and mix on low to combine, about 10 seconds. Add a third of the flour mixture and mix on low for 5 seconds. Continuing to mix on low, add ½ cup water, then another third of the flour, and mix for 5 seconds. Add the remaining ½ cup water and the remaining flour and mix for 5 seconds. Add the pecan halves and raisins and mix on low for 30 seconds. Remove the bowl from the mixer and mix thoroughly with a rubber spatula.

Pour the batter into the prepared pan, spreading evenly. Place the loaf pan in the preheated oven and bake until a toothpick inserted in the center of the bread comes out clean, 75 to 80 minutes. Allow the bread to cool in the pan for 15 minutes. Remove from the pan and allow to cool to room temperature before slicing.

The Chef's Touch

Although many of our fruit breads are served year-round, this particular bread is only offered in October and November, during the harvest season.

This bread may be prepared using canned pumpkin. The recipe requires 1¼ cups of pumpkin purée. It is important to use solid pack pumpkin, rather than the "pumpkin pie filling" which is available in similar packaging but has more ingredients (spices, etc.) than simply pumpkin.

Rather than combining raisins and nuts in this bread, one or the other may be used singly; use a total of 1½ cups. Other nuts, such as cashews or peanuts, may be used as well.

If a table-model electric mixer is not available, this recipe may be prepared using a hand-held mixer (mixing time may increase slightly).

Apricot Almond Bread

Yields 1 loaf (16 half-inch slices)

9 medium apricots, unpeeled,
   pitted, and each cut into 8 slices
1½ cups granulated sugar
¾ cup water
½ cup sliced almonds
1 teaspoon vegetable shortening
3 cups plus 1 tablespoon all-
   purpose flour

12 tablespoons unsalted butter
3 eggs
1 teaspoon cinnamon
1 teaspoon almond extract
2 teaspoons baking powder
1 teaspoon baking soda
½ teaspoon salt
½ cup sour cream

EQUIPMENT: *Paring knife, cutting board, French knife, measuring cup, 2½-quart saucepan, medium-gauge strainer, two stainless-steel bowls (one large), baking sheet, 9 × 5 × 3-inch loaf pan, measuring spoons, electric mixer with paddle, rubber spatula*

Heat two-thirds of the sliced apricots with ½ cup sugar and ¾ cup water in a 2½-quart saucepan over medium high heat. Bring to a boil, then adjust the heat and simmer for 5 minutes. Remove from the heat and drain through the strainer, discarding the liquid. Transfer to a stainless-steel bowl, then cool in an ice water bath (see page 315). When the blanched apricots are cool, stir in the remaining apricots.

Preheat the oven to 325 degrees.

Toast the almonds on a baking sheet in the preheated oven until golden brown, 10 to 12 minutes. Remove from the oven and keep at room temperature until needed. Do not turn off the oven.

Lightly coat the loaf pan with the vegetable shortening. Flour the pan with 1 tablespoon flour and shake out the excess.

Combine the remaining 1 cup sugar and the butter in the bowl of an electric mixer fitted with a paddle. Beat the mixture on medium for 4 minutes, then scrape down the sides of the bowl. Beat on high for 3 minutes, then again scrape down the bowl. Beat on high until thoroughly creamed, about 3 minutes. Scrape down the bowl a final time.

Operating the mixer on high speed, add the eggs, one at a time, beating for 20 seconds and scraping down the bowl after adding each egg.

Add the toasted almonds, apricot mixture, cinnamon, and almond extract, and mix on high for 30 seconds. Add the baking powder (see page 319), baking soda (breaking up any lumps), and salt and mix for 15 to 20 seconds.

Add the remaining 3 cups flour and mix on low speed for 20 seconds. Add the sour cream and mix on low for 20 more seconds. Remove the bowl from the mixer. Use a rubber spatula to finish mixing the batter until it is smooth and thoroughly combined.

Pour the batter into the prepared pan, spreading evenly. Place in the preheated oven and bake until a toothpick inserted in the center of the bread comes out clean, 60 to 70 minutes. Allow the bread to cool in the pan for 15 minutes. Remove from the pan and allow to cool to room temperature before slicing.

The Chef's Touch

Nine medium apricots should yield 3 cups sliced apricots.

To prepare this bread using canned apricots, replace the apricot preparation with a 1-pound can of unpeeled apricot halves. Be sure to drain the apricots well, but there is no need to chop them.

If a table-model electric mixer is not available, this recipe may also be prepared using a hand-held mixer (mixing time may increase slightly).

Country Wheat Bread

Yields 2 round loaves

1 tablespoon granulated sugar	$1/2$ cup whole wheat flour
$1/2$ cup warm water	2 teaspoons salt
2 tablespoons active dry yeast	$1/2$ teaspoon minced fresh garlic
$2^{1}/4$ cups plus 1 tablespoon all-purpose flour	4 tablespoons unsalted butter, melted
$1/2$ cup coarse cracked wheat	$1/4$ cup sour cream

EQUIPMENT: *Paring knife, cutting board, French knife, sauté pan, measuring cup, measuring spoons, stainless-steel bowl, whisk, electric mixer with paddle, 100% cotton kitchen towel, baking sheet, parchment paper*

In the bowl of an electric mixer, dissolve the sugar in $1/2$ cup warm water (see page 318). Add the yeast and stir gently to dissolve. Allow the mixture to stand until it begins to foam, 2 to 3 minutes.

Place the mixing bowl on a mixer fitted with a paddle. Add $2^{1}/4$ cups all-purpose flour, the cracked wheat, whole wheat flour, salt, and minced garlic; mix on low for 30 seconds. Add the melted butter and sour cream; mix on low for 1 minute. Scrape down the sides of the bowl and mix on low for 1 additional minute.

Flour a clean, dry work surface with $1/2$ tablespoon flour. Knead the dough on the floured work surface for 3 to 4 minutes. Transfer to a stainless-steel bowl and cover with a damp towel. Place in a warm location and allow the dough to rise until it has doubled in volume, 20 to 25 minutes.

Preheat the oven to 350 degrees.

Flour a clean, dry work surface with the remaining $1/2$ tablespoon flour. Punch down the dough to its original size and divide the dough into 2 equal portions. Knead each portion into a round loaf, about 4 inches across and 2 inches tall. Transfer to a baking sheet lined with parchment paper. Cover with a damp towel. Allow the loaves to rise in a warm location until doubled in size, 20 to 25 minutes.

Remove the towel and bake the loaves in the preheated oven for 25 to 35 minutes. Allow to cool to room temperature before slicing.

The Chef's Touch

This bread was developed specifically for a luncheon sandwich of charred raw tenderloin of beef served with roasted peppers and whole-grain mustard.

Coarse cracked wheat is milled from unpolished whole wheat berries. Many supermarkets sell cracked wheat in bulk or in 1-pound boxes in the health-food section rather than where flour is displayed. The addition of cracked wheat to this bread gives it a unique and attractive rough-textured appearance.

Yeast must have a warm environment to produce the carbon dioxide necessary to make bread dough rise. Depending upon the relative characteristics of the dough, this proofing can be done in a variety of environments. For this particular dough, a warm place should be about 70 to 80 degrees (just about normal room temperature) and it should be free from cold drafts (away from heating and air-conditioning vents).

The sour cream and melted butter in the dough are sufficient to keep the dough from drying out during the proofing process if it is covered with a damp cotton towel.

To test the bread for doneness, lightly tap the bottom of the loaf; a hollow sound will indicate that the bread is done.

If a table-model electric mixer is not available, this recipe may also be prepared by hand (mixing time may double).

AUTUMN

Black Pepper Brioche

Yields 1 loaf (16 half-inch slices)

4 cups all-purpose flour
2 teaspoons salt
4 teaspoons freshly cracked black
   peppercorns
2 tablespoons granulated sugar
½ cup warm water

2 tablespoons active dry yeast
4 eggs
12 tablespoons plus 1 teaspoon
   unsalted butter, softened
1 tablespoon cold water

EQUIPMENT: *Measuring cup, sifter, wax paper, measuring spoons, two stainless-steel bowls, electric mixer with dough hook, rubber spatula, 100% cotton kitchen towel, 9-inch pie tin, film wrap, 9 × 5 × 3-inch loaf pan, whisk, pastry brush*

Sift the flour onto wax paper. Remeasure 4 cups sifted flour (there will be more sifted flour than the necessary 4 cups; reserve the remainder for later use). Sift the remeasured 4 cups together with the salt. Add the cracked black peppercorns to the sifted flour and salt and set aside.

In the bowl of an electric mixer, dissolve the sugar in ½ cup warm water (see page 318). Add the yeast and stir gently to dissolve. Allow the mixture to stand until it begins to foam, 2 to 3 minutes.

Add the sifted flour mixture and 3 eggs to the dissolved sugar and yeast. Combine on the low speed of an electric mixer fitted with a dough hook for 1 minute. Scrape down the sides of the bowl, then continue to mix on low speed until the dough forms a ball, about 2 minutes. Adjust the mixer speed to medium, and begin to add 12 tablespoons butter, a tablespoon at a time, being certain each tablespoon is thoroughly incorporated before adding the next. (If the dough attaches itself to the dough hook, stop the mixer and pull the dough off the hook.) Continue to add the butter until all 12 tablespoons have been incorporated into the dough, 12 to 14 minutes.

Transfer the dough to a stainless-steel bowl, cover with a towel, place in a warm location, and allow to rise until the dough has doubled in volume, about 1 hour. Punch down the dough to its original size, transfer to a pie tin, cover with film wrap, and place in the freezer for 15 minutes.

Preheat the oven to 325 degrees.

Flour a clean, dry surface with 1 tablespoon of the reserved sifted flour. Divide the dough into 3 equal pieces. Using your hands, roll each piece into long, ropelike strands about 14 to 15 inches long and 1½ inches thick. Braid the 3 pieces of dough together. Coat the loaf pan with the remaining teaspoon butter. Place the braided dough into the loaf pan. Place in a warm location and allow the dough to rise until it has doubled in volume, about 30 minutes. Whisk the remaining egg with 1 tablespoon cold water, then gently and lightly brush the top of the dough with this egg wash.

Bake for 30 minutes in the preheated oven. Allow the baked loaf to cool in the pan for 15 minutes before removing. Remove the bread from the loaf pan and allow to cool to room temperature before slicing.

The Chef's Touch

BRIOCHE VARIATIONS:

Plain: Omit black pepper.

Raisin: Add ¾ cup raisins in place of the black pepper.

Unbraided: Cool the dough in the refrigerator for 10 to 15 minutes rather than placing it in the freezer. Remove from the refrigerator, knead until smooth, place in a buttered loaf pan, press the dough into the corners of the pan, and allow to rise; then proceed as described for the braided loaf.

Individual: Change the ingredients to 13 tablespoons unsalted butter. Use 1 tablespoon butter to coat 8 individual oven-proof 8- to 10-ounce ceramic crocks instead of using a loaf pan. Divide the chilled dough into 8 equal portions. Pinch off ¼ ounce (about ½ tablespoon) dough from each portion. Knead each larger portion into a smooth, rounded ball. Make a ½-inch-deep impression in each dough ball, then place each dough ball in a crock, with the impression facing up. Shape each ¼-ounce dough portion into the configuration of a pear. Dip the smaller end of the pear shape into cold water, then place that end into the impression. Allow the dough to rise in a warm location (70 to 80 degrees) until the dough fills up the crock, about 50 minutes. Brush with egg wash and bake in a preheated 325-degree oven for 20 minutes.

To proof brioche dough inside an oven, the oven should not be heated. Place a roasting pan of hot tap water on the floor of the oven, then set the dough on the middle rack and close the oven door. The dough should proof in the required time.

To test the bread for doneness, gently remove the loaf from the baking pan. Lightly tap the bottom of the loaf; a hollow sound will indicate that the bread is done.

Sautéed Rapini with Oven-roasted Cherry Tomatoes and Pine Nuts

Serves 8

1 pint cherry tomatoes
Salt and pepper to season
$1/2$ cup pine nuts
2 pounds rapini (broccoli rabe)
2 tablespoons olive oil

EQUIPMENT: *Paring knife, cutting board, two baking sheets with sides, parchment paper, measuring cup, French knife, stainless-steel bowl, measuring spoons, large non-stick sauté pan, slotted spoon*

Preheat the oven to 200 degrees.

Cut the cherry tomatoes in half. Generously season with salt and place, cut side up, on a baking sheet covered with parchment paper. Roast the tomatoes in the preheated oven for 3 hours. Remove from the oven and allow to cool to room temperature, then cut each roasted tomato in half (cooled oven-roasted tomatoes may be placed in a covered container and kept in the refrigerator for several days). Raise the oven temperature to 300 degrees.

Toast the pine nuts on a baking sheet in the 300-degree oven for 15 minutes. Remove from the oven and keep at room temperature until needed.

Separate the rapini into individual stalks. Remove all leaves and flowery tops and discard. Slice the rapini stalks on an angle into $1/8$-inch-thick slices.

Heat the olive oil in a large non-stick sauté pan over medium high heat. When hot, add the rapini, season with salt and pepper, and sauté until hot, 4 to 5 minutes. When hot, add the oven-roasted cherry tomatoes and sauté just to combine. Adjust the seasoning with salt and pepper. Portion the rapini mixture into individual serving dishes and sprinkle the pine nuts over the top of each portion. Serve immediately.

The Chef's Touch

My first taste of rapini was at the Ristorante Il Sorso Preferito while on a sojourn in the south of Italy. Located in the seaport town of Bari, on the Adriatic coast, this crowded and noisy restaurant was the scene of a hectic but very satisfying dinner for a group of food lovers accompanying Giuliano Bugialli. All the food served that evening was very authentic and possessed a gusto seldom savored in Italian restaurants in America. The one item that particularly stands out in memory was a serving of tiny little ear-shaped pasta called *orecchiette*. The pasta had been combined with a sauté of rapini, sun-dried tomatoes, anchovies, and lots of garlic. Delicious Italian soul food!

Rapini has many names—almost all of them difficult to pronounce. Elizabeth Schneider's encyclopedic book *Uncommon Fruits and Vegetables* lists seven different appellations for this uncommonly delicious vegetable. When requesting rapini from produce vendors it may be helpful to know that it is also recognized by many as broccoli rabe. Rapini has an assertive flavor that is best described as slightly bitter and very interesting.

If rapini is not available, use cooked broccoli stems.

Sun-dried tomatoes packed in olive oil are an adequate substitute for oven-roasted tomatoes. They should be well drained on paper towels and cut into thin strips before use. Add the sun-dried tomatoes to the sauté pan at the same time as the rapini.

Crispy Potato Cakes

Yields 6 five-ounce cakes or 8 four-ounce cakes

3 pounds Idaho baking potatoes
   Salt and pepper to season
1 egg, lightly beaten

1 cup clarified butter (see
   page 312)

EQUIPMENT: *5-quart saucepan, tongs or slotted spoon, two stainless-steel bowls, paring knife, mandolin, whisk, two baking sheets with sides, one large non-stick sauté pan, metal spatula*

Cook the unpeeled potatoes in boiling salted water for 35 minutes. Drain the potatoes and transfer to a stainless-steel bowl. Cool under slowly running water for 10 minutes. When the potatoes are cool, drain and refrigerate for 25 to 30 minutes.

Peel the cooled potatoes and cut into strips 1/8 inch by 3/8 inch using a mandolin (see page 320) or a French knife. Place the strips in a stainless-steel bowl and season with salt and pepper. Add the beaten egg to the potatoes and gently combine by hand. Divide into the desired number of portions. Form the portions into 3/4-inch-high cakes. Transfer the cakes to a baking sheet.

Preheat the oven to 350 degrees.

Heat 1/2 cup clarified butter in a large non-stick sauté pan over medium high heat. When hot, fry 3 or 4 potato cakes until evenly golden brown, 3 1/2 to 4 minutes on each side. Transfer to a baking sheet and hold at room temperature. Discard any remaining butter from the pan, wipe the pan dry, and repeat the cooking procedure with the remaining 3 or 4 cakes. When all the cakes have been fried, place the baking sheet in the preheated oven for 10 minutes. Serve hot and crispy.

The Chef's Touch

These cakes are terrific as a side dish (served with almost any meat or poultry item), appetizer (see Crispy Potato Cakes with Irish Smoked Salmon, Leeks, and Cream, page 25), or as the centerpiece for a main course (see Whole Stuffed Quail with Crispy Potato Cakes and Wild Mushroom Sauce, page 156). Serve them hot and crispy on the outside and warm and moist on the inside!

After 35 minutes of boiling, the potatoes will be properly cooked. They should still be slightly firm; otherwise, they will not cut well and will lose the textural quality needed to form attractive potato cakes.

Uncooked potato cakes may be kept refrigerated, covered, for up to twenty-four hours before cooking.

Black-eyed Pea Cakes

Serves 8

1 pound dried black-eyed peas,
  washed and picked over
1 tablespoon salt
1 tablespoon unsalted butter,
  softened
1/2 cup minced onion
  Salt and pepper to season
1 teaspoon minced garlic
1/2 cup plus 2 tablespoons all-
  purpose flour

1 egg yolk
1 teaspoon chopped fresh parsley
1 teaspoon chopped fresh spinach
1 teaspoon chopped fresh thyme
  (or a pinch of dried)
1/2 cup clarified butter (see
  page 312)

EQUIPMENT: *Colander, 5-quart saucepan, measuring cup, measuring spoons, two non-stick sauté pans (one large), wooden spoon, food processor, rubber spatula, stainless-steel bowl, two baking sheets, parchment paper, film wrap, metal spatula*

Place the washed peas in a 5-quart saucepan and cover with 4 cups cold water; allow to soak at room temperature for 2 hours. Drain the liquid and rinse the peas. Return the peas to the saucepan and cover with 6 cups fresh cold water. Add 1 tablespoon salt. Place the saucepan over medium high heat and cook until tender, about 25 minutes. Drain, then cool under running water.

Heat 1 tablespoon unsalted butter in a non-stick sauté pan over medium heat. When hot, add the onion, season with salt and pepper, and sauté for 1 minute. Add the garlic and 2 tablespoons flour and cook, stirring, for 4 to 5 minutes, being careful not to scorch the flour. Remove from the heat.

Put 3 cups of the cooled black-eyed peas in a food processor fitted with a metal blade. Add the onion and flour mixture and purée for 1 1/2 to 2 minutes. Add the egg yolk and pulse to combine.

Place the remaining 3 cups black-eyed peas in a stainless-steel bowl and crush by hand. Add the puréed peas and fresh herbs. Season with salt and pepper and mix well.

Form the black-eyed pea mixture into 8 cakes of equal dimensions. Each cake will require slightly more than $1/2$ cup of the mixture and should weigh about $4^{1}/_2$ ounces. The cakes should be $1/2$ inch tall and 4 inches in diameter. Place the cakes on a baking sheet lined with parchment paper as they are formed. Cover the sheet with film wrap and refrigerate at least 1 hour.

Preheat the oven to 350 degrees.

Heat $1/4$ cup clarified butter in a large non-stick sauté pan over medium high heat. Coat the pea cakes lightly with the remaining $1/2$ cup flour, patting the cakes gently to remove the excess. When the butter is hot, season with salt and pepper and then fry 4 cakes until browned, about 2 minutes per side. Once the cakes are fried, transfer to a baking sheet. After the first 4 cakes have been removed from the pan, pour out the butter, wipe the pan dry, and heat the remaining $1/4$ cup butter until hot. Repeat the cooking procedure with the remaining 4 pea cakes. When all of the cakes have been fried, place the baking sheet in the preheated oven until all of the cakes are hot, 4 to 5 minutes. Serve very hot.

The Chef's Touch

What food has a closer tie to the South than black-eyed peas? When I tell someone that I am a chef from Virginia, I am immediately asked if I prepare grits and black-eyed peas.

This particular recipe was developed after reading a passage describing field peas (as they were more likely to be called in the eighteenth century) in Mary Randolph's *The Virginia House-wife*.

The cakes can be made a day or two in advance, but *must* sit for at least one hour after being formed and before being fried; otherwise, they have a tendency to fall apart while cooking.

There are many condiments with which these cakes could be served. On the more casual side, try Marinated Chopped Tomatoes (see page 199). For a more expensive treatment, serve the cakes with Wild Mushroom Sauce (see page 156) and a sprinkling of country ham or crisp roasted slab bacon.

Serve these cakes as a side dish. They are particularly good with grilled wild fowl.

Cranberry Bread

Yields 1 loaf (16 half-inch slices)

½ pound whole cranberries
1 teaspoon vegetable shortening
3 cups plus 1 tablespoon all-purpose flour
1¼ cups granulated sugar

2 teaspoons baking soda
2 teaspoons baking powder
3 eggs
3 tablespoons vegetable oil
1 cup fresh orange juice

EQUIPMENT: *Measuring cup, food processor, measuring spoons, 9 × 5 × 3-inch loaf pan, electric mixer with paddle, two stainless-steel bowls, whisk, rubber spatula*

Chop the cranberries in a food processor fitted with a metal blade, then pulse for 10 to 15 seconds. Keep the cranberries at room temperature until needed.

Lightly coat a loaf pan with 1 teaspoon vegetable shortening. Dust the pan with 1 tablespoon flour and shake out the excess.

Combine the remaining 3 cups flour and the sugar, baking soda (breaking up any lumps), and baking powder (see page 319) in the bowl of an electric mixer fitted with a paddle.

Preheat the oven to 325 degrees.

Whisk the eggs in a stainless-steel bowl until foamy. Add the vegetable oil and the orange juice and combine thoroughly.

With the mixer on low, slowly pour in the egg mixture. Mix on low until the flour has been thoroughly moistened, about 20 seconds. Remove the bowl from the mixer. Use a rubber spatula to finish mixing the batter until it is smooth and thoroughly combined. Then fold in the chopped cranberries.

Pour the batter into the prepared pan, spreading it evenly. Place the loaf pan in the preheated oven and bake until a toothpick inserted in the center of the bread comes out clean, 65 to 75 minutes. Allow the bread to cool in the pan for 15 minutes. Remove from the pan and allow to cool to room temperature before slicing.

The Chef's Touch

Don't let the dessert-like texture and appearance of this bread fool you; it has a great deal of compatibility with many entrées. At The Trellis during the winter season, it particularly complements such dishes as roast pork, turkey, and grilled chicken.

Frozen cranberries may be used in the preparation of this bread; use the same quantity.

It is important when chopping cranberries (whether in a food processor or with a knife) that each cranberry be cut in two. The mouth-wrenching sensation of an uncut berry is quite unpleasant.

The best way to serve this bread is in half slices, as we do at The Trellis. Cut the whole loaf in half lengthwise, then cut ½-inch-thick slices.

This bread may be frozen after slicing and kept for two to three weeks in the freezer. Remove only as many slices as needed and toast in the oven or in a toaster.

If a table-model electric mixer is not available, this recipe may also be prepared using a hand-held model (mixing time may increase slightly), or the mixing can be done by hand, using a wire whisk (mixing time may double).

Toasted Walnut Bread

Yields 1 loaf (16 half-inch slices)

1 cup walnut pieces	4 cups all-purpose flour
1¼ cups milk	1 cup whole wheat flour
2 tablespoons granulated sugar	1 egg
1 tablespoon salt	1 tablespoon water
2 tablespoons active dry yeast	
5 tablespoons unsalted butter, softened	

EQUIPMENT: *Baking sheet, 2½-quart saucepan, measuring cup, measuring spoons, whisk, electric mixer with dough hook, instant-read test thermometer, non-stick sauté pan, stainless-steel bowl, rubber spatula, 100% cotton kitchen towel, 9 × 5 × 3-inch loaf pan, pastry brush, cake spatula*

Preheat the oven to 300 degrees.

Toast the walnut pieces on a baking sheet in the preheated oven for 15 minutes. Remove from the oven and allow to cool to room temperature. Lightly crush with the bottom of a sauté pan. Keep at room temperature until needed.

Heat the milk in a 2½-quart saucepan over medium high heat. When hot, add the sugar and salt and whisk to dissolve. Bring to a boil, then transfer to the bowl of an electric mixer. Cool the milk to 110 degrees, which should take about 6 minutes (do this at room temperature; occasionally whisk to help the milk cool in the suggested time). When the milk reaches the proper temperature, add the yeast and stir gently to dissolve. Allow the mixture to stand until it begins to foam (see page 318), 2 to 3 minutes.

Coat a loaf pan with ½ tablespoon butter. Coat a stainless-steel bowl with ½ tablespoon butter. Melt the remaining 4 tablespoons butter in a non-stick sauté pan over medium heat.

Place the mixing bowl on a mixer fitted with a dough hook. On top of the milk and yeast, add the all-purpose flour, whole wheat flour, crushed walnuts, and melted butter. Combine on medium speed for 2 minutes. Scrape down the sides of the bowl, then continue to mix on medium speed until the dough begins to form a ball, about 30 seconds. Transfer the dough to a lightly floured work surface.

Knead the dough by hand for 5 minutes. Place in the buttered bowl, wiping the bowl with the dough. Turn the dough over so that the buttered portion is facing up. Cover the bowl with a towel. Allow the dough to rise in a warm location until doubled in volume, about 1 hour.

When the dough has doubled, punch it down to its original size. Form into a loaf and place in the buttered loaf pan. Cover with a towel and place in a warm location. Allow the dough to rise until it reaches the top of the loaf pan, about a half hour.

Preheat the oven to 350 degrees.

Whisk the egg with 1 tablespoon water. Lightly brush the top of the dough with this egg wash. Bake the loaf in the preheated oven for 35 to 45 minutes. Allow the bread to cool in the loaf pan for 15 minutes before removing. Remove the bread from the loaf pan and allow to cool to room temperature before slicing.

The Chef's Touch

This bread, which we suggest as an accompaniment to chilled Shiitake Mushroom Pâté (see page 18), has also been served at The Trellis with such items as a smoked salmon, goat cheese, and pickled red onion sandwich and a roulade of rabbit and country ham appetizer.

This particular bread should be proofed (see page 205) in a warm (about 70 to 80 degrees), dry place, away from any cool drafts.

To test the bread for doneness, gently remove the loaf from the baking pan. Lightly tap the bottom of the loaf; a hollow sound will indicate that the bread is done.

If a table-model electric mixer is not available, this recipe may also be prepared by hand (mixing time may double).

SUMMER

Curly Endive, Spinach, Fresh Corn, and Roasted Peppers with Smoked Bacon Dressing (PAGE 63)

SUMMER

Chilled Lump Backfin Crabmeat on Sun-dried Tomato Fettucine and Chive Fettucine (PAGE 12)

SUMMER

Yellow Squash, Green Beans, and Scallions with Herb Vinaigrette (PAGE 65)

SUMMER

LOWER FRONT *Grilled Tuna and Grilled Potatoes with Tomatoes, Green Beans, and Onion Dressing* (PAGE 116) UPPER REAR *Grouper, Shrimp, and Scallops with Snow Peas, Tomatoes, and Tarragon Butter* (PAGE 114)

SUMMER

FRONT *Grilled Pork Tenderloin with Corn and Smoked Chili Salsa on "Hot" Pepper Fettucine* (PAGE 125)
CENTER RIGHT *Sautéed Rabbit with Cabbage, Apples, Pearl Onions, and Plums* (PAGE 128)
REAR *Loin Lamb Chops with Peppers, Onions, Tomatoes, Mushrooms, and Mint* (PAGE 123)

SUMMER

FRONT *Balloon of Summer Melon, Berries, and Grapes with Port Wine Ice* (PAGE 262)
LOWER RIGHT *Espresso–Pecan Fudge Ice Cream Terrine* (PAGE 268)
REAR *Chocolate–Mint Chocolate Chip Ice Cream Cake* (PAGE 264)

AUTUMN

Death by Chocolate (PAGE 281)

AUTUMN

Whole Stuffed Quail with Crispy Potato Cakes and
Wild Mushroom Sauce (PAGE 156)
Sautéed Butternut Squash and Salsify (PAGE 216)

WINTER

Braised Tenderloin of Beef with Mushrooms, Raisins, Figs, and Red Wine (PAGE 188)

AUTUMN

FRONT *Grilled Medallions of Pork with Sweet Potatoes, Cranberries, and Pine Nuts* (PAGE 151)
REAR *Pan Roast of Oysters with Wild Mushrooms, Spinach, Leeks, and Cream* (PAGE 134)

WINTER

LOWER FRONT *Grilled Medallions of Veal with Apples, Mushrooms, and Cream on Buckwheat Fettucine* (PAGE 182)
UPPER RIGHT *Fresh Herb Tagliatelle with Oranges, Red Onions, and Black Pepper Butter* (PAGE 21)

THE TRELLIS STAFF

FRONT *Andrew O'Connell, Marcel Desaulniers*
BACK LEFT TO RIGHT *Jeff Duncan, Jonathan Zearfoss, John Twichell, Giselle Hicks,*
Philip Delaplane, Clementine Darden, Michael Gyetvan

Chili Corn Bread

Yields 1 loaf (16 half-inch slices)

1 tablespoon granulated sugar
½ cup warm water
2 tablespoons active dry yeast
3 cups plus 2 tablespoons all-purpose flour
½ cup corn flour (masa harina)
½ cup yellow cornmeal
1 tablespoon salt
4 eggs
4 tablespoons plus 1 teaspoon unsalted butter, softened
1 tablespoon vegetable oil
1 teaspoon minced fresh garlic

½ cup minced onion
Salt and pepper to season
1 small jalapeño pepper, roasted (see page 314), seeded, and minced
1 medium red bell pepper, roasted (see page 315), seeded, and minced
1 medium green bell pepper, roasted, seeded, and minced
½ cup cooked corn
1 tablespoon water

EQUIPMENT: *Electric mixer with dough hook, two stainless-steel bowls, measuring cup, measuring spoons, 100% cotton kitchen towel, paring knife, cutting board, French knife, non-stick sauté pan, rubber spatula, 9 × 5 × 3-inch loaf pan, whisk, pastry brush*

In the bowl of an electric mixer, dissolve the sugar in the warm water (see page 318). Add the yeast and stir gently to dissolve. Allow the mixture to stand until it begins to foam, 2 to 3 minutes.

Place the mixing bowl on an electric mixer fitted with a dough hook. On top of the water and yeast mixture, add 3 cups all-purpose flour, the corn flour, cornmeal, and 1 tablespoon salt. Place 3 eggs on top of the dry ingredients. Combine the ingredients on low until the dough begins to form a ball, about 1½ minutes. Continue to mix on low. Add 4 tablespoons butter, 1 tablespoon at a time, at 10-second intervals. Knead on low speed until the butter is completely incorporated and the dough is smooth, about 4 minutes. Transfer the dough to a stainless-steel bowl and cover with a towel. Allow the dough to rise in a warm place until it has doubled in volume, about 2 hours.

While the dough is rising, heat 1 tablespoon vegetable oil in a non-stick sauté pan over medium high heat. When hot, add the garlic and sauté for 5 seconds. Add the onion, season with salt and pepper, and sauté for 1½ to 2 minutes. Add the minced jalapeño, sauté for 10 seconds, then add the minced bell peppers, season with salt and pepper, and sauté for 2 minutes. Add the corn and sauté to combine. Transfer the mixture to a stainless-steel bowl and refrigerate until cold.

Coat a loaf pan with the remaining teaspoon butter. When the dough has doubled in volume, punch it down to its original size. Place the dough on a clean, dry surface that has been floured with the remaining 2 tablespoons flour. Use your hands to form a bowl-like indentation in the center of the dough. Place the chilled sautéed vegetables in the indentation. Fold the dough over to cover the vegetables. Knead until the vegetables have been completely incorporated into the dough, 2½ to 3 minutes. Form the dough into a loaf and place in the prepared loaf pan. Cover with the towel and allow the dough to rise until it reaches the top of the loaf pan, about 1 hour.

Preheat the oven to 350 degrees.

Whisk the remaining egg with 1 tablespoon water. Lightly brush the top of the dough with this egg wash. Bake the loaf in the preheated oven for 40 to 45 minutes. Allow to cool in the loaf pan for 15 minutes. Remove the bread from the loaf pan and allow to cool to room temperature before slicing.

The Chef's Touch

Our interest in the cuisine of the Southwest inspired the creation of this bread. Several of the recipes which this bread has accompanied are in this book. Other favorites that we have featured on our menu include pan-fried oysters with country ham on toasted chili corn bread and a luncheon sandwich of roast turkey and Oregon Tillamook Cheddar with spicy mayonnaise.

Corn flour, also known as masa harina, is readily available in most major supermarkets, usually in the same location as other flours. If corn flour is not available, replace the ½ cup corn flour with an additional ¼ cup all-purpose flour.

For this recipe, blanch 1 medium ear of corn for 1 minute in 3 quarts boiling salted water. Drain the corn, then cool under cold running water. When the corn is cool enough to handle, cut away the kernels. Frozen or canned corn may also be used. Thaw and drain frozen corn thoroughly before sautéing. Rinse canned corn under cold running water until the water runs clear, then drain thoroughly before sautéing.

Add a dash or two of Tabasco sauce to the sautéed vegetables for increased "heat."

For this particular dough, proofing (see page 205) should be done at a temperature of between 70 and 80 degrees and away from cold drafts. This corn bread dough is delicate and should not be disturbed during the proofing stage, especially during the second rising.

To test the bread for doneness, gently remove the loaf from the baking pan. Lightly tap the bottom of the loaf; a hollow sound will indicate that the bread is done.

If a table-model electric mixer is not available, this recipe may also be prepared by hand, using a wire whisk (mixing time may double).

DESSERTS

Strawberry and Papaya Sorbet

Yields 1³/₄ quarts

3 cups water
2¹/₂ cups granulated sugar
1³/₄ pounds papayas, ends trimmed, peeled, halved, seeded, and cut into 1-inch chunks

1 pint strawberries, stems removed
2 tablespoons fresh lemon juice

EQUIPMENT: *2¹/₂-quart saucepan, measuring cup, whisk, paring knife, food processor, rubber spatula, two stainless-steel bowls (one large), measuring spoons, instant-read test thermometer, ice cream freezer, 2-quart plastic container with lid*

Heat the water and sugar in a 2¹/₂-quart saucepan over medium high heat. Whisk to dissolve the sugar. Bring to a boil and allow to boil until slightly thickened and reduced to 3¹/₂ cups, about 15 minutes.

While the sugar and water are reducing, in a food processor fitted with a metal blade, purée the papayas until smooth, 45 to 60 seconds. Transfer the puréed papayas to a stainless-steel bowl. Purée the strawberries in the food processor for 30 seconds. Combine with the papayas.

Pour the boiling syrup over the puréed fruit. Cool the mixture in an ice water bath (see page 315) to a temperature of 40 to 45 degrees, about 15 minutes.

When cool, add the lemon juice. Freeze in an ice cream freezer, following the manufacturer's instructions. Transfer the semifrozen sorbet to a plastic container, securely covered, then place in the freezer for several hours before serving. Serve within 3 days.

The Chef's Touch

Unfortunately, most papayas sold in this country have not been tree-ripened. The delicate tropical-floral taste of this fruit is best appreciated when eating ripened fruit, so look for slightly firm, yellow-fleshed fruit with only slight traces of green (the greener the fruit, the less likely it is to have good flavor). Papayas will develop most of their flavor potential and will continue to ripen if stored at room temperature, although this type of ripening will not yield the flavor intensity of tree-ripened fruit. Storing at temperatures under 45 degrees will inhibit any further ripening.

If very ripe papayas are used, it may be necessary to add an additional tablespoon of lemon juice to create the proper acid balance; otherwise, a cloyingly sweet sorbet may result.

Caramel–Macadamia Nut Ice Cream Cake

Serves 8 to 12

Caramel Ice Cream
1³/₄ cups heavy cream
1¹/₂ cups half-and-half
1 cup granulated sugar
¹/₂ cup egg yolks
¹/₈ teaspoon fresh lemon juice

Macadamia Nut Cake
1¹/₂ cups macadamia nuts
2 teaspoons vegetable shortening
1³/₄ cups plus 1 tablespoon all-purpose flour
2 teaspoons baking soda

¹/₂ teaspoon cinnamon
¹/₂ teaspoon salt
1 cup tightly packed light brown sugar
4 tablespoons unsalted butter
¹/₂ pound cream cheese, softened
3 eggs
1 teaspoon pure vanilla extract

Caramel Sauce
2 cups granulated sugar
¹/₂ teaspoon fresh lemon juice
1¹/₂ cups heavy cream

EQUIPMENT: *Measuring cup, two 2¹/₂-quart saucepans, whisk, electric mixer with paddle, rubber spatula, instant-read test thermometer, three stainless-steel bowls (one large), wooden spoon, measuring spoons, ice cream freezer, 2-quart plastic container with lid, food processor, 9 × 3-inch springform pan, sifter, parchment paper, 12-inch serrated slicer, metal spoon, aluminum foil, large 100% cotton kitchen towel*

Make the custard for the ice cream by heating 1¹/₂ cups heavy cream and 1¹/₂ cups half-and-half in a 2¹/₂-quart saucepan over medium high heat. When hot, add ¹/₄ cup sugar. Stir to dissolve and bring the mixture to a boil. This should take 5 to 7 minutes.

While the cream is heating, place ¹/₂ cup egg yolks and ¹/₄ cup sugar in the bowl of an electric mixer fitted with a paddle. Beat the eggs on high for 2 to 2¹/₂ minutes, then scrape down the sides of the bowl. Beat, on high, until slightly thickened and lemon colored, an additional 2¹/₂ to 3 minutes. At this point, the cream should be boiling. If not, adjust the

249

mixer speed to low and continue to mix until the cream boils. If this is not done, the egg yolks will develop undesirable lumps.

Pour the boiling cream into the beaten egg yolks and whisk to combine. Return to the saucepan and heat over medium high heat, stirring constantly, until the cream reaches a temperature of 185 degrees, 2 to 4 minutes. Remove from the heat and transfer to a stainless-steel bowl. Cool this custard in an ice water bath (see page 315) for about 15 minutes.

While the custard is cooling, prepare the caramel. Heat the remaining 1/2 cup sugar in a 2 1/2-quart saucepan over medium heat. Caramelize the sugar for 5 to 6 minutes, stirring constantly with a wooden spoon to break up any lumps (the sugar will first turn clear as it liquefies, then brown as it caramelizes). Add 1/8 teaspoon lemon juice and stir to combine. (Be careful when adding lemon juice to melted sugar: it spurts and can burn.) Remove the saucepan from the heat, carefully add the remaining 1/4 cup heavy cream, and stir to combine (the mixture will steam and boil rapidly as the cream is added). Pour the caramel into the custard and stir gently to blend; continue to cool in an ice water bath to a temperature of 40 to 45 degrees, about 10 minutes.

When cold, freeze in an ice cream freezer following the manufacturer's instructions. Transfer the semifrozen ice cream to a 2-quart plastic container. Securely cover the container, then place in the freezer for at least 4 hours.

Preheat the oven to 325 degrees.

To make the cake, toast the macadamia nuts on a baking sheet in the preheated oven for 12 to 15 minutes. Remove from the oven and cool to room temperature. Do not turn off the oven. Chop the cooled nuts in a food processor fitted with a metal blade by pulsing for 15 to 20 seconds. Keep at room temperature until needed.

While the nuts are toasting, coat a 9- by 3-inch springform pan with 2 teaspoons vegetable shortening. Flour the pan with 1 tablespoon flour and shake out the excess. Set aside until needed.

Combine together in a sifter 1 3/4 cups flour, 2 teaspoons baking soda, 1/2 teaspoon cinnamon, and 1/2 teaspoon salt. Sift onto parchment paper and set aside. Combine 1 cup brown sugar and 4 tablespoons butter in the bowl of an electric mixer fitted with a paddle. Beat on medium for 2 minutes, then scrape down the sides of the bowl. Add 1/2 pound cream cheese and beat on medium for 1 minute, then scrape down the bowl. Beat on high for 1 minute, then add the 3 eggs, one at a time, beating on high for 15 seconds and scraping down the bowl after each addition. After the eggs are added, beat on high for 2 minutes. Add 1 teaspoon vanilla extract, beat on high for 5 seconds, and scrape down the bowl.

Remove the bowl from the mixer. Use a rubber spatula to fold in the chopped nuts, then fold in the sifted flour mixture. Continue to mix until the cake batter is thoroughly combined. Pour into the prepared pan, spreading the batter evenly. Bake in the 325-degree oven until a tooth-pick inserted in the center of the cake comes out clean, about 50 minutes. Remove the cake from the oven and allow to cool in the pan for 30 minutes at room temperature. Remove the sides of the springform pan and allow the cake to cool for an additional 1½ hours at room temperature, then refrigerate the macadamia nut cake for 1 hour.

To assemble the cake, remove the bottom of the springform pan from the cake, then reassemble the pan. Slice the cake, horizontally, into three equal layers. Place the bottom layer of cake in the springform pan, portion half the ice cream on top of the cake layer, and spread the ice cream evenly over the cake. Place the center section of cake on top of the layer of ice cream. Portion the remaining ice cream over the cake and spread evenly. Place the top portion of the cake on top of the ice cream layer and gently press down on the cake. Cover the springform pan with aluminum foil and freeze the cake for at least 12 hours before serving.

After the cake has been in the freezer for 12 hours, prepare the caramel sauce. Heat 2 cups sugar in a 2½-quart saucepan over medium high heat. Caramelize the sugar for 12 to 15 minutes, constantly stirring with a wooden spoon to break up the lumps. Add ½ teaspoon lemon juice and stir to combine. Remove the saucepan from the heat, carefully add 1½ cups heavy cream, and stir to combine. Transfer to a stainless-steel bowl and hold at room temperature until needed.

To remove the cake from the springform pan, first remove the aluminum foil. Wrap a damp, hot towel around the sides of the pan (the towel should be large enough to completely wrap around and cover the sides of the pan). Hold the towel tightly around the pan for 1 minute, then release the springform and remove the cake.

To serve, cut the caramel–macadamia nut ice cream cake into the desired number of portions. Heat the blade of a serrated slicer under hot running water before slicing the cake. Repeat after making each slice. Portion 3 to 4 tablespoons caramel sauce onto each plate. Place a cake slice on each sauced plate. Allow the servings to temper at room temperature for 5 to 7 minutes before serving.

The Chef's Touch

The sweet, buttery flavor of the macadamia nut places it instantly in the dessert category without further enhancement. Restraint with such ingredients is not, however, indicative of the style of Trellis desserts!

Use several toothpicks inserted in the sides of the cake as guides to accurately slice the cake into 3 layers.

If the ice cream is hard-frozen, allow it to temper at room temperature for 10 minutes before attempting to assemble the cake.

To spread the ice cream, use a large metal spoon that has been heated in a bowl of hot water. Reheat the spoon frequently during the ice cream spreading procedure. Shake the excess water off the spoon immediately after dipping it in the hot water.

If the caramel sauce becomes too firm, or if it is prepared the day before it is to be served (and kept refrigerated after it had cooled to room temperature), bring it back to the desired consistency by placing it, in its container, in another bowl partially filled with very hot water. Allow to stand until soft, 10 to 15 minutes.

If a table-model electric mixer is not available, this recipe may also be prepared using a hand-held model (mixing time may increase slightly) or by hand, using a wire whisk (mixing time may double).

For a final touch, garnish the cake with unsweetened whipped cream and toasted whole macadamia nuts.

Chocolate Pecan Cake

Serves 8 to 12

3¹/₂ cups pecan halves

1 pound plus 1¹/₂ teaspoons
 unsalted butter

12 ounces semisweet chocolate,
 broken into ¹/₂-ounce pieces

6 ounces unsweetened chocolate,
 broken into ¹/₂-ounce pieces

¹/₂ cup plus 2 tablespoons all-
 purpose flour

10 eggs, separated into 10 yolks, 5
 whites, and 4 whites

2 cups granulated sugar

EQUIPMENT: *Measuring cup, baking sheet, sauté pan, two double boilers, film wrap, electric mixer with balloon whip and paddle, rubber spatula, two stainless-steel bowls, whisk, 9 × 3-inch springform pan, parchment paper, cake plate, instant-read meat thermometer, 12-inch serrated slicer, cake spatula, pastry bag, #2 star tip*

Preheat the oven to 325 degrees.

Toast the pecan halves on a baking sheet in the preheated oven for 10 to 12 minutes. Cool to room temperature. Reserve 8 to 12 halves (based on the anticipated number of servings). Crush the remaining nuts with the bottom of a sauté pan (the pieces should be ¹/₄ inch or smaller). Keep all the nuts at room temperature until needed.

Heat 1 inch of water in the bottom half of a double boiler over medium heat. Place ¹/₄ pound butter, 8 ounces semisweet chocolate, and 2 ounces unsweetened chocolate in the top half of the double boiler (see page 317). Tightly cover the top with film wrap and allow to heat for 10 to 12 minutes. Remove from the heat, stir until smooth, and hold at room temperature.

Coat the bottom and sides of a springform pan with 1 teaspoon butter. Line the pan with a 7- by 7-inch piece of parchment paper. Coat the parchment paper with ¹/₂ teaspoon butter. Flour the pan with 2 table-spoons flour, shaking out the excess. Set aside.

Place the 10 yolks and 1 cup sugar in the bowl of an electric mixer

257

fitted with a paddle. Beat on medium speed for 5 minutes. Scrape down the bowl and beat for 10 additional minutes.

While the yolks are beating, whisk 5 egg whites in a large stainless-steel bowl until soft peaks form, 5 to 6 minutes.

Add the melted chocolate mixture to the beaten egg yolk mixture and beat on high speed for 30 seconds. Remove the bowl from the mixer. Use a rubber spatula to fold in 2 cups crushed pecans, gently fold in a quarter of the whisked egg whites, and then fold this mixture into the remaining egg whites. Fold in ½ cup flour. Pour the mixture into the prepared springform pan, spreading evenly. Bake in the preheated oven until a toothpick inserted in the center comes out clean, about 1 hour. Remove the cake from the oven and allow to cool in the pan for 15 minutes. Release the springform and remove the cake; invert onto a cake plate. Remove the parchment paper and refrigerate the cake for 1½ hours.

While the cake is cooling, prepare the icing. Heat 1 inch of water in the bottom half of a double boiler over medium heat. Place the remaining chocolate in the top half of the double boiler. Tightly cover with film wrap and heat for 10 to 12 minutes. Remove from the heat and stir until smooth. Keep at room temperature.

Heat 1 inch of water in the bottom half of a double boiler over medium high heat. Place the remaining 4 egg whites and 1 cup sugar in the top half of the double boiler. Whisk the egg whites and sugar together to dissolve the sugar. Heat to a temperature of 120 degrees, about 5 minutes. Stir occasionally while heating. Transfer the whites to an electric mixer fitted with a balloon whip. Whisk the egg whites on high for 2 to 2½ minutes. Scrape down the bowl and whisk until stiff, an additional 5 minutes. Transfer the whisked egg whites to a stainless-steel bowl and hold at room temperature.

Place ¾ pound butter in the bowl of an electric mixer fitted with a paddle. Beat the butter on low speed for 1 minute, on medium speed for 2 minutes, and on high for 1½ to 2 minutes, until smooth. Add the melted chocolate and beat on high for 30 seconds. Scrape down the sides of the bowl and beat for an additional 30 seconds. Remove the bowl from the mixer. Fold the chocolate butter mixture into the egg whites and refrigerate the icing for 20 minutes.

Turn the cake over. Using a slicer, trim off just enough of the top of the cake to make an even surface. Slice the cake horizontally into three equal layers. Place a dab of icing in the center of a cake plate. Place the bottom layer of the cake onto the plate, gently pressing down on the cake so that the icing will hold it in place. Evenly spread 1½ cups icing over the bottom layer. Place the center layer on top of the iced bottom layer. Evenly spread 1½ cups icing over the center layer. Place the top layer (trimmed side up) on top of the iced center layer. Evenly spread 1 cup icing on the top of the cake, then evenly spread 1 cup icing over the sides of the cake. Press the crushed nuts into the icing on the sides of the cake, coating evenly. Place the cake in the freezer for 5 minutes, or in the refrigerator for 10 minutes (refrigerate the remaining icing during this time).

Fill a pastry bag fitted with a star tip with the remaining icing. Pipe a circle of 8 to 12 stars (depending on the number of reserved pecans) evenly spaced around the outside edge of the top of the cake. Press a pecan half into each star. Refrigerate the cake for 2 hours before serving.

Cut the cake with a serrated slicer, heating the blade of the slicer under hot running water before making each slice. Allow the slices of chocolate pecan cake to temper at room temperature for 10 to 15 minutes before serving.

The Chef's Touch

My son Marc has recently become a chocophile. His newfound predilection toward all things chocolate has him adding two scoops of dark chocolate ice cream to accompany this elegant but subtle cake.

Preparation of this cake may be spread out over two days. Day 1: Prepare the cake and icing and refrigerate until assembly. Day 2: Remove the icing from the refrigerator at least one hour before assembly so it may temper at room temperature (making it easier to spread). Assemble the cake and refrigerate for two hours before cutting for service.

This cake would work well made with several other nuts: walnuts, hazelnuts, or cashews.

A quarter of the egg whites *must be gently folded* into the chocolate and egg yolk mixture to lighten the batter, followed by *gently folding* this mixture into the remaining egg whites. If *gentle folding* does not occur, the air in the mixture will be dissipated and the baked volume of the cake will be diminished.

The baked cake should be about 2 inches high. After trimming the top to achieve an even surface, mark the cake with toothpicks to indicate slices of about 1/2 inch in thickness. Professional pastry chefs often use 2 flat metal bars (of the desired height) on either side of the cake as a guide for cutting to a specific thickness.

The total yield of icing should be 6 cups. If less, reduce accordingly the amount used for icing each layer, being certain to reserve the 1 cup necessary for garnishing the top of the cake with stars.

SUMMER

Banana Sorbet

Yields 1³/₄ quarts

2 cups water
1¹/₂ cups granulated sugar

3 pounds medium-size bananas,
    unpeeled
2 tablespoons fresh lemon juice

EQUIPMENT: *2¹/₂-quart saucepan, measuring cup, whisk, two stainless-steel bowls (one large), slotted spoon, instant-read test thermometer, measuring spoons, ice cream freezer, rubber spatula, 2-quart plastic container with lid*

Heat the water and sugar in a 2¹/₂-quart saucepan over medium high heat. Whisk to dissolve the sugar. Bring the mixture to a boil and allow to boil until slightly thickened and reduced to 2¹/₄ cups, about 15 minutes.

While the sugar and water are reducing to a syrup, peel the bananas. Smash them to a rough-textured consistency in a stainless-steel bowl, using a slotted spoon (the yield should be about 3 cups).

Pour the boiling syrup over the smashed bananas. Cool in an ice water bath (see page 315) to a temperature of 40 to 45 degrees, about 15 minutes.

When cold, add the lemon juice. Freeze in an ice cream freezer following the manufacturer's instructions. Transfer the semifrozen sorbet to a plastic container, securely cover the container, then place in the freezer for several hours before serving. Serve within 3 days.

The Chef's Touch

The creamy smoothness of the bananas in this sorbet creates a culinary *trompe bouche*. The recipe contains no cream or eggs, yet the palate perceives these rich ingredients.

Essentially, the flavor of the sorbet will be that of the bananas used to prepare the sorbet. For the best-tasting sorbet, purchase bananas with skins that are uniformly yellow in color. Avoid bananas whose skin has green streaks (underripe) or brown patches (overripe).

The sugar syrup must be thick enough to coat the back of a spoon before it is added to the smashed bananas. If the syrup is too thin, the sorbet will freeze too hard.

Balloon of Summer Melon, Berries, and Grapes with Port Wine Ice

Serves 8

2 cups dry red wine
1 cup port wine
2 cups water
1 cup granulated sugar
1 small orange, juiced
1 lemon, juiced
1 medium honeydew melon, peeled, seeded, and cut into ¹/₂-inch pieces
1 medium cantaloupe, peeled, seeded, and cut into ¹/₂-inch pieces

³/₄ pound red seedless grapes, stemmed and washed
1 pint strawberries, stemmed and quartered
1 pint blueberries, stemmed and washed
1 pint blackberries

EQUIPMENT: *Two 2¹/₂-quart saucepans, measuring cup, two whisks, medium-gauge strainer, two stainless-steel bowls (one large), rubber spatula, instant-read test thermometer, ice cream freezer, 2-quart plastic container with lid, serrated slicer, cutting board, French knife, paring knife, ice cream scoop*

Heat the red wine and port wine in a 2¹/₂-quart saucepan over medium high heat. Bring to a boil and allow to boil for 10 minutes, whisking occasionally.

While the wine is heating, heat the water and sugar in a separate 2¹/₂-quart saucepan over medium high heat. Bring to a boil and allow to boil until slightly thickened, about 5 minutes.

Place the orange and lemon juices in a stainless-steel bowl. Add the hot wine mixture and hot sugar syrup and whisk to combine. Cool in an ice water bath (see page 315) to a temperature of 40 to 45 degrees, about 15 minutes. When cold, freeze in an ice cream freezer, following the manufacturer's instructions.

Transfer the semifrozen port wine ice to a plastic container, securely cover the container, then place in the freezer for several hours before serving.

Combine the honeydew, cantaloupe, grapes, strawberries, and blueberries in a stainless-steel bowl. Portion the fruit mixture into 8 large (16-ounce) balloon wineglasses. Portion 1 or 2 scoops of port wine ice onto the fruit. Finish by garnishing each balloon with 4 to 6 blackberries. Serve immediately.

The Chef's Touch

Port wine ice should be served within twenty-four hours of freezing. Other delicious melons (available from midsummer through early fall) are the crenshaw and casaba, which could also be used in this recipe.

Other berries to consider would be boysenberries, loganberries, and, of course, raspberries.

Although grapes are available year-round, the peak of the production starts in July. There are many varieties available, both seedless and seeded. If you purchase seeded, split the grapes in half, then remove the seeds before serving.

Chocolate–Mint Chocolate Chip Ice Cream Cake

Serves 8 to 12

Mint Chocolate Chip Ice Cream
- 2 cups heavy cream
- ¾ cup chopped fresh mint
- 1 cup granulated sugar
- 1½ cups half-and-half
- ½ cup egg yolks
- 1 cup chocolate chips

Chocolate Cake
- 3 ounces unsweetened chocolate, broken into ½-ounce pieces
- 1 ounce semisweet chocolate, broken into ½-ounce pieces
- 2 teaspoons vegetable shortening
- 2 cups plus 1 tablespoon all-purpose flour
- 1½ teaspoons baking soda
- ½ teaspoon salt
- 1 cup (½ pound) tightly packed light brown sugar
- ¼ pound unsalted butter, cut into 8 pieces
- 2 eggs
- 2 teaspoons pure vanilla extract
- 1 cup water
- 1 cup sour cream

Chocolate Ganache
- ¾ cup heavy cream
- 2 tablespoons granulated sugar
- 2 tablespoons unsalted butter
- 6 ounces semisweet chocolate, broken into ½-ounce pieces

EQUIPMENT: *Three stainless-steel bowls (one large), film wrap, medium-gauge strainer, ladle, measuring cup, double boiler, 2½-quart saucepan, whisk, electric mixer with paddle, rubber spatula, instant-read test thermometer, ice cream freezer, 2-quart plastic container with lid, sifter, wax paper, 9 × 3-inch springform pan, measuring spoons, 12-inch serrated slicer, baking sheet with sides, metal spoon, aluminum foil, large 100% cotton kitchen towel, cake spatula*

Twelve hours in advance of preparing the ice cream, combine 1 cup heavy cream, ¾ cup chopped mint, and ¼ cup sugar in a stainless-steel bowl. Tightly cover with film wrap and refrigerate.

Strain the cream and mint mixture through a fine strainer into a 2½-

quart saucepan. Use a ladle to gently press down on the mint leaves to extract as much flavor as possible. Add the remaining cup heavy cream and 1½ cups half-and-half and heat over medium high heat. When hot, add ¼ cup sugar and stir to dissolve. Bring the mixture to a boil.

While the cream is heating, place ½ cup egg yolks and the remaining ½ cup sugar in the bowl of an electric mixer fitted with a paddle. Beat the eggs on high for 2 to 2½ minutes. Scrape down the sides of the bowl. Beat on high until slightly thickened and lemon colored, an additional 2½ to 3 minutes. (At this point, the cream should be boiling. If not, adjust the mixer speed to low and continue to mix until the cream boils. If this is not done, the egg yolks will develop undesirable lumps.)

Pour the boiling cream into the beaten egg yolks and whisk to combine. Return to the saucepan and heat over medium high heat, stirring constantly. Bring to a temperature of 185 degrees, 2 to 4 minutes. Remove from the heat and transfer to a stainless-steel bowl. Cool in an ice water bath (see page 315) to a temperature of 40 to 45 degrees, about 15 minutes.

When cold, fold in the chocolate chips and freeze in an ice cream freezer, following the manufacturer's instructions. Transfer the semi-frozen ice cream to a 2-quart plastic container. Securely cover the container, then place in the freezer for at least 4 hours.

Preheat the oven to 325 degrees.

Begin to prepare the cake. Heat 1 inch of water in the bottom half of a double boiler over medium heat. Place 3 ounces unsweetened chocolate and 1 ounce semisweet chocolate in the top half of the double boiler (see page 317). Heat for 5 to 6 minutes, remove from the heat, and stir until smooth.

Coat a 9- by 3-inch springform pan with 2 teaspoons vegetable shortening. Flour the pan with 1 tablespoon flour, shaking out the excess. Combine together in a sifter 2 cups flour, 1½ teaspoons baking soda, and ½ teaspoon salt. Sift onto wax paper and set aside.

Combine 1 cup brown sugar and ¼ pound butter in the bowl of an electric mixer fitted with a paddle. Beat on low for 2 minutes, then on high for 1½ minutes. Scrape down the sides of the bowl, then beat on high for an additional 2 minutes. Add 1 egg and beat on high for 15 seconds; scrape down the bowl. Add the remaining egg, beat on high for 15 seconds, and scrape down the bowl. Beat on high for 2 minutes. Add the melted chocolate and 2 teaspoons vanilla extract. Beat on low for 30 seconds, then scrape down the bowl.

Heat 1 cup water to a boil. Operate the mixer on low speed while adding a third of the sifted flour and ½ cup sour cream; allow to mix for 30 seconds. Add another third of the flour and the remaining ½ cup sour cream and mix for another 30 seconds. Add the remaining sifted flour and the cup of boiling water and mix for an additional 30 seconds before removing the bowl from the mixer. Use a rubber spatula to finish mixing the batter until it is smooth and thoroughly combined.

Pour the cake batter into the prepared pan, spreading the batter evenly. Bake in the preheated oven until a toothpick inserted in the center of the cake comes out clean, 1 hour. Remove the cake from the oven and cool in the pan for 30 minutes at room temperature. Remove the sides of the springform pan and allow the cake to cool for an additional 1½ hours at room temperature. Refrigerate the chocolate cake for 1 hour.

Remove the bottom of the springform pan from the cake, then reassemble the pan. Cut the cake, horizontally, into three equal slices. Place the bottom slice of the cake in the springform pan, portion half the ice cream on top of the bottom cake slice, and spread the ice cream evenly over the cake. Place the center slice of cake on top of the layer of ice cream. Portion the remaining ice cream over the cake and spread evenly. Place the top slice of the cake on top of the ice cream layer and gently press down on the cake. Cover the entire pan with aluminum foil and freeze the cake for at least 12 hours before completing the assembly.

After the cake has been in the freezer for 12 hours, prepare the chocolate ganache. Heat ¾ cup heavy cream, 2 tablespoons sugar, and 2 tablespoons butter in a 2½-quart saucepan over medium high heat; bring to a boil. Place 6 ounces semisweet chocolate in a stainless-steel bowl. Pour the boiling cream over the chocolate and allow to stand for 3 to 4 minutes. Stir until smooth. Keep at room temperature until ready to use.

To remove the cake from the springform pan, first remove the aluminum foil. Wrap a damp, hot towel around the sides of the pan (the towel should be large enough to completely wrap around and cover the sides of the pan). Hold the towel tightly around the pan for 1 minute, then release the springform and remove the cake. Place the cake on a baking sheet. Pour the ganache over the cake and use a cake spatula to spread the ganache evenly over the top and sides. Place the cake in the freezer for 15 minutes.

Cut the chocolate–mint chocolate chip ice cream cake into the desired number of servings. Heat the blade of a serrated slicer under hot running water before making each slice. Place the ice cream cake portions on chilled plates and allow them to temper at room temperature for 5 to 7 minutes before serving.

The Chef's Touch

Three cups of washed, dried, and loosely packed mint leaves will yield the necessary ¾ cup chopped mint leaves.

Use several toothpicks inserted into the sides of the cake as guides to accurately slice the cake into 3 layers.

If the ice cream is too hard to spread evenly, allow it to temper at room temperature for about 10 minutes before attempting to assemble the cake.

To spread the ice cream, use a large metal spoon that has been heated in a bowl of hot water. Reheat the spoon frequently during the ice cream spreading procedure. Shake the excess water off the spoon immediately after dipping it in the hot water.

Be certain that the cream and egg mixture is very cold before adding the chocolate chips; otherwise, the chips will melt.

If a table-model electric mixer is not available, this recipe may also be prepared using a hand-held model (mixing time may increase slightly), or by hand, using a wire whisk (mixing time may double).

Espresso–Pecan Fudge Ice Cream Terrine

Serves 8

2 cups finely ground espresso
  coffee
4 cups heavy cream
1¹/₂ cups half-and-half
1¹/₂ cups whole milk
1¹/₂ cups pecan pieces
4 tablespoons unsalted butter

1 cup tightly packed dark brown
  sugar
1³/₄ cups granulated sugar
2 cups unsweetened cocoa, sifted
¹/₄ teaspoon salt
³/₄ cup egg yolks

EQUIPMENT: *8 × 24-inch 4-ply cheesecloth, string, measuring cup, two 2¹/₂-quart saucepans (one with lid), measuring spoons, baking sheet, sifter, whisk, metal spoon, electric mixer with paddle, instant-read test thermometer, three stainless-steel bowls (one large), ice cream freezer, 9 × 5 × 3-inch loaf pan, parchment paper, rubber spatula, aluminum foil, double boiler, cake spatula, serrated slicer*

Preheat the oven to 300 degrees.

Place the ground espresso in the center of the cheesecloth, fold the sides over, and securely tie with string. Heat 2 cups heavy cream, the half-and-half, milk, and the cheesecloth-wrapped espresso in a 2¹/₂-quart saucepan over medium high heat. Bring the mixture to a boil. While the cream is heating, use a metal spoon to occasionally press down on the wrapped espresso. As soon as the mixture comes to a boil, remove from the heat, cover, and allow to stand for 1 hour.

While the espresso is steeping in the cream, toast the pecans in the preheated oven for 15 minutes. Remove from the oven and cool to room temperature. Crush the pecans into approximately ¹/₄-inch pieces with the bottom of a sauté pan. Keep at room temperature until needed.

Prepare the fudge. Heat the remaining 2 cups heavy cream and the butter in a 2¹/₂-quart saucepan over medium high heat. When hot, add the brown sugar and 1 cup granulated sugar. Stir to dissolve. Bring to a boil and allow to boil until the sugar has dissolved, 2 to 3 minutes. Remove from the heat and cool at room temperature for 5 minutes.

Whisk the sifted cocoa, ¼ cup at a time, into the cooled cream and sugar mixture. Add the salt and continue to whisk until the fudge is smooth. Refrigerate 2 cups to use as sauce. Combine the remaining fudge with the crushed pecans and hold at room temperature until needed.

After the espresso has steeped for 1 hour, remove it from the cream and gently squeeze the liquid from it back into the cream. Return the espresso-flavored cream to medium high heat. When hot, add ¼ cup granulated sugar and stir to dissolve. Bring to a boil.

While the cream is heating, place the egg yolks and remaining ½ cup sugar in the bowl of an electric mixer fitted with a paddle. Beat the eggs on high for 2 to 2½ minutes. Scrape down the sides of the bowl, then beat on high until slightly thickened and lemon colored, 2½ to 3 minutes. (At this point, the cream should be boiling. If not, adjust the mixer speed to low and continue to mix until the cream boils. If this is not done, the egg yolks will develop undesirable lumps.)

Pour the boiling cream into the beaten egg yolks and whisk to combine. Return to the saucepan and heat over medium high heat, stirring constantly. Bring to a temperature of 185 degrees, 2 to 4 minutes. Remove from the heat and cool in an ice water bath (see page 315) to a temperature of 40 to 45 degrees, about 15 minutes.

When the mixture is cold, freeze in an ice cream freezer following the manufacturer's instructions.

Line the bottom and narrow sides of a loaf pan with a strip of parchment paper 4 inches wide and 18 inches long. Spoon half the semifrozen ice cream into the loaf pan, making an even layer. Evenly spread the pecan fudge over the ice cream layer. Spoon the remaining ice cream over the fudge and spread evenly. Cover the loaf pan with aluminum foil and freeze the ice cream terrine for 12 hours before serving.

Heat 1 inch of water in the bottom half of a double boiler over medium high heat. Place the reserved fudge in the top half of the double boiler and heat for 10 minutes. Occasionally stir until it has returned to its original consistency. Remove the double boiler from the heat and allow to stand while completing the steps for serving the terrine.

To remove the frozen terrine from the loaf pan, first remove the aluminum foil. Briefly dip (for a few seconds) the pan in a sink containing 1 inch of very hot water. Unmold the terrine by inverting it onto a baking sheet lined with parchment paper. Return to the freezer for 5 minutes.

Flood the base of each 10-inch plate with ¼ cup warm fudge sauce.

Slice the ends from the terrine (keep frozen for an emergency!); cut the terrine into 8 slices about 1 inch thick. Place a slice of terrine in the center of each sauced plate and serve immediately.

The Chef's Touch

A quarter pound of espresso coffee beans will yield the necessary 2 cups ground espresso. High-quality ground espresso under the Medaglia D'Oro label is available in supermarkets.

It is important to use 4-ply cheesecloth; lesser-ply cloth will result in espresso grounds escaping into the cream. In the event this situation does occur, strain the cream through a strainer fine enough to remove the grounds.

After the sugar is dissolved in the cream, the mixture is allowed to cool for 5 minutes before the sifted cocoa is whisked in. This is done to prevent the cocoa from scorching, which would occur if it were added to the boiling cream.

Apply the warm fudge sauce to barely warm plates. The fudge sauce itself should not be too hot when portioned onto the plates. It should be warm enough to flow yet not so warm that it would immediately melt the ice cream.

The egg yolks and sugar may also be prepared using a hand-held mixer (mixing time may increase slightly) or by hand, using a wire whisk (mixing time may double).

Caramel Apple Sorbet

Yields 1 quart

1¹/₄ pounds Granny Smith apples
1 tablespoon plus ¹/₈ teaspoon
  fresh lemon juice

2³/₄ cups water
1³/₄ cups granulated sugar

EQUIPMENT: *Food processor with grating disk or hand grater, measuring spoons, rubber spatula, two stainless-steel bowls (one large), two 2¹/₂-quart saucepans, measuring cup, whisk, wooden spoon, instant-read test thermometer, ice cream freezer, 2-quart plastic container with lid*

Core and quarter the apples (do not peel). Grate the apple quarters, then place the grated apple in a stainless-steel bowl and toss with 1 tablespoon lemon juice. Refrigerate until needed.

Heat the water and 1¹/₄ cups sugar in a 2¹/₂-quart saucepan over medium high heat. Whisk to dissolve the sugar. Bring to a boil and allow to boil until slightly thickened and reduced to 2 cups, about 10 minutes.

About 4 minutes into the boiling of the sugar and water, start the caramel. Heat the remaining ¹/₂ cup sugar in a 2¹/₂-quart saucepan over medium heat. Caramelize the sugar, constantly stirring with a wooden spoon to break up any lumps, for 5 to 6 minutes (the sugar will first turn clear as it liquefies, then light brown as it caramelizes). Add the remaining ¹/₈ teaspoon lemon juice and stir to combine (be careful when adding the lemon juice to the melted sugar; it spurts and can burn). Remove from the heat.

Carefully pour the sugar syrup into the caramelized sugar, stirring to combine. Pour the hot sugar mixture over the grated apple and stir. Cool in an ice water bath (see page 315) to a temperature of 40 to 45 degrees, about 15 minutes.

When cold, freeze in an ice cream freezer following the manufacturer's instructions. Transfer the semifrozen sorbet to a plastic container, securely cover the container, then freeze for several hours before serving. Serve within 3 days.

The Chef's Touch

Granny Smith apples have just the right tartness and firm texture desired for this sorbet. Other varieties such as Gravensteins and Newton Pippins could also be used, as well as Golden Delicious, although the latter is sweeter and usually does not have quite as firm a texture.

Whichever apple is used, the necessary amount needed for this recipe is 2 cups grated. Be certain that the grated apple is well combined with the lemon juice to prevent oxidation (which would result in darkened apples).

Chocolate Cashew Dacquoise

Serves 8 to 12

1 cup egg whites
¹/₈ teaspoon cream of tartar
¹/₈ teaspoon salt
1¹/₄ cups granulated sugar
2 tablespoons cocoa, sifted
2 tablespoons cornstarch
2 cups cashew pieces
1¹/₄ pounds plus 2 tablespoons
   unsalted butter, softened

1¹/₂ cups confectioners' sugar
6 egg yolks
1 pound semisweet chocolate,
   broken into ¹/₂-ounce pieces
¹/₄ cup brewed full-strength coffee
1 cup heavy cream

EQUIPMENT: *9-inch cake plate, three baking sheets with sides, parchment paper, measuring cup, measuring spoons, electric mixer with balloon whip and paddle, sifter, rubber spatula, two pastry bags with straight tips, film wrap, French knife, cutting board, double boiler, three stainless-steel bowls, serrated knife, cake spatula, #2 star tip, 12-inch serrated slicer*

Using a 9-inch cake plate as a guide, trace a circle on each of three sheets of parchment paper (cut to fit baking sheets) with a pencil. Turn each sheet of parchment paper over and place with the trace mark down on a baking sheet.

Preheat the oven to 250 degrees.

Whisk 1 cup egg whites on medium speed in the bowl of an electric mixer fitted with a balloon whip. Whisk until frothy, about 1 minute. Add ¹/₈ teaspoon cream of tartar and ¹/₈ teaspoon salt, increase speed to high, and whisk until the egg whites begin to stiffen, about 1¹/₂ to 2 minutes. Gradually add ¹/₂ cup granulated sugar while continuing to whisk on high speed. Stop the mixer and scrape down the sides of the bowl. Gradually add the remaining ³/₄ cup sugar while whisking on high speed until soft peaks form, about 3 minutes. Remove the bowl from the mixer and use a rubber spatula to fold in 2 tablespoons cocoa and 2 tablespoons cornstarch.

Fill a pastry bag (with no tip) with about a third of the meringue. Pin down each corner of the parchment paper with a dab of meringue. Fill each traced circle with meringue; start in the center and pipe a ¹/₂-inch wide spiral toward the outside of the circle. Repeat this procedure with each of the two remaining circles (each circle should be filled with about a third of the original amount of meringue). Place the meringues in the preheated oven and bake for 15 minutes. Reduce the oven temperature to 225 degrees and bake for 2 hours. Remove from the oven and allow to cool on baking sheets for 45 minutes before handling. Raise the oven temperature to 300 degrees.

Toast the cashew pieces on a baking sheet in the 300-degree oven until golden, 15 to 18 minutes. Remove from the oven and allow to cool to room temperature. Chop ¹/₂ cup toasted cashew pieces by hand, or in a food processor fitted with a metal blade, into pieces no larger than ¹/₈ inch. Place the chopped cashews and cashew pieces into separate containers, cover with film wrap, and keep at room temperature until needed.

Cut ¹/₂ pound butter into 8 equal pieces and place in the bowl of an electric mixer fitted with a paddle. Beat on low speed for 1 minute. Add ³/₄ cup confectioners' sugar, beat on medium for 1¹/₂ minutes, then beat on high for an additional 1¹/₂ minutes. Scrape down the bowl. With the mixer on high, add 3 egg yolks, one at a time, and beat for 30 seconds. Scrape down the bowl, then beat for 1 additional minute. Add the chopped cashews and beat on high for 30 seconds. Scrape down the bowl, then beat on high for 30 more seconds. Transfer the cashew icing to a stainless-steel bowl, cover with film wrap, and keep at room temperature until needed.

Heat 1 inch of water in the bottom half of a double boiler over medium high heat. Place 4 ounces semisweet chocolate and ¹/₄ cup brewed coffee in the top half of the double boiler (see page 317). Tightly cover the top with film wrap. Heat until just melted, 6 to 8 minutes. Remove from the heat and stir until smooth. Cover with film wrap and hold at room temperature until needed.

Cut ³/₄ pound butter into 12 equal pieces and place in the bowl of an electric mixer fitted with a paddle. Beat on low speed for 1 minute. Add the remaining ³/₄ cup confectioners' sugar, beat on medium for 1¹/₂ minutes, then beat on high for an additional 1¹/₂ minutes. Scrape down the bowl. With the mixer on high, add the remaining 3 egg yolks, one at a time, and beat for 30 seconds. Scrape down the bowl, then beat for 1 additional minute. Add the melted chocolate and beat on high for 30 seconds. Scrape down the bowl, then beat on high for 30 more seconds, until thoroughly combined. Transfer the chocolate icing to a stainless-steel bowl, cover with film wrap, and keep at room temperature until needed.

Heat 1 inch of water in the bottom half of a double boiler over medium high heat. Place the remaining 12 ounces semisweet chocolate, remaining 2 tablespoons butter, and 1 cup heavy cream in the top half of the double boiler. Tightly cover the top of the pot with film wrap. Heat until just melted, 8 to 10 minutes. Remove from the heat, stir until smooth, then transfer to a stainless-steel bowl. Cover the ganache with film wrap and hold at room temperature until needed.

Trim each meringue with a serrated knife so that it will fit perfectly on a 9-inch cake plate. Place a dab of icing in the center of the plate. Place a meringue, top side up, on the plate, gently pressing down on the meringue so that the icing will hold it in place. Reserve and refrigerate $1/2$ cup cashew icing and $3/4$ cup chocolate icing. Place the remainder of each of the icings in separate pastry bags with no tips. Pipe a $1/2$-inch-wide ring of chocolate icing along the outside edge of the meringue. Pipe a similar ring of cashew icing alongside the chocolate ring. Continue to pipe out alternating rings of icing until the surface of the meringue is covered.

Place a second meringue, top side up, onto the rings of icing and gently press down on the meringue; repeat the procedure of piping out alternate rings of icing until the second meringue is covered with icing.

Place the third meringue, bottom side up, onto the rings of icing, once again gently pressing down on the meringue. Using a cake spatula, spread the reserved cashew icing in a smooth and even layer over the top and sides of the dacquoise. Put the dacquoise in the freezer for 20 minutes or in the refrigerator for 40 minutes.

Place the well-chilled dacquoise on a baking sheet. Pour half the ganache on top of the dacquoise. Use a cake spatula to spread the ganache evenly and smoothly over the top and sides of the dacquoise. Refrigerate the dacquoise for 10 minutes to set the ganache, then repeat the procedure with the remaining amount of ganache. Remove the dacquoise from the baking sheet and refrigerate for 5 minutes. Press the cashew pieces into the sides of the dacquoise. Freeze the dacquoise for 10 minutes or refrigerate for 20 minutes.

Fill a pastry bag fitted with a #2 star tip with the reserved chocolate icing. Pipe a circle of 8 to 12 stars (depending upon the desired number of servings) along the outside edge of the top of the dacquoise. Refrigerate the dacquoise for 4 hours before serving.

Place in the freezer for an additional 30 minutes, if the 4 hours of refrigeration was not sufficient to chill the dacquoise properly. The dacquoise should not be cut unless it is very cold. Cut the dacquoise with a serrated slicer, heating the blade of the slicer under hot running water before making each slice. Allow the sliced dacquoise to temper at room temperature for 10 to 15 minutes before serving.

The Chef's Touch

It is better to bake the meringues on separate shelves. If the oven has only two shelves, you may place two baking sheets, slightly overlapping each other, on the same shelf. If this is done, it will be necessary to rotate the baking sheets once or twice while the meringues are baking in order to assure that they are uniformly baked.

Baked meringues may be baked a day or two in advance of assembling the dacquoise. Store baked meringues in a closed container in a dry place at room temperature.

Baked meringues are brittle: handle with care. A sharp serrated knife is the best tool to use to trim the meringues so they will fit exactly onto a 9-inch cake plate. Be very careful to press down gently on the meringues when assembling the dacquoise layers. If the layers of meringue are not sufficiently pressed into the icing, the finished dacquoise will have noticeable holes between the layers when sliced. On the other hand, if the meringues are not *gently* pressed into the icing they will surely break, causing an unattractive appearance.

If a table-model electric mixer is not available, this recipe may also be prepared using a hand-held mixer (mixing time may increase slightly).

Death by Chocolate

Serves 12

Cocoa Meringue
4 egg whites
¹/₈ teaspoon cream of tartar
¹/₈ teaspoon salt
1¹/₄ cups granulated sugar
2 tablespoons cocoa, sifted
1 tablespoon cornstarch

Chocolate Mousse
6 ounces semisweet chocolate,
 broken into ¹/₂-ounce pieces
1¹/₂ cups heavy cream
3 egg whites
2 tablespoons granulated sugar

Chocolate Ganache
22 ounces semisweet chocolate,
 broken into ¹/₂-ounce pieces
1¹/₂ cups heavy cream
3 tablespoons unsalted butter

Chocolate Brownie
3 ounces semisweet chocolate,
 broken into ¹/₂-ounce pieces
4 tablespoons plus 1 teaspoon
 unsalted butter, softened
1¹/₂ ounces unsweetened chocolate,
 broken into ¹/₂-ounce pieces
3 eggs
³/₄ cup granulated sugar

1 teaspoon pure vanilla extract
8 tablespoons plus 1 teaspoon
 all-purpose flour
¹/₂ teaspoon salt
¹/₂ teaspoon baking powder
2 tablespoons sour cream

Mocha Mousse
14 ounces semisweet chocolate,
 broken into ¹/₂-ounce pieces
4 ounces unsweetened chocolate,
 broken into ¹/₂-ounce pieces
¹/₂ cup water
¹/₄ cup instant coffee granules
2 tablespoons cocoa, sifted
2 egg yolks
5 egg whites
2 tablespoons granulated sugar
³/₄ cup heavy cream

Chocolate Rum Sauce
¹/₄ pound unsalted butter, softened
1 cup granulated sugar
1 cup heavy cream
¹/₃ cup cocoa, sifted
2 teaspoons Myers' dark rum
¹/₈ teaspoon salt
1 tablespoon instant coffee
 granules
1 teaspoon pure vanilla extract

EQUIPMENT: *Measuring cup, measuring spoons, sifter, electric mixer with balloon whip, rubber spatula, two baking sheets, parchment paper, 9-inch cake plate, pastry bag, #7 straight tip, double boiler, cutting board, French knife, film wrap, four stainless-steel bowls, two whisks, 9 × 1¹/₂-inch cake pan, 12-inch serrated slicer, 9 × 3-inch springform pan, ladle, serrated knife, large metal spoon, cake spatula, #4 star tip, 2¹/₂-quart saucepan*

Preheat the oven to 225 degrees.

Prepare the cocoa meringue. Whisk 4 egg whites on medium speed in the bowl of an electric mixer fitted with a balloon whip. Whisk until frothy, about 1 minute. Add ¹/₈ teaspoon cream of tartar and ¹/₈ teaspoon salt, increase speed to high, and whisk until the egg whites begin to stiffen, 1¹/₂ to 2 minutes. Gradually add ¹/₂ cup sugar while continuing to whisk on high speed. Stop the mixer and scrape down the bowl. Gradually add the remaining ³/₄ cup sugar while whisking on high speed until soft peaks form, about 3 minutes. Remove the bowl from the mixer and use a rubber spatula to fold in 2 tablespoons cocoa and 1 tablespoon cornstarch.

Using a 9-inch cake plate as a guide, with a pencil trace a circle on a sheet of parchment paper cut to fit a baking sheet. Turn the paper over and, with the trace mark down, place on a baking sheet. Fill a pastry bag fitted with a straight tip with cocoa meringue. Pin down each corner of the parchment paper with a dab of meringue. Fill the traced circle with meringue: start in the center and pipe a ³/₄-inch-wide spiral toward the outside of the circle.

Place the meringue in the preheated oven and bake for 15 minutes. Reduce the oven temperature to 200 degrees and bake for 2 hours and 45 minutes. Remove from the oven and allow the cocoa meringue to cool on the baking sheet for 45 minutes before handling. Adjust the oven temperature to 325 degrees.

While the meringue is baking, prepare the chocolate mousse. Heat 1 inch of water in the bottom half of a double boiler over medium heat. Place 6 ounces semisweet chocolate in the top half of the double boiler (see page 317). Tightly cover the top with film wrap. Allow the chocolate to melt slowly, about 10 minutes. Remove the pot from the heat and keep at room temperature until needed.

Place 1¹/₂ cups heavy cream in the well-chilled bowl of an electric mixer fitted with a well-chilled balloon whip. Whisk on high speed for 1¹/₂ minutes, scrape down the sides of the bowl, and whisk on high for 1 additional minute, until peaks form. Refrigerate until needed.

Whisk 3 egg whites in a stainless-steel bowl until soft peaks form, about 3 minutes. Add 2 tablespoons sugar and continue to whisk until stiff peaks form, 1 to 1½ minutes. Whisk the melted chocolate until smooth. Add a quarter of the whipped cream to the chocolate and whisk quickly and vigorously, then add to the egg whites, followed by the remaining whipped cream. Fold all together gently but thoroughly. Refrigerate the chocolate mousse until needed.

Prepare the ganache. Heat 1 inch of water in the bottom half of a double boiler over medium high heat. Place 22 ounces semisweet chocolate, 1½ cups heavy cream, and 3 tablespoons butter in the top half of the double boiler. Tightly cover the top with film wrap. Allow to heat for 3 minutes, remove the film wrap, and stir the mixture. Continue to stir while heating the mixture for 2 additional minutes. Remove from the heat and stir until smooth, then transfer to a stainless-steel bowl. Cover with film wrap and keep the ganache at room temperature until needed.

Prepare the chocolate brownie. Heat 1 inch of water in the bottom half of a double boiler over medium high heat. Place 3 ounces semisweet chocolate, 4 tablespoons butter, and 1½ ounces unsweetened chocolate in the top half of the double boiler. Tightly cover the top with film wrap. Heat for 6 to 7 minutes, remove from the heat, and stir until smooth.

Whisk together 3 eggs, ¾ cup sugar, and 1 teaspoon vanilla in a stainless-steel bowl until slightly thickened, about 3 minutes. Coat a 9 × 1½-inch cake pan with 1 teaspoon butter. Flour the pan with 1 teaspoon flour, shaking out the excess. Fold the chocolate mixture into the egg mixture. Into this combined mixture, fold 8 tablespoons flour, ½ teaspoon salt, and ½ teaspoon baking powder. In a separate bowl, vigorously whisk 2 tablespoons sour cream. Thoroughly fold the sour cream into the brownie mixture. Pour into the prepared cake pan, spreading evenly. Place the pan in the 325-degree oven and bake the chocolate brownie until a toothpick inserted in the center comes out clean, about 30 minutes.

Remove the brownie from the oven and allow to cool in the pan at room temperature for 5 minutes. Turn out onto a cake plate and place in the freezer for 10 minutes. Remove the brownie from the freezer and cut in half horizontally. Allow the brownie to stand at room temperature while preparing the mocha mousse.

Prepare the mocha mousse. Heat 1 inch of water in the bottom half of a double boiler over medium high heat. Place 14 ounces semisweet chocolate, 4 ounces unsweetened chocolate, ½ cup water, ¼ cup instant coffee, and 2 tablespoons cocoa in the top half of the double boiler. Tightly cover the top with film wrap. Heat for 5 to 7 minutes, remove the film wrap, and stir the mixture until smooth. Add 2 egg yolks and continue to stir until smooth. Transfer the mixture to a stainless-steel bowl. Allow to stand at room temperature while whisking the egg whites. In the bowl of an electric mixer, whisk the 5 egg whites on high speed until soft peaks form, 2 to 3 minutes. Continue to whisk while gradually adding 2 tablespoons sugar. Whisk until stiff, about 2 minutes.

Whip ¾ cup heavy cream in a well-chilled stainless-steel bowl until stiff. Fold a quarter of the egg whites into the melted chocolate mixture, then fold in the whipped cream. Now fold in the remaining egg whites. Hold the mocha mousse at room temperature.

Assemble Death by Chocolate. Place a closed springform pan on a baking sheet. Set the top half of the chocolate brownie inside the pan, top side up. Ladle 1½ cups ganache into the pan over the chocolate brownie. Trim the cocoa meringue with a serrated knife so that it will fit tightly into the pan. Place the trimmed cocoa meringue, top side up, inside the pan on top of the ganache, pressing down gently on the cocoa meringue to eliminate air pockets. Spoon the mocha mousse on top of the cocoa meringue, spreading evenly. Place the remaining chocolate brownie half, bottom side up, on top of the mocha mousse. Chill the cake in the freezer for 30 minutes, or refrigerate for 1 hour.

Remove the cake from the freezer and cut around the edges to release from the springform pan. Pour the remaining ganache over the cake and use a cake spatula to spread the ganache evenly over the top and sides of the cake. Refrigerate the cake for 10 to 15 minutes to set the ganache.

Fill a pastry bag fitted with a #4 star tip with the chocolate mousse. Pipe a circle of stars (each touching the other) along the outside edge of the top of the cake. Continue to pipe out circles of stars until the top of the cake is covered. Refrigerate the Death by Chocolate for at least 4 hours and preferably 12 hours before cutting.

Prepare the chocolate rum sauce (the sauce can be prepared just prior to service or several hours in advance). Heat ¼ pound butter in a 2½-quart saucepan over medium heat. When hot, add 1 cup sugar, 1 cup heavy cream, ⅓ cup sifted cocoa, 2 teaspoons rum and ⅛ teaspoon salt. Bring to a boil, then adjust the heat and allow to simmer for 5 minutes. Remove the saucepan from the heat and stir in 1 tablespoon instant coffee and 1 teaspoon vanilla extract. Allow to cool to room temperature before using.

To serve, cut the Death by Chocolate into the desired number of servings. Heat the blade of a serrated slicer under hot running water before making each slice. Flood the base of each 10-inch dinner plate with the chocolate rum sauce and place a piece of Death by Chocolate in the center of each plate. Serve immediately.

The Chef's Touch

You will not find the recipe for Death by Chocolate in a culinary lexicon. It is a contemporary concoction, an amalgam of cocoa meringue, chocolate mousse, chocolate ganache, chocolate brownie, and mocha mousse, structured in an extraordinary, albeit sound, manner.

A fair warning must be issued that this is a time- and money-consuming recipe.

It is best to start work on this cake very early in the day if it is to be served that evening. Death by Chocolate may be held for two to three days under refrigeration, *but it is at its best served within twenty-four hours of completion.* The preparation in one day of all the chocolate components for this cake might seem overwhelming. To prepare in advance, spread the production out over a period of three days. Day 1: Prepare the chocolate brownie and keep refrigerated until cake assembly. Day 2: Bake the cocoa meringue and store in a dry place at room temperature (between 68 and 78 degrees). Prepare the chocolate rum sauce, refrigerate until two hours before service, then bring to room temperature. Day 3: Prepare the chocolate mousse, mocha mousse, and ganache. Assemble cake.

Use the 9-inch bottom of the springform pan to trace the circle onto the parchment paper.

Be certain that the meringue completely fills the traced circle. If the meringue is not large enough, the sides of the cake will be uneven. Do not be concerned if the meringue slightly overlaps the circle; any excess may be trimmed off after the meringue has been baked.

Baked meringues are very brittle; handle with care. Use a very sharp serrated knife to trim the meringue; otherwise, the meringue will break apart.

If the mocha mousse is prepared several hours in advance of the assembly of the cake, it should be refrigerated until 1 to 1½ hours before assembly, at which time it should be allowed to temper at room temperature (if it is too cold it will be difficult to spread evenly over the delicate mocha meringue).

If the ganache solidifies, place the bowl containing the ganache in a pan of hot water and stir until the texture is correct for pouring.

Use several toothpicks inserted in the sides of the chocolate brownie as guides to accurately halve the brownie horizontally.

The preparations may also be completed using a hand-held mixer, but preparation time may increase slightly.

For organizational and shopping convenience the following is a compilation of all the ingredients needed to produce Death by Chocolate:

2 pounds, 13 ounces semisweet
  chocolate
5¹/₂ ounces unsweetened chocolate
4³/₄ cups heavy cream
3¹/₄ cups granulated sugar
15 eggs
15 tablespoons plus 1 teaspoon
   (almost ¹/₂ pound)
   unsalted butter
10 tablespoons cocoa
8 tablespoons plus 1 teaspoon all-
  purpose flour

¹/₂ cup water
5 tablespoons instant coffee
2 tablespoons sour cream
1 tablespoon cornstarch
2 teaspoons pure vanilla extract
2 teaspoons dark rum
³/₄ teaspoon salt
¹/₂ teaspoon baking powder
¹/₈ teaspoon cream of tartar

Total weight of ingredients: about 10 pounds, 2¹/₂ ounces. Total cost of ingredients: it may be less expensive to visit The Trellis!

Chocolate Praline Ice Cream Terrine

Serves 8

Praline
1 cup pecan pieces
1 teaspoon unsalted butter, softened
1 cup granulated sugar
¹/₈ teaspoon fresh lemon juice
¹/₄ cup heavy cream

Chocolate Ice Cream
6 ounces semisweet chocolate, broken into ¹/₂-ounce pieces

2 ounces unsweetened chocolate, broken into ¹/₂-ounce pieces
2¹/₂ cups whole milk
1 cup heavy cream
¹/₂ cup granulated sugar
¹/₂ cup egg yolks

Caramel Sauce
2 cups granulated sugar
¹/₂ teaspoon fresh lemon juice
1¹/₂ cups heavy cream

EQUIPMENT: *Measuring cup, baking sheet, measuring spoons, 9 × 1¹/₂-inch cake pan, two 2¹/₂-quart saucepans, wooden spoon, film wrap, double boiler, French knife, cutting board, whisk, two stainless-steel bowls (one large), rubber spatula, electric mixer with paddle, instant-read test thermometer, ice cream freezer, 9 × 5 × 3-inch loaf pan, parchment paper, aluminum foil, cake spatula, serrated slicer*

Preheat the oven to 300 degrees.

Toast the pecans on a baking sheet in the preheated oven for 15 minutes. Remove from the oven and allow to cool to room temperature. Coat a 9- by 1¹/₂-inch cake pan with 1 teaspoon butter. Spread the cooled pecans over the bottom of the cake pan.

Heat 1 cup sugar in a 2¹/₂-quart saucepan over medium heat. Caramelize the sugar for 7 to 8 minutes, constantly stirring with a wooden spoon to break up any lumps (the sugar will first turn clear as it liquefies, then brown as it caramelizes). Add ¹/₈ teaspoon lemon juice and stir to combine. (Be careful when adding the lemon juice to the melted sugar; it spurts and can burn.) Remove the saucepan from the heat and add ¹/₄ cup heavy cream; stir to combine (the mixture will steam and boil rapidly as the cream is added). Pour the caramel mixture over the pecans and stir with a wooden spoon to combine and completely coat the pecans with caramel; spread the mixture evenly over the bottom of the pan. Freeze the praline for 1½ hours. Remove from the freezer. Place the cake pan in a larger pan containing ½ inch of very hot water. Allow the cake pan to stand in the hot water for a few seconds, long enough to loosen the praline from the pan. Remove the praline from the pan, cover with film wrap, and store in the freezer until needed.

Heat 1 inch of water in the bottom half of a double boiler over medium high heat. Place 6 ounces semisweet chocolate, 2 ounces unsweetened chocolate, and ½ cup milk in the top half of the double boiler. Tightly cover the top with film wrap. Heat for 8 to 10 minutes, then transfer to a stainless-steel bowl and stir until smooth.

Heat the remaining 2 cups milk and 1 cup heavy cream in a 2½-quart saucepan over medium high heat. When hot, add ¼ cup sugar and stir to dissolve. Bring the cream to a boil.

While the cream is heating, place ½ cup egg yolks and the remaining ¼ cup sugar in the bowl of an electric mixer fitted with a paddle. Beat the eggs on high for 2 to 2½ minutes. Scrape down the sides of the bowl. Then beat on high until slightly thickened and lemon colored, 2½ to 3 minutes. (At this point, the cream should be boiling. If not, adjust the mixer speed to low and continue to mix until the cream boils. If this is not done, the egg yolks will develop undesirable lumps.)

Pour the boiling milk and cream into the beaten egg yolks; whisk to combine. Return to the saucepan and heat over medium high heat, stirring constantly. Bring to a temperature of 185 degrees, 2 to 4 minutes. Remove from the heat and cool in an ice water bath (see page 315) to a temperature of 40 to 45 degrees, about 15 minutes.

While the custard is cooling, chop the praline into ¼-inch pieces. When the custard is cold, stir in the chopped praline and freeze in an ice cream freezer, following the manufacturer's instructions.

Line the bottom and narrow sides of a loaf pan with a 4-inch-wide by 18-inch-long strip of parchment paper. Transfer the semifrozen ice cream to the loaf pan, spreading evenly. Cover the loaf pan with aluminum foil and freeze the ice cream terrine for 12 hours before serving.

Heat 2 cups sugar in a 2½-quart saucepan over medium high heat. Caramelize the sugar for 12 to 15 minutes, constantly stirring with a wooden spoon to break up any lumps. Add ½ teaspoon lemon juice and stir to combine. Remove the saucepan from the heat and add 1½ cups heavy cream; stir to combine. Transfer the caramel sauce to a stainless-steel bowl and allow to cool to room temperature, 10 to 15 minutes.

To remove the frozen terrine from the loaf pan, briefly dip (for a few seconds) the pan in a sink or large pan filled with 1 inch of very hot water. Unmold the terrine by inverting it onto a baking sheet lined with parchment paper. Return to the freezer for 5 minutes.

Flood the base of each 10-inch plate with 1/4 cup caramel sauce. Slice the ends from the terrine (freeze and save for a midnight snack). Cut the terrine into 8 slices about 1 inch thick. Place a slice of terrine in the center of each sauced plate and serve immediately.

The Chef's Touch

Chocolatier magazine uses a rating key of one to three chocolate "kisses" to alert their readers to the preparation time, as well as the general culinary skills, required to prepare the recipes featured in its delicious pages. Recipes that rate three kisses are described as "stunning creative chocolate masterpieces that may require advance preparation and several steps to complete, but well worth the effort." Our chocolate praline ice cream terrine rated three kisses when it appeared in the May 1987 issue of *Chocolatier*. We agree!

The praline is returned to the freezer after being released from the cake pan. Then it is removed from the freezer and chopped. This is done to ensure that the praline is not the least bit tacky when it is chopped. It must be very hard to facilitate the chopping.

If the caramel sauce becomes too firm or if it is prepared the day before it is to be served (keep the sauce refrigerated after it cools to room temperature), bring it back to the desired consistency by placing the bowl containing the sauce into another bowl partially filled with very hot water. Allow the sauce to stand for 10 to 15 minutes.

The caramel sauce should be served at room temperature or slightly warmer. Be careful that the sauce is not too warm; otherwise, the ice cream terrine will begin to melt as soon as it is placed on the sauced plates.

The egg yolks and sugar may also be prepared using a hand-held mixer (mixing time may increase slightly) or by hand, using a wire whisk (mixing time may double).

For a final touch, garnish the plates with toasted pecan halves and white and dark chocolate curls.

Pear Fritters with Toasted Pecan Ice Cream and Pear Custard Sauce

Serves 8

Toasted Pecan Ice Cream

1¼ cups pecan pieces
2¼ cups heavy cream
1½ cups half-and-half
1 cup firmly packed light brown sugar
¾ cup egg yolks

Pear Custard Sauce

3 ripe pears, unpeeled
1 cup water
½ cup granulated sugar
1 teaspoon fresh lemon juice
1 cup heavy cream
1 cup half-and-half
4 egg yolks
2 teaspoons cornstarch

Pear Fritters

1½ cups all-purpose flour
½ cup granulated sugar
½ cup grated Cheddar cheese
4 tablespoons baking powder
2 teaspoons cornstarch
1 teaspoon salt
1 teaspoon cinnamon
½ cup heavy cream
2 eggs
1 cup Budweiser beer
3 tablespoons fresh lemon juice
6 ripe pears
3 cups vegetable oil
2 tablespoons confectioners' sugar

EQUIPMENT: *Measuring cup, two baking sheets, sauté pan, two 2½-quart saucepans, whisk, electric mixer with paddle, rubber spatula, instant-read test thermometer, four stainless-steel bowls (one large), ice cream freezer, 2-quart plastic container with lid, paring knife, cutting board, French knife, measuring spoons, wooden spoon, film wrap, vegetable peeler, corer, deep fat fryer or heavy-duty 5-quart saucepan, candy/deep-frying thermometer, paper towels, tongs, ice cream scoop*

Preheat the oven to 300 degrees.

Toast 1¼ cups pecan pieces on a baking sheet in the preheated oven for 15 minutes. Remove from the oven and allow to cool to room temperature. Crush the pecan pieces with the bottom of a sauté pan and keep at room temperature until needed.

Heat 2¹/₄ cups heavy cream and 1¹/₂ cups half-and-half in a 2¹/₂-quart saucepan over medium high heat. When hot, add ¹/₂ cup brown sugar and stir to dissolve. Bring the mixture to a boil.

While the cream is heating, place ³/₄ cup egg yolks and the remaining ¹/₂ cup brown sugar in the bowl of an electric mixer fitted with a paddle. Beat on high for 2 to 2¹/₂ minutes. Scrape down the sides of the bowl. Then beat on high until slightly thickened and lemon colored, an additional 2¹/₂ to 3 minutes. (At this point, the cream should be boiling. If not, adjust the mixer speed to low and continue to mix until the cream boils. If this is not done, the egg yolks will develop undesirable lumps.)

Pour the boiling cream into the beaten egg yolks; whisk to combine. Return to the saucepan and heat over medium high heat, stirring constantly. Bring to a temperature of 185 degrees, 2 to 4 minutes. Remove from the heat and transfer to a stainless-steel bowl. Add the crushed pecans and stir to combine. Cool the mixture in an ice water bath (see page 315) to a temperature of 40 to 45 degrees, about 15 minutes.

When cold, freeze in an ice cream freezer, following the manufacturer's instructions. Transfer the semifrozen ice cream to a 2-quart plastic container. Securely cover and freeze for several hours.

Core, quarter, and chop 3 pears into ¹/₄-inch pieces (do not peel). Combine the chopped pears, 1 cup water, ¹/₂ cup sugar, and 1 teaspoon lemon juice in a 2¹/₂-quart saucepan and heat over medium high heat. Bring to a boil, then adjust the heat and allow to simmer until the pears are translucent, about 30 minutes. Transfer the mixture to a stainless-steel bowl and cool in an ice water bath for 15 minutes.

While the pears are cooling, heat 1 cup heavy cream and 1 cup half-and-half in a 2¹/₂-quart saucepan over medium high heat and bring to a boil.

While the cream is heating, whisk 4 egg yolks with 2 teaspoons cornstarch in a stainless-steel bowl for 3 minutes. Pour the boiling cream into the egg yolk mixture; using a wooden spoon, stir gently to combine. Stir in the cooled chopped pear mixture. Cool the pear custard sauce in an ice water bath for 12 to 15 minutes. Refrigerate until needed.

Prepare the fritter batter about 1 hour before serving this dessert. In a stainless-steel bowl, combine 1¹/₂ cups flour, ¹/₂ cup granulated sugar, ¹/₂ cup grated Cheddar cheese, 4 tablespoons baking powder, 2 teaspoons cornstarch, 1 teaspoon salt, and 1 teaspoon cinnamon. In a separate stainless-steel bowl, whisk together ¹/₂ cup heavy cream and 2 eggs; then whisk in 1 cup beer and 2 tablespoons lemon juice. Pour the wet ingredients into the dry ingredients; use a rubber spatula to thoroughly mix. Cover the bowl tightly with film wrap and keep at room temperature.

Acidulate 1 quart water with the remaining tablespoon lemon juice. Peel and core 6 pears; slice them into ¼- to ⅜-inch-thick slices (each pear should yield 6 slices) and immediately place in the acidulated water.

Preheat the oven to 200 degrees.

Heat 3 cups vegetable oil in a deep fat fryer (or heavy-duty 5-quart saucepan) to a temperature of 365 to 375 degrees. Rinse the pear slices under cold running water, then drain thoroughly. Place the pear slices on paper towels and pat dry. Dip 4 pear slices into the batter. Drop batter-coated slices into the hot oil and fry until golden brown, about 15 seconds per side. Transfer the fritters to a baking sheet lined with paper towels. Hold warm in the 200-degree oven while repeating the battering and frying procedure with the remaining pear slices, 4 at a time.

Portion 6 tablespoons pear custard sauce onto each of eight 10-inch plates. To one side of each plate, place 3 scoops ice cream. Remove the fritters from the oven and dust them with confectioners' sugar. Set 3 or 4 fritters (each one slightly overlapping the previous one) opposite the ice cream scoops on each plate and serve immediately.

The Chef's Touch

Toasted pecan ice cream may be prepared up to five days before this dessert is served. The pear custard sauce may be prepared a day in advance, leaving only the pear fritters to be dealt with near service time. The batter for the fritters may be prepared up to two hours before service. The batter must be held at room temperature; if it is refrigerated, the fried coating on the pears will not be delicate and crisp. It may be necessary to stir the batter occasionally, as it will have a tendency to increase in volume if it stands at room temperature for more than half an hour.

The egg yolks and sugar may also be prepared using a hand-held mixer, or by hand with a wire whisk. If prepared by hand, additional time should be allowed.

BASICS,
TECHNIQUES,
EQUIPMENT,
AND
SOURCES

BASICS

Chicken Stock

Yields 3 quarts (12 cups)

5 pounds chicken bones,
   uncooked backs, necks, and
   wings
1 medium onion, chopped
2 stalks celery, chopped
2 medium leeks, white part only,
   chopped

4 quarts cold water
1¹/₂ tablespoons salt
2 teaspoons fresh thyme
   (or 1 teaspoon dried)
1 teaspoon whole black
   peppercorns
6 sprigs parsley

EQUIPMENT: *Large stockpot (about 8 to 10 quarts), paring knife, cutting board, French knife, measuring cup, stirring spoon, measuring spoon, colander, large stainless-steel bowl, fine strainer*

Place the chicken bones in a large stockpot. Wash the bones under cold running water until the water in the pot is clear. Drain the water from the pot.

Add the chopped onion, celery, leeks, and 4 quarts cold water to the pot. Heat over medium high heat until the water begins to simmer. Add the salt, thyme, peppercorns, and parsley sprigs. Adjust the heat so that the water will simmer slowly for 3¹/₂ to 4 hours.

Carefully pour the stock through a colander into a large stainless-steel bowl, leaving the bones and the vegetables in the pot. Pour the stock through a fine strainer.

Cool the chicken stock in an ice water bath (see page 315). Refrigerate for 2 to 3 days or freeze (see page 318).

The Chef's Touch

This chicken stock recipe produces a mild-flavored stock. If a more intensely flavored stock is desirable, reduce the strained stock by half of its volume to intensify the flavor yet preserve the clear, light color.

The intensity of the stock flavor may also be increased by using whole raw chickens (use the cooked meat for salads, hash, etc.) or bones from chickens that have been roasted. In either case, the stock will be flavorful, albeit darker in color.

For the sake of time or water conservation, it may not be practical to wash the chicken bones as directed. There are two alternate methods to clean the bones of blood: cover the bones with cold water, bring to a boil, discard the water, then re-cover the bones with cold water and proceed as directed; or when the water first comes to a simmer, use a skimmer or a large metal spoon to skim any accumulated scum before adding the vegetables and proceeding as directed in the recipe.

Fish Stock

4 pounds flatfish bones
1 small onion, chopped
2 stalks celery, chopped
2 medium leeks, white part only,
  chopped

3 quarts cold water
1 lemon, juiced
1 tablespoon salt
^{1}/$_2$ teaspoon whole black
  peppercorns

EQUIPMENT: *5-quart saucepan, paring knife, cutting board, French knife, measuring cup, measuring spoons, colander, large stainless-steel bowl, fine strainer*

Place the fish bones in a 5-quart saucepan. Wash the fish bones under cold running water until the water in the saucepan is clear, about 5 minutes. Drain the water from the saucepan.

Add the chopped onion, celery, leeks, and 3 quarts cold water to the pan. Heat over medium high heat until the water begins to simmer. Add the lemon juice, salt, and peppercorns. Adjust the heat so the water will simmer slowly for 45 to 50 minutes. *Do not stir.*

Carefully pour the stock through a colander into a large stainless-steel bowl, leaving the bones and the vegetables in the saucepan. Pour the stock through a fine strainer.

If not to be used immediately, cool the fish stock in an ice water bath (see page 315) and refrigerate for 2 to 3 days or freeze (see page 318).

The Chef's Touch

Flounder bones make excellent fish stock. Other flatfish such as halibut, sole, and turbot also make excellent stock. The general rule is to use non-oily fish, so the bones from red snapper and grouper are also very desirable. Do not use the bones from oily fish such as bluefish, mackerel, salmon, swordfish, goldfish, or tuna. Use the bones, but not the heads and gills, as these parts are particularly perishable. Wash the bones thoroughly to remove any organs or blood.

This fish stock is light in flavor, thereby making it very versatile. It is the stock that should be used to prepare the recipes that call for fish stock in this cookbook. For a more intensely flavored stock, add additional salt and pepper, 2 bay leaves, 1 teaspoon fresh thyme, and a few parsley sprigs to the simmering water. After straining, allow the clear stock to simmer slowly, until it has reduced by half of its volume.

Vegetable Stock

Yields 2 quarts (8 cups)

3 quarts cold water

2 medium onions, chopped

4 stalks celery, chopped

1 medium potato, scrubbed and cut into 1-inch pieces

1 medium carrot, scrubbed and chopped

2 medium leeks, white part only, chopped

1 medium tomato, cored and chopped

1 tablespoon salt

2 medium garlic cloves, peeled

1 teaspoon chopped fresh parsley

1/2 teaspoon whole black peppercorns

EQUIPMENT: *Paring knife, vegetable peeler, cutting board, French knife, 5-quart saucepan, measuring cup, measuring spoon, wooden spoon, colander, stainless-steel bowl, fine strainer*

Heat 1/2 cup water in a 5-quart saucepan over medium high heat. When hot, add the chopped onions, celery, potato, carrot, leeks, tomato, and salt. Steam for 5 minutes, stirring occasionally.

Add the remaining water along with the garlic, parsley, and peppercorns. When the mixture begins to simmer, adjust the heat and continue to simmer for 2 hours.

Carefully pour the stock through a colander into a stainless-steel bowl, leaving the vegetables in the saucepan. Pour the stock through a fine strainer.

If the vegetable stock is not to be used immediately, cool in an ice water bath (see page 315), then refrigerate for 2 to 3 days or freeze (see page 318).

The Chef's Touch

The mixture of vegetables listed in this recipe will produce a mild and versatile stock. Of course, other vegetables, such as fennel, artichokes, and asparagus, may be considered—as well as mushrooms; however, the flavor and the color will be more assertive.

The mildness of this stock makes it adaptable to a variety of preparations. Consider using it to prepare many of the soups listed in this cookbook. To render a soup such as Wild Mushroom authentically vegetarian, low in saturated fat, and cholesterol-free yet still delicious, use vegetable stock rather than chicken stock, and vegetable oil instead of butter to prepare the roux, and omit the cream.

The herbs used to prepare this vegetable stock should not overwhelm the overall flavor of the stock. For that reason I have suggested a relatively small quantity (1 teaspoon) of chopped fresh parsley. Certain herbs, such as thyme, will both darken the stock and impart a distinct flavor. Of course, this may be compatible with the intended recipe. For example, consider using 1 to 2 teaspoons fresh thyme in the preparation of a vegetable stock that in turn would be utilized in preparing a thyme-flavored rice pilaf.

Trellis Vinaigrette

Yields 2 cups

6 tablespoons cider vinegar
3 tablespoons fresh lemon juice
4 teaspoons Dijon-style mustard
1¹/₂ teaspoons salt

¹/₄ teaspoon freshly ground black
   pepper
1¹/₂ cups vegetable oil

EQUIPMENT: *Stainless-steel bowl, measuring spoons, whisk, measuring cup, 1-pint glass jar with lid*

In a stainless-steel bowl, whisk together the vinegar, lemon juice, mustard, salt, and black pepper. Combine thoroughly. Slowly whisk in the vegetable oil until the dressing is well combined.

Transfer to a glass jar, cover tightly, and refrigerate for at least 1 hour before serving.

The Chef's Touch

Since our opening, this vinaigrette has been used to dress the mixed seasonal salads offered at lunch at The Trellis. It also serves as an excellent marinade for pasta and for grilled vegetables.

Use an oil which has not been hydrogenated and is low in saturated fat, such as safflower oil. Olive oil, which we use in many dressings, is too distinct for a light vinaigrette such as this. Your favorite mustard will lend a personal touch to this recipe.

This vinaigrette will keep for several days, covered and refrigerated. Whisk vigorously before using.

Clarified Butter

2 pounds unsalted butter

EQUIPMENT: *2¹/₂-quart saucepan, ladle, stainless-steel container with lid*

Melt the butter in 2¹/₂-quart saucepan over very low heat for about 30 minutes. When melted, use a ladle to skim as much of the white frothy matter (which is primarily water) off the top as possible without removing the clear yellow liquid (the fat).

Adjust the heat to medium. Continue to heat, occasionally skimming additional white solids as necessary until the top of the butter appears clear, about 45 minutes. Remove from the heat. Let stand at room temperature for 10 minutes.

Skim any remaining solids. Carefully pour the clear yellow fat into a stainless-steel container, discarding the watery bottom layer.

The Chef's Touch

The benefit of clarified over whole butter is that it can sustain substantially higher temperatures without burning. For this reason, clarified butter is ideal for sautéing: it does not burn (when used as directed) and will impart a buttery flavor.

Clarified butter may be stored covered in the refrigerator for two weeks or in the freezer for up to one month. Longer storage will affect the structure of the butter and it may evaporate when heated.

TECHNIQUES

TABLE OF VOLUME AND WEIGHT RELATIONSHIPS
FOR SPECIFIC FOODS UTILIZED IN THIS COOKBOOK

All of the recipes contained in this book were tested in my own home kitchen by Trellis assistant chef Jonathan Zearfoss, pastry chef Andrew O'Connell, and myself. During the eight months of testing, it became apparent that one person's medium head of Bibb lettuce may be another person's large head. For that reason, we decided to weigh many of the ingredients in order to establish an average weight for a specified size. It was also decided in the recipes to list some items by volume where weight was not critical; on the other hand, where a specific weight was necessary in order to achieve a successful recipe, we in fact listed those items by weight. In hopes of avoiding confusion I offer in this table some of the more frequently specified food items in this cookbook by weight and volume.

WHOLE NUTS:

	¹/₄ cup	*¹/₂ cup*	*1 cup*
Almonds	1 oz	2 oz	4 oz
Cashews	1¹/₄ oz	2¹/₂ oz	5 oz
Hazelnuts	1¹/₄ oz	2¹/₂ oz	5 oz
Macadamia Nuts	1¹/₂ oz	3 oz	6 oz
Peanuts	1 oz	2 oz	4 oz
Pecans	1 oz	2 oz	4 oz
Pine Nuts	1¹/₂ oz	3 oz	6 oz
Walnuts	1 oz	2 oz	4 oz

VEGETABLES:
(*As Purchased*)

	Small	*Medium*	*Large*
Arugula (bunch)	¹/₄ lb	¹/₂ lb	³/₄ lb
Bell Peppers (each)	¹/₄ lb	6 oz	¹/₂ lb
Cabbage, Green (head)	2 lb	2¹/₂ lb	3 lb
Carrots (each)	¹/₄ lb	6 oz	³/₄ lb
Chicory or Curly Endive (head)	¹/₄ lb	³/₄ lb	1 lb

313

VEGETABLES:
(*As Purchased*)

	Small	Medium	Large
Cucumber (each)	——	½ lb	¾ lb
Fennel Bulb (each)	¼ lb	½ lb	1 lb
Lettuce (head)			
Bibb	¼ lb	½ lb	1 lb
Red Leaf	½ lb	¾ lb	1 lb
Romaine	½ lb	1 lb	1½ lb
Onion, Red (each)	¼ lb	6 oz	½ lb
Onion, White (each)	¼ lb	½ lb	¾ lb
Spinach, Flat Leaf (bunch)	——	——	¾ lb
Watercress (bunch)	——	¼ lb	6 oz
Zucchini (each)	——	½ lb	¾ lb

MISCELLANEOUS:

Cheese—1 ounce of Parmesan will yield ½ cup loosely packed grated cheese.

   1 ounce of Monterey Jack or Tillamook Cheddar will yield ⅓ cup loosely packed grated cheese.

Corn—1 medium ear of white shoe peg corn will yield ⅓ cup kernels.

   1 medium ear of yellow corn will yield ½ cup kernels.

Eggs—All eggs used are "large."

Shrimp—Large = 26 to 30 count per pound

   Jumbo = 12 to 15 count per pound

Tomatoes—All tomatoes used are medium.

   10 medium tomatoes = about 4 pounds

   1 peeled and seeded medium tomato will yield ⅔ cup chopped tomato.

ZESTING CITRUS FRUIT:

Use a zester or a vegetable peeler to zest citrus fruit. The zester has the advantage of removing only the desired rind in very thin strips. If using a vegetable peeler, be careful when cutting the skin away from the fruit to remove only the colored skin and not the bitter white pith which lies beneath the skin. After removing the rind with a vegetable peeler, cut the rind into thin strips with a sharp French knife.

JALAPEÑO PEPPERS:

For roasted jalapeño peppers, char the peppers over a gas flame, charcoal fire, or electric range element until black. When the peppers are thoroughly black, rinse under cold running water to remove the skin.

Cut each pepper in half lengthwise and rinse under running water to remove the seeds.

Handle jalapeño peppers with care. The oils from the peppers, and especially the seeds, can irritate the skin and the eyes, causing a burning sensation. Use plastic gloves or wash hands immediately after handling peppers. Aloe vera gel will alleviate skin irritation if preventive steps are not successful.

ROASTING BELL PEPPERS:
Peppers may be roasted in several different ways: for 6 to 8 minutes over a very hot charcoal or wood fire, for 8 to 10 minutes over a gas flame, or for 12 to 15 minutes under the broiler element of an electric range. Turn the peppers frequently while charring, and roast until the skin is uniformly charred and blistered. Immediately cool and rinse roasted peppers under cold running water to stop the cooking action and to remove the charred skin.

CUTTING PASTA:
If the pasta dough is too moist, it may not cut properly on the pasta machine (the strands will stick together). If this occurs, air-dry the pasta for 10 to 15 minutes before cutting. Fresh-cut pasta may be refrigerated for 24 to 48 hours. In addition to the suggested pasta cut, all of the pasta doughs may be cut into a variety of shapes. Fettuccine, tagliatelle, spaghetti, and capellini are but a few of the dozens of interesting pasta possibilities. Toss freshly cut pasta with cornmeal to prevent sticking.

COOKING PASTA:
Before cooking fresh pasta, be certain to shake off any cornmeal. Fresh-cut pasta cooks very quickly: you should frequently taste a strand to determine the degree of doneness, as pasta should be cooked only until it is tender but still firm to the bite (*al dente*).

PROPER COOLING OF SOUPS, STOCKS, AND OTHER FOODS:
In order to quickly lower the temperature of foods, it is advisable to use an ice water bath.

To reduce the development of food-spoiling bacteria, hot foods that are to be refrigerated *must* be cooled quickly before refrigeration. Depending upon the volume of food to be cooled, the ice water bath may be set up in the kitchen sink or in a stainless-steel bowl large enough to hold the container of food to be cooled. There should be sufficient space in the sink or bowl to place enough ice and water to surround most of the outside surface area of the container. Place a stainless-steel ladle or stirring spoon in the container of food and stir frequently during the cooling process to promote rapid cooling.

Certain items, such as ice cream and sorbet bases, need to be cooled before they are placed in an ice cream freezer to facilitate the freezing process.

PEELING AND SEEDING TOMATOES:

To peel tomatoes, first core the tomatoes. Turn each tomato over and make a small **X** on the bottom end, cutting just through the skin but not into the flesh. Place the cored tomatoes in boiling water for 40 to 50 seconds. Remove from the hot water and immediately plunge into ice water. When the tomatoes are cold, remove from the water and peel with a paring knife, starting from the **X**. The skin should slip off easily.

To seed the peeled tomatoes, cut them in half horizontally, then seed by holding each tomato half under cold running water, gently squeezing, and allowing the water to flush out the seeds from the internal tomato sections.

HOW TO FLATTEN MEAT OR POULTRY:

Place the meat or poultry to be flattened between 2 sheets of lightly oiled aluminum foil. Using the flat side of a meat cleaver or the bottom of a heavy-duty sauté pan, pound the meat until it is uniformly flat. If the aluminum foil tears immediately, you are probably pounding the meat with too much force. Replace the sheets of aluminum foil as needed. Meat is flattened to give it a uniform thickness and, in some cases, to tenderize.

HOW TO DRESS LIVE SOFT-SHELL CRABS:

Rinse each live crab under cool running water to remove any eel grass, seaweed, or other packing materials. Place the crab on its back on a cutting board; gently pull the large claws away from the face of the crab. Use a sharp knife to cut away the eye-and-mouth section of the crab. Gently press downward on the center portion of the crab to remove the yellow bile. Pull away and remove the apron (female crabs have a **V**-shaped apron while male crabs have an inverted **T**-shaped apron). Turn the crab right side up. Lift up the soft shell flap on each end and remove the spongy gill tissue. Rinse the crab under cool running water and pat dry with paper towels.

BONING FOWL:

To skin and bone leg and thigh sections, remove each leg and thigh section from the carcass. Use your fingers to separate the skin from the flesh. After the skin has been removed, cut the leg away from the thigh, at the joint. Cut the tip off each leg. Push down on the leg meat to reveal the bone. Using a knife, scrape the leg meat from the bone. Cut and scrape the meat away from the thigh bones. Remove any remaining fat, cartilage, or sinewy membranes from the meat.

To skin and remove breasts from the carcass, remove the skin from the breast area by making an incision along the breast bone. Then, using your fingers, separate the skin from the flesh. After the skin is removed, use a sharp, thin boning knife to make an incision on either side of the breast bone, the length of the bone. Carefully cut the breasts away from the carcass by guiding the blade of the knife parallel with the breast plate and away from the flesh.

PREPARING ARTICHOKES:

To prepare artichokes for cooking, first remove the outer leaves. Slice straight across the flower about ³/₄ inch above the point where the stem meets the choke. Using a sharp-edged soup spoon or a grapefruit spoon, remove the purple and white thistle from the center of the cut artichoke. Cut away all but ¹/₄ inch of the stem. Place the artichokes, as soon as you cut and trim each one, directly into enough acidulated cold water to cover, using 1 tablespoon lemon juice for every 3 cups water. The artichokes should be cooked soon after they have been placed in the acidulated water, as prolonged immersion will result in a sour-tasting artichoke. Drain the artichokes well before placing them in the cooking water.

It is necessary to use stainless-steel knives when working with artichokes. In addition, the holding and cooking vessels should be stainless-steel or glass. Otherwise, the artichokes will become unattractively discolored. Also be certain that the artichokes are cooked through or they will discolor.

PEELING BUTTERNUT SQUASH:

Peel the butternut squash with a vegetable peeler. Split the squash in half widthwise at the point where the straight-sided top portion and the bulbous bottom portion come together. Trim the end from the bulbous portion, split in half lengthwise, remove the seeds, then cut into the desired shape. Trim the end from the straight-sided top portion, cut in half lengthwise, then cut into the desired shape.

MELTING CHOCOLATE:

Double boilers are very important for working with chocolate. If you do not own an authentic double boiler (see page 322), use a stainless-steel bowl that will cover the circumference of the top of the pot (so that steam cannot escape), yet remain several inches away from the bottom. The bowl in which the chocolate is being melted should not touch the boiling water; if it does, the chocolate may get grainy and stiff.

DISSOLVING YEAST:

In all of the yeast bread recipes in this cookbook, sugar and yeast are dissolved in warm water or milk. The temperature of the liquid should be between 100 and 110 degrees. The dissolved sugar and yeast mixture should foam in 2 to 3 minutes. If this foaming action does not occur within 5 minutes, the yeast is probably inactive. Discard and start this procedure again with fresh ingredients.

FREEZING STOCK:

When freezing stock, be certain it is thoroughly cooled before freezing. Freeze about 3 cups prepared stock in each 1-quart container. Stock will expand during freezing, thus necessitating the larger volume of the containers versus the actual amount of stock. Seal container tightly and mark with the date; use within 1 month.

COOKIES FOR CRUMB CRUST:

To prevent cookies from baking unevenly, rotate the baking sheets (switch sheets from one rack to the other and turn sheets 180 degrees) after the first 8 minutes of baking.

Cookies may be baked several days ahead and kept fresh in a securely covered plastic container.

In order to achieve a uniform and attractive crumb crust, the application of the crust to a springform pan should be done in the following manner. First press the crumb mixture onto the buttered sides of the pan. Use your fingers to even the crumbs along the lower edge of the sides, so that the crumb crust is square along the lower edge rather than rounded. Again using your hands, press the remaining crumbs to a uniform and level thickness on the bottom of the pan.

WHIPPING HEAVY CREAM:

It is important that the bowl and whisk used for whipping heavy cream be very cold. The best way to do this is by placing clean and dry utensils in the freezer. If lack of space prohibits this, then fill the bowl with ice water several minutes before using (also place the whisk in ice water). *Thoroughly dry* the bowl and whisk, before adding and whisking the cream.

LEAVENING AGENTS:

The leavening agents baking powder and baking soda begin acting as soon as they are moistened. For this reason, it is very important that no time be wasted getting the pan of batter into the oven as soon as it is prepared. If any time is lost, the finished product may be smaller in size and dense instead of light.

ICE CREAM:

A hand-held electric mixer may be used to prepare the egg yolks for ice cream. Use the same technique as described for the table-model mixer. Also, the egg yolks may be beaten by hand with a whisk. They will not, however, be quite as light. If the egg yolks are whisked by hand, wait until the cream has come to a boil before beginning to whisk the yolks. Adjust the heat so the cream does not scald and yet stays boiling hot while you whisk the eggs.

BAKING CHEESECAKES:

Constant controlled heat is a critical factor in producing a top-quality cheesecake. Initially, the temperature needs to be high enough to set the filling so that it does not leach into the crumb crust. Subsequently, the temperature must be low to minimize the moisture loss from the filling. Too high a baking temperature will cause moisture to escape quickly, resulting in unattractive cracks in the top surface of the cake. Try to monitor the progress of the cake without opening the oven door (ovens with windows are desirable) or to open the door only once after the first 30 minutes or so. If the cake appears to be rising too quickly and if small cracks appear, lower the suggested baking temperature (additional baking time will be necessary). The surest indicator of doneness is an internal temperature of exactly 160 degrees. Use an instant-read meat thermometer (see page 322) to obtain this reading.

EQUIPMENT

MANDOLIN:

The mandolin is an invaluable piece of equipment in the Trellis kitchen. We have several and use them every day for one slicing task or another. Using the mandolin results in uniformity of thickness and length. Cucumbers and other vegetables can be cut into long or short strands; potatoes and other vegetables can be sliced into uniform slices or cut into an attractive waffle cut.

Mandolins may be purchased at kitchen supply stores and from cookware catalogs such as Williams-Sonoma (see page 325).

"LITTLE CHIEF" SMOKER:

Home smoking can be easy and economical. The "Little Chief" electric smoker which we use at The Trellis is the same piece of equipment used by thousands of home cooks. Although professional-size smokers with precise temperature controls are available, we chose the "Little Chief" over five years ago because of its economy and simplicity of operation. A note of caution: restrict the use of the smoker to an outside area, an open garage, or a porch, and certainly never use inside your home. The "Little Chief" smoker is available from Luhr-Jensen and Sons (see page 325).

PASTA MACHINE:

Although pasta can be produced entirely by hand, a pasta machine will make life much simpler. With a manually operated pasta machine the pasta dough can be kneaded, rolled into sheets, then cut into the desired shape. All of the pasta recipes in this book were tested using an all-stainless-steel Atlas brand pasta machine which retails for about $30. These pasta machines are easy to operate, produce a high-quality pasta, and can be cleaned very quickly. At The Trellis, we use a professional-size manually operated pasta machine, the Imperia 220 (see page 326), which is a king-size version of the smaller Atlas machine, and with which we produce the same high-quality pasta. Electrically operated machines are available, but it is our experience that they frequently malfunction. Additionally, this type of machine is usually more difficult to operate as well as to clean, especially if the machine extrudes the dough.

RUBBER SPATULA:

Usually thought of as a tool to be used by a home cook rather than a professional, a rubber spatula is a valuable piece of equipment in any kitchen. By using a rubber spatula, every ounce of sauce, soup, butter, or other ingredients can be quickly, efficiently, and entirely removed from a bowl, saucepan, or vessel, no matter the size or configuration. The recipes in this book are designed so as not to produce excess product over the amount needed for assembly. It is therefore important to transfer ingredients completely from one container to another.

NON-STICK SAUTÉ PANS:

Teflon or Silverstone-coated pans have been used in home kitchens for a number of years. The primary allure for the home cook has been that these so-called non-stick pans are easy to clean because foods will not adhere to the cooking surface. In fact, this depends upon which foods are being cooked and at what temperature. The use of non-stick pans in professional kitchens has become more prevalent in the last few years. For obvious reasons, many chefs prefer these pans for preparing various egg dishes. At The Trellis, we have a number of non-stick pans. Using these pans allows us to sauté foods in a minimum amount of butter or oil (a small amount of oil or butter is necessary to help develop the essences of the foods being cooked), which allows the flavor of the food being cooked or warmed to stand on its own. Additionally, it is a more healthful manner of cooking.

JAPANESE TURNING SLICER:

With the exception of our ice cream freezer, I cannot think of another piece of equipment in our kitchen that is as much fun to operate as the Japanese turning slicer. With this manually operated machine, vegetables can be cut into thin, seemingly endless strands. The unusual appearance of vegetables cut on the turning slicer is a source of amusement to our cooks and guests alike. The best vegetables to cut on the turning slicer are solid ones without interior seeds, such as carrots and beets. Do not use heavily seeded vegetables such as zucchini and cucumbers. Peel the vegetables before turning. Japanese turning slicers are usually available from cookware catalogs such as Williams-Sonoma (see page 325).

INSTANT-READ TEST THERMOMETER:
Several recipes in this book require that an accurate temperature reading be obtained either during the cooking process or during cooling. The most widely available thermometer we have found for these purposes is an instant-read test thermometer. To get a temperature reading with this type of thermometer, the stainless-steel sensor is momentarily inserted into the food being prepared. An easy-to-read dial displays an accurate temperature in a matter of seconds. For general testing, a thermometer with a range of 0 degrees to 220 degrees is recommended. This type of thermometer is designed for instant readings only; it is *not* for oven use. Taylor brand thermometers are the standard of the industry. The same high-quality Taylor thermometer sold to food service professionals is also available in hardware stores and kitchen supply stores and retails for about $12. For more information on thermometers, write:

> Mr. Earl D. Vaught
> Manager, Marketing Communications
> Thermometer Corporation of America
> 95 Glenn Bridge Road
> Arden, North Carolina 28704

DOUBLE BOILER:
A double boiler is a two-sectioned pot. The bottom section holds water, while the top section, when completely inserted into the bottom section, fits snugly on the sides but does not extend completely to the bottom. The top section holds the food to be heated or cooked. The advantage of a double boiler is that the food in the top section may be cooked or held warm without the surface of the pot being in direct contact with the heating element. This is particularly important when holding a delicate food, such as a cream reduction, warm, as well as when melting chocolate.

Double boilers are available in a variety of sizes and in various materials. A double boiler with a ceramic insert is particularly suitable for melting chocolate, holding sauces, and keeping soups warm, while those fashioned from aluminum or stainless steel are more appropriate for cooking foods such as wild rice.

An adequate double boiler can be simply fashioned by inserting a smaller pot into a larger pot that has been partially filled with water. Be careful when using this type of double boiler, especially when melting chocolate, that the top section does not come into contact with the water in the bottom section. Also, be careful that steam does not escape from the bottom section and condense onto the chocolate. Both instances would adversely affect the texture and eating quality of the chocolate.

ICE CREAM FREEZER:

Ice cream and sorbet sales account for almost half of the desserts sold at The Trellis. Fortunately, we have a large-batch freezer which produces 24 quarts of incomparably delicious ice cream at a time. Many freezers, electrically or manually operated, are available for home use. To test the recipes for this cookbook, pastry chef Andrew O'Connell used the Il Gelataio 1600 manufactured by the Simac Appliance Corporation. This is an excellent, easy-to-use, electrically operated machine. The Il Gelataio 1600 produces 1½ to 2 quarts of ice cream or sorbet per batch. The only major drawback to this machine is that the freezing chamber cannot be removed, which makes cleaning a bit difficult. More up-to-date models with removable freezing chambers are available. For more information about ice cream freezers write:

Simac Appliance Corporation
145 West Commercial Avenue
Moonachie, New Jersey 07074

SAUCEPANS:

High-quality equipment in good working order is elemental to the end results of any recipe. This, however, does not always mean that this equipment must be expensive. In the initial stages of planning the testing of the recipes for this book, I requested that assistant chef Jonathan Zearfoss purchase non-professional saucepans. I was surprised and somewhat chagrined when he returned from his shopping foray with what appeared, to me, to be highly inadequate cookware. As it turned out, the saucepans were inexpensive and of impeccable quality. Almost all of the recipes in this book specifying 2½-quart or 5-quart saucepans were prepared using Visions cookware. Manufactured by Corning Glass Works, these transparent glass-ceramic pans have three advantages: they can be subjected to temperature extremes, they are easy to clean, and compared to other high-quality saucepans, they are very inexpensive.

TONGS:

The equipment listing for many recipes in this cookbook includes tongs. At The Trellis we use 9-inch stainless-steel tongs. They are a handy piece of equipment to use for a variety of tasks: removing blanched vegetables from boiling water to transfer to ice water; turning foods on a charcoal grill or in a sauté pan; holding a pepper while charring over a gas or charcoal fire. Tongs enable a cook to touch foods without damaging their texture or piercing the flesh, as may happen when a fork is used. Tongs also enable a cook to handle many hot foods with a minimum risk of being burned.

SOURCES

FOOD AND EQUIPMENT SOURCES

COUNTRY HAMS; HICKORY-SMOKED SLAB BACON; SURRY SAUSAGE
S. Wallace Edwards & Sons, Inc.
P.O. Box 25
Surry, Virginia 23883
804-294-3121 or toll-free outside Virginia 800-222-4267
MasterCard/Visa or American Express

FRESH WILD MUSHROOMS; QUAIL
Flying Foods International
43–43 Ninth Street
Long Island City, New York 11101
718-706-0820

QUAIL; PHEASANT
Foodtech International, Inc.
5717 A. Edsall Road
Alexandria, Virginia 22304
703-751-7777
MasterCard/Visa
Freight charge for orders under $100

UNSALTED VIRGINIA PEANUTS
Peanut Shop of Williamsburg
P.O. Box G N
Williamsburg, Virginia 23187
804-253-0060
MasterCard/Visa

FRESH-CUT HERBS
Wilson's Savory Farm
Route 2, Box 753
Donalds, South Carolina 29638
803-379-8021
Orders shipped via Express Mail ($15 shipping and handling charge),
next-day delivery

MAYTAG BLUE CHEESE
Maytag Dairy Farms
P.O. Box 806
Newton, Iowa 50208
515-792-1133 or toll-free outside Iowa 800-247-2458

SMOKED SALMON
Ducktrap River Fish Farms, Inc.
P.O. Box 378
Lincolnville, Maine 04849
207-763-3960
MasterCard/Visa
Write for free catalog

SHIITAKE MUSHROOMS
Weaving Run Mushrooms
Route 1, Box 393-C-10
Hague, Virginia 22469
804-472-3548
Write or call for information

"LITTLE CHIEF" ELECTRIC SMOKERS
Luhr-Jensen and Sons
P.O. Box 297
Hood River, Oregon 97031
503-386-3811

STAINLESS-STEEL MANDOLINS; JAPANESE TURNING SLICERS
Williams-Sonoma
Mail Order Department
P.O. Box 7456
San Francisco, California 94120
415-421-4242

or

The Chef's Catalog
3215 Commercial Avenue
Northbrook, Illinois 60062
312-480-9400

PROFESSIONAL PASTA MACHINES (Imperia 220)
E. Rossi & Co., Inc.
191 Grand Street
New York, New York 10013
212-226-9254

INDEX